35.-

Adoption and Financial Assistance

ADOPTION AND FINANCIAL ASSISTANCE

Tools for Navigating the Bureaucracy

Rita Laws
and
Tim O'Hanlon

Foreword by Jeanette Wiedemeier Bower

BERGIN & GARVEY
Westport, Connecticut • London

Library of Congress Cataloging-in-Publication Data

Laws, Rita, 1956–
  Adoption and financial assistance : tools for navigating the
bureaucracy / by Rita Laws and Tim O'Hanlon ; foreword by Jeanette
Wiedemeier Bower.
    p. cm.
  Includes bibliographical references (p.) and index.
  ISBN 0–89789–668–8 (alk. paper)
  1. Special needs adoption—United States. 2. Federal aid to child
welfare—United States. 3. Adoption—Law and legislation—United
States. 4. Foster children—Legal status, laws, etc.—United
States. 5. United States. Adoption and Safe Families Act of 1997.
  I. O'Hanlon, Tim. II. Title.
HV875.55.L38 1999
362.73'4'0973—dc21   98–55901

British Library Cataloguing in Publication Data is available.

Library of Congress Catalog Card Number: 98–55901
ISBN: 0–89789–668–8

First published in 1999

Bergin & Garvey, 88 Post Road West, Westport, CT 06881
An imprint of Greenwood Publishing Group, Inc.
www.greenwood.com

Printed in the United States of America

The paper used in this book complies with the
Permanent Paper Standard issued by the National
Information Standards Organization (Z39.48–1984).

10 9 8 7 6 5 4 3 2 1

To the parent advocates and adoption activists who help waiting and adopted children who have special needs.

Give up on building a house if you like, or completing a crossword puzzle, but whatever you do, never stop advocating for children. They can't challenge the bureaucracy. Only adults can do that.

Contents

Part III: Document Appendices

Part IV: Information Resources

Foreword

In my experience in working with adoption and foster care issues, it has always struck me that individuals who choose to parent children with special needs are a particularly special type of people. Even if they did not know the specific nature of their child's condition at the time of the adoption, they rose to the occasion when the need presented itself—through the therapies, medical appointments, surgeries, behavior outbreaks, and more. They did so for the love of their children.

Public and private agencies throughout the country have always been pleased to recruit these adoptive parents, but many—certainly not all—are less willing and often unprepared to provide the ongoing support services that will keep these families strong and together. Therefore, parents find themselves at odds with the very people who helped create their precious families. Many parents find it difficult under these circumstances to "rock the boat." Others want to advocate for their children but do not even know the first step in doing so.

Adoption and Financial Assistance: Tools for Navigating the Bureaucracy provides a useful how-to framework for advocating for children with special needs and does so in an easy-to-read fashion. The book outlines step-by-step strategies for negotiating with your agency, organizing through a parent support group, and obtaining valuable adoption subsidies both prior to and after finalization.

Parents will find themselves identifying with the many stories throughout the book and saying out loud, "That's happened to me before!" And the reason parents will be able to relate to the book is because of the authors and their backgrounds. Dr. O'Hanlon writes from the perspective of an administrator within the system who has spent his career advocating for services for children with special needs. Dr. Laws is the parent of eight special needs children and has spent her adult life fighting different states for services and resources for her children. I find *Adoption and Financial Assistance: Tools for Navigating the Bureaucracy* a refreshing resource for new and veteran parents alike.

Jeanette Wiedemeier Bower
North American Council on Adoptable Children

Preface

When it comes to special needs adoption and money, the authors want the reader to know several things right up front:

- Nothing in this book should be used as a substitute for the counsel of an attorney in an adoption assistance court action. Parents should seek legal advice from a qualified adoption-assistance-experienced attorney.
- Regardless of parental income, and thanks to PIQ 92–02, it is almost never too late to seek adoption assistance and retroactive payments.
- The federal government has committed the money to make special needs adoption affordable for all Americans who want to get a child out of foster care for good. However, accessing these funds is not easy or simple. When it comes to financial requests that are in the best interests of adopted children, parents should never take no for an answer—at first.
- Parents who believe they have not been dealt with fairly have options in a process called the fair hearing, and hiring legal help is not required for this informal type of appeal.
- The state adoption bureaucracy is not impossible to understand.
- Adoption assistance payments and service subsidies make special needs adoption possible for millions of families and thousands of waiting children. Permanency is better for children than foster care because adoption creates productive citizens. In the long run, even subsidized adoptions save the taxpayer money. Parents who advocate financially for their children are not just helping their children and their families, they are making a stronger nation.
- In writing this book, we drew on research, personal experience, and the experience gained assisting thousands of other families. One of the authors of this book is an adoptive parent and advocate, and the other is an adoption advocate and

a former state adoption bureaucrat. The examples chosen are composites of real-life stories with details changed to protect the privacy of families and, especially, of children.

- In most cases, we do not identify states by name because state laws change so rapidly. What's true today in a certain state can be totally different tomorrow. Readers must inform themselves of current law and adoption policy in their own state. There is more about how to obtain the most up-to-date information in Parts III and IV.

- This book was written to encourage special needs adoption and to help families who adopt children with special needs to better meet their children's needs. The safety and best interests of the child is the goal, and financial advocacy is the means.

Some of the chapters in this book began as articles for *Adoptive Families* magazine, published by Adoptive Families of America, Inc. (AFA), Minneapolis, Minnesota, and edited by Linda Lynch. Thank you, Linda. Some of the research cited within appears courtesy of the North American Council on Adoptable Children (NACAC) in St. Paul, Minnesota. NACAC leads the way in adoption assistance research and advocacy.

Friends and fellow-advocates at the following special needs adoption organizations offered their support, ideas, and encouragement: Adoptive Families of America, North American Council on Adoptable Children, and the National Adoption Center.

When people work on behalf of a just cause, and especially when it benefits a defenseless group such as children, they tend to become deeply involved with their work. Such people are hard working, serene, confident, doggedly determined, caring, and they have a certain kind of gleam in the eye that identifies them as child-centered. The following people who helped us review the contents of this book have just such eyes and their generous help is much appreciated: L. Anne Babb, Ph.D.; Jeanette Wiedemeier Bower, M.P.A.; John Hamilton, Esq.; Deb Harder; Linda Lynch; and Ann McCabe.

We also wish to thank Lynn Taylor, at Greenwood Publishing Group, for her encouragement; L. Anne Babb for her many ideas; and Jeanette Wiedemeier Bower for a beautiful Foreword. Love and gratitude to Tim's wife, Nancy, and son, Matthew O'Hanlon, and to Rita's children, Samantha, Tim, Tony, Joaquin, Jesse, Kelly, John, Eli, Jamie, George, and Geoffrey, and granddaughter, Adriana Laws. Finally, Rita wants to thank her parents, Nancy and Sam Laws, and NACAC state representative DWe Williams, for their support and inspiration.

Acronyms

AAP	Adoption Assistance Payments
AASK	Adopt a Special Kid
ADD	Attention Deficit Disorder
ADHD	Attention Deficit Hyperactivity Disorder
AFA	Adoptive Families of America
AFDC	Aid to Families with Dependent Children
APWA	American Public Welfare Association
ASFA	Adoption and Safe Families Act
CFR	Code of Federal Regulations
DHS	Department of Human Services
FFP	Federal Financial Participation
MARE	Massachusetts Adoption Resource Exchange
NAC	National Adoption Center
NACAC	North American Council on Adoptable Children
NAIC	National Adoption Information Clearinghouse
OURS	Organization for a United Response
PIQ	Policy Interpretation Question
SSI	Supplemental Security Income
TANF	Temporary Aid to Needy Families

PART I

ADOPTION AND THE BUREAUCRACY

1

Adoption ABCs: Advocacy, Bureaucracy, and Children

The full value of this life can only be got by fighting.
—G. K. Chesterton (1874–1936)

VROOM, VROOM!

If someone gave you every part required to build a brand new car, but only some of the assembly instructions and tools, could you build the car? If you built it, would it run? Unless you are gifted mechanically and experienced in auto assembly, chances are you would not be able to build or use that car. PL 96–272, the adoption assistance law that is also called Title IV-E, or ASFA IV-B, is like that pile of auto parts, although its potential to do good is far greater than that of a new automobile.

PL 96–272 is designed to make special needs adoption, both the process and the child rearing, financially affordable for virtually every American who wants to open his or her home to a waiting child. It has already had a profoundly positive effect on waiting children by encouraging thousands of adoptions that could otherwise not have happened (Gilles & Kroll, 1992; Bower, 1998; Marindin, 1998). And as a bonus, this law is reforming foster care and saving tax dollars in the long run (O'Hanlon, 1995). It encourages the more cost-effective process of adoption while shrinking the numbers of children in expensive foster care. A 1993 study by Westat, Incorporated, found that this law has saved the U.S. taxpayer billions of dollars. In fact, Title IV-E is the most important and effective adoption legislation in the history of the United States.

Like the pile of auto parts, PL 96–272 is limited by its complexity. This law had to strike a balance between encouraging birth family reunification, where possible, and adoption, where possible, while discouraging foster care drift. Additionally, this law's intent is not well understood, applied, or explained by most state bureaucracies. Without full instructions and good tools, waiting and adopted children with special needs and their new families cannot benefit fully from the legislation.

Currently, experienced foster and adoptive parents and families who work closely with adoption advocates and support groups are among the few who are able to make Title IV-E work for children as it should. Some private and state agencies do an excellent job, as well, but they are few and far between.

This book is designed to give all adoptive and potential adoptive parents a complete set of assembly instructions and at least some of the tools needed to assemble PL 96–272 into a working machine. This book also strives to explain how the state bureaucracy charged with implementing Title IV-E functions, why it works the way it does, and how parents can work within that system more effectively. The extensive resources and federal documents in Parts III and IV are some of the best tools available anywhere.

THE NEED FOR ADVOCACY

Special needs adoption is challenging. This is not to say adoption can't be positive. Special needs adoption can be and should be joyful. After all, it is the ultimate win-win situation: Child who needs parent gets parent, and parent who wants child gets child. But the joy that comes from a successful adoption is not bestowed automatically on the family. Successful special needs adoptions are the result of hard work on the part of the parents and their support network, and most of that work can be summed up in one word: advocacy.

Advocacy is the process of pressing a cause or issue with an authoritative body. In the case of adoption, the cause is the best interest of the child and the family. A parent-advocate is firm and calm, knowledgeable, a good listener, and somewhat stubborn. Put another way, an advocate must have the three Ps: patience, persistence, and pluck (courage).

The authoritative body the advocate negotiates with is the same organization that has the potential to be the parents' best ally or worst nemesis— the state adoption bureaucracy. Often called the Department of Human Resources or Services (DHS), or the Division of Child and Family Services or an equivalent name, the state bureaucracy is made up of the people who administer state adoption policy.

Too often, these administrators have little or no personal contact with the adoptive parents, the child, or the family. This lack of one-on-one contact can create distance and indifference. The goal of detached bureaucrats is to maintain a status quo with as little distraction is possible. "Keep it simple" and "Don't rock the boat" are their unwritten twin mantras. By contrast, the goal of child-centered bureaucrats who put children first is to maintain the focus on children's needs.

Adoptive parents often have a difficult time understanding and then remembering that the state may or may not always act for the child's welfare. For people who grew up without reason to mistrust government or bureaucracy, this is a particularly difficult concept to grasp and hang on to. But sometimes, the state (or city or county or federal agency) acts only in its own best interests or at least appears to be doing so.

Fortunately, parents are not alone. There are many child advocates, volunteer support group volunteers, and adoption professionals who are happy to assist with the advocacy process. Parts III and IV of this book have more information about locating them.

The social worker who places the child and supervises the placement is the bridge between the parent and the system. She or he is neither advocate nor bureaucrat but rather a hybrid of both. (State social workers who are total advocates are likely to burn out, get transferred, or start their own adoption agencies.) Depending on this person's level of experience, dedication, and child-centeredness, the social worker will either make the job of the parents easier or tougher. Since parents can't predict what kind of social worker they will be assigned, every adoptive mom and dad should be prepared and must learn the fine art of advocacy.

THE CHILDREN WHO WAIT

In this complex system of parent, bureaucrat, and social worker, the waiting and adopted children are the ultimate beneficiaries, or victims. A waiting child is a child who has spent time in the foster care system waiting to be adopted. Healthy babies and new-to-the-system healthy toddlers who have hundreds of couples lined up and vying to adopt them are not waiting children. Waiting children have special needs that make adoption more challenging. Currently 100,000 of the 500,000 foster children in the United States are waiting to be adopted.

Special needs is a term coined in the seventies to describe adoptable children who are waiting. The term's definition is important because only children with special needs are eligible for the special state and federal programs that reimburse parents for the cost of the adoption and that pay for some of the children's medical and maintenance expenses after the adoption. The federal government defines a child with special needs as one who has one or more special needs or factors, such as

- sibling status (must remain with one or more siblings)
- minority race (this is not a special need or a requirement but a placement factor)
- age (older children)
- mild, moderate, or severe physical, mental, or emotional challenges
- risk factors for problems that could show up later (prenatal exposure to drugs, a family history of mental illness, abuse, neglect, a difficult birth, multiple care-givers, unknown paternity, and others).

Special needs waiting children can be healthy looking infants who were exposed to heroin prenatally, a two-year-old with asthma, or a seventeen and one-half-year-old who simply wants a real family before he or she graduates from high school. Quite often, they are sibling groups with two to seven or more members who need to be adopted together by one family.

The definition of the term *special needs* is not fixed because each state has the flexibility to determine its own definition based on the population of waiting children. For example, in one state, a healthy minority race child may not be considered to have special needs until after age three, whereas in another state, that same child may qualify at age two years. In places where girls are in higher demand, girls may qualify as special needs at ages older than that of boys.

A Law By Any Other Name . . .

On November 19, 1997, PL 96–272, or Title IV-E, was amended in positive ways that further help children with special needs. The amendments came about as a result of passage of ASFA, an acronym child advocates and adoptive parents will come to know very well in the years ahead. ASFA stands for the Adoption and Safe Families Act, otherwise known as Public Law 105–89, or H.R.867.

Because of ASFA, PL 96–272 is now officially called the Adoption and Safe Families Act of 1997, Title IV, Part B—Child and Family Services. In time, this new name will take hold, but it won't happen overnight. For now, it is important to note that the day is coming when PL 96–272, or Title IV-E, will probably be more commonly referred to ASFA, IV-B or PL 105–89.

There is more information throughout this book on what ASFA contains, and the text of the law can be found in Part III. The American Bar Association Web site (American Bar Association, 750 N. Lake Shore Dr., Chicago, IL 60611, (312)988–5000) http://www.abanet.org mailto:info@abanet.org has both a copy of the text of ASFA and an interesting hybrid article anyone can access. It is a copy of 1980's PL 96–272 with all of the modifications of 1997's ASFA added, including strikeout font showing the deleted sections and italic font for the added parts. This document is an invaluable resource for people who may not understand how ASFA is impacting adoption law. For example, one of the many positive changes due to ASFA is that children who experience disrupted or dissolved adoptions can now retain their IV-E eligibility into the next placement.

A BIT OF HISTORY

So what are these federal programs that make special needs adoption affordable for the average American, and where did they come from? In short, the original activists in the special needs adoption movement are responsible.

As with many modern-day social movements, this one can be traced to the end of World War II. Adoption was an oft-heard word after the war. Worldwide, there were millions of war orphans, and Americans opened their hearts and homes to many of them.

At the same time, the harsh stigma attached to out-of-wedlock births began to soften a little. This lowered the number of healthy white infants available for adoption. Over the next four decades, the stigma lost its sting while more effective forms of birth control and legalized abortion caused the number of such infants to drop more sharply. Ironically, this was coupled with an increase in marital infertility that created a larger demand for healthy white babies.

As the number of healthy infants available for adoption dropped, the number of waiting children with special needs grew. Drugs, poverty, and unemployment, along with better social work methods and increased awareness of child abuse, brought more and more children into the foster care system. Courts took little interest in terminating the parental rights of older and disabled foster children because Americans were not clamoring to adopt such children anyway. But some Americans believed that all children are adoptable, and they started educating the public one community at a time.

The 1950s saw the first wave of true adoption activists. These were ordinary people, many of them foster parents and foster care workers, who believed that all foster children had the right to permanency. These people knew by experience and instinct what many scientific studies would prove in later decades: Adopted children have much better adult outcomes than foster children (Bower, 1998).

The Family Nobody Wanted

In 1954, a book based on the true-life story of a special needs adoptive family became a national best-seller. The cover jacket contained photo ovals of twelve children and two adults who looked nothing alike and, yet, they were a family. The title was *The Family Nobody Wanted*, and the author was Helen Doss. The photo on the back of the cover created a stir. It featured two human staircases. At one end was the father with six sons standing in front of him in order of height. On the other side of the photo was the mother of this clan, with six daughters cascading downward in front of her. Everyone was smiling.

The Family Nobody Wanted was the story of how Carl and Helen Doss adopted twelve children from cultures and national backgrounds including Korea, Japan, the Philippines, Spain, France, Malaya, Burma, Cheyenne, Chippewa, and Blackfoot. They also tried, but failed, to adopt an African-American child. For their time, even today, creating a multirace family, especially a large family, through special needs adoption was a radical thing to do.

Why did they do it? They loved children. They wanted to parent a large family, and it made sense to adopt children who needed forever parents. How did they do it? With strong faith (Carl was also a Methodist minister), hard work, and advocacy skills. Years later, studies would show that the most successful special needs adoptive parents are likely to go to church weekly and have a strong faith in God.

A description of Mrs. Doss' book on the cover jacket summed up their attitude well by comparing it to another radical idea called democracy: "The Dosses have been called radical for their solution to the problem of helping 'the ones needing love to find people who have it.' But as Carl pointed out . . . 'it is radical to say that all men are created equal, and that all men are brothers—and that the individual is important.'"

The Family Nobody Wanted inspired an entire generation of people to take a closer look at the ways we as a society can help our waiting children. Many people became foster and adoptive parents as a result of reading this book.

RADICAL IDEAS

Foster parents and adoptive parents banded together in various support groups during the sixties and seventies in an effort to help waiting children and the families who care for them. They proposed new ideas that were child-centered and based on the radical notion put forward by the Child Welfare League of America at their 1955 convention: Laws governing children should always work for the "best interests" of the child. Today, this may sound like common sense, but prior to this time, adoption was primarily a means for solving adult problems, that is, allowing infertile couples to adopt or making it possible to adopt an heir. If a child benefited from such an arrangement, it was simply coincidental. After 1955, the idea that adoption existed primarily to benefit the child began to take hold.

Just as the word *radical* was used to describe the famous Doss family who adopted twelve transracial children, the word *militant* was used to describe the pioneers of the North American Council on Adoptable Children (NACAC) and its founders, Peter and Joyce Forsythe (Cole & Donley, 1990). NACAC maintained that there was no such person as an unadoptable child. Its members advocated moving all waiting children out of institutions and the foster care system and into permanent adoptive homes.

Also, in the late sixties, six couples met at a Minnesota airport to welcome home their newly adopted children, all born in Korea. Under Betty Kramer's direction, they formed an adoptive parent support group called Parents of Korean and Korean-American Children. In 1968, they changed their name to OURS, an acronym for Organization for a United Response. In 1989, the nonprofit group changed its organizational name one last time to Adoptive Families of America, Incorporated (AFA). Over time, AFA made a conscious effort to represent all types of adoptive families, not just those adopting internationally. This influential organization today publishes the adoption magazine with the highest circulation nationally, *Adoptive Families*.

About the same time, on the West Coast, Bob and Dorothy DeBolt, parents to twenty children through birth and adoption, founded AASK, Adopt A Special Kid. Because of AASK, thousands of children have found permanent families, and their families have found a support system as well. Currently, AASK is headquartered in Oakland, California.

TV and Foster Children

The influence of the early special needs adoption pioneers slowly crept into the public consciousness in many ways, even through television. For example, many people today who watch reruns of an old show called "My Three Sons" starring Fred MacMurray don't realize that the character named Ernie, the youngest of the three sons, originally joined the show's family as a foster child.

In a compelling early episode of the popular series, Ernie and Chip come home from school upset because the other children have labeled Ernie "a secondhand child." These child peers had also criticized Mr. Douglas and his brother, Uncle Charlie, for accepting foster care board payments on Ernie's behalf.

Uncle Charlie becomes very upset that the other children could tease Ernie in such a "cruel way" and asks his brother to legally adopt the child. Mr. Douglas explains that he has already asked the social worker, Ernestine, about this and has been denied because the adoption rules require the presence of a woman in the house, that is, mother, aunt, or grandmother. Here is a clear case of a well-intended rule that is acting against the best interests of a particular child. Mr. Douglas, his advocacy skills in full bloom, pleads with Ernestine to find a way around this "strict" rule, for Ernie's sake. Ernestine, who knows how well Ernie is doing in this home, promises to try.

In the next scene, Ernie waits nervously outside a judge's chambers while all of the adults in his life talk within. The judge, on strong recommendation from Ernestine and her supervisor, has decided to allow a "legal fiction" into the record. A legal fiction, the judge explains, is a lie that is deemed acceptable because it exists for an important reason, in this case, to allow the adoption of a waiting child by his committed foster family. The legal fiction is that Uncle Charlie, with his cooking, sewing, and gruff but caring child-rearing practices, is the "woman of the house." The adoption is allowed and in the tear-jerking ending, a delighted Ernie starts calling Mr. Douglas "Dad."

A single male parent adoption in the 1960s? It may be television, but it accurately portrays the power of advocacy.

AN IMPORTANT TOOL IN THE SPECIAL NEEDS ADOPTION MOVEMENT

The activists knew they needed a way to tell ordinary people about the individual children who waited for permanency. Massachusetts developed such a tool. This progressive state, which had been the first to institute child labor and adoption statutes, was one of the first to publish a photolisting book. In the mid-fifties, it began MARE, the Massachusetts Adoption Resource Exchange. By 1970, MARE was pairing photographs with the created biographies of the state's waiting children and then used the waiting-child catalogs to recruit adoptive families for the children. MARE is going strong today, still matching children with families.

The CAP Book in Rochester, New York, a successful national photolisting book, soon followed, and within a decade there were dozens of state and regional photolisting services advertising waiting children to prospective parents. Some of these books reverse the process and also list waiting adoptive families for social workers to read about and match to the children in their caseloads.

Photolisting remains a popular and important recruiting tool for matching waiting children and prospective families but something even better has grown from it. Today, thousands of children are photolisted on the Web by various states and such groups as the National Adoption Center (NAC). See Part IV of this book for a list of World Wide Web sites. These electronic photolistings of waiting U.S. children draw a much larger response than printed listings, perhaps because anyone with a personal computer and modem can access them. One social worker in Texas offered that she receives two dozen "hits" (inquiries) for an on-line photolisting for every one inquiry received for the same printed photolisting distributed in the Texas photolisting book.

A BIG ROADBLOCK IS REMOVED PERMANENTLY

Photolisting created the means to let the public know about individual waiting children. This created a demand for the adoption of such children. Next, many states began dropping restrictions that kept millions of Americans from being considered as adoptive parents. This easing of eligibility requirements for adoptive parents resulted in thousands of special needs adoptions that would have been impossible before. Factors such as race, handicap, marital status, income, home ownership, gender, and religion no longer kept Americans from adopting children with special needs. Age was usually not a factor unless the youngest parent in a couple would be older than sixty-five by the time the adopted child was eighteen (Nelson, 1985). More and more, adoption agencies were working with people interested in transracial adoption and also working with qualified gay men and lesbians who wanted to adopt waiting children with special needs.

THE BIGGEST ROADBLOCK TO ADOPTION

The movement grew. Special needs adoptive parent support groups grew in number and influence, and they demanded the deinstitutionalization of all waiting children and real permanency planning. This was the beginning of the permanency planning movement (Nelson, 1985). In 1978, a revolutionary new federal law called the Adoption Opportunities Act (Public Law 95–266) was passed to help remove obstacles to adoption. The act also provided for ways to match waiting children to families and to create regional Adoption Resource Centers. Finally, the U.S. Congress had sent a clear message that waiting children are a valuable resource in this society and need our attention.

In the seventies, astute child advocates discovered that the biggest roadblock to adoption was money. It takes a lot of money to raise children with special needs, a fact foster parents knew all too well. In those days, some states wouldn't allow foster parents to adopt their charges under any circumstances, and if it was allowed, it was strongly discouraged due to the financial practices of the time.

The monthly foster care board payment was often what made foster care financially possible. Families with big hearts and tight budgets could afford to help a foster child if they received monthly board payments and if the foster child had Medicaid or other types of medical insurance. The problem arose when that same family asked to adopt the child.

In those states where foster parents were allowed to adopt their charges, the board payments and medical assistance were discontinued after the adoption. Insurance companies sometimes refused to add the child or to pay for preexisting conditions after adoption, a problem that is rare today. Families were faced with the heartbreaking choice of adopting their beloved special needs foster child and face economic ruin or taking the chance that the foster relationship would not be abruptly terminated by the state agency.

Some families got around these heartless rules by adopting their adult foster children, but even this was not the optimum arrangement for the child. Children need and want permanency, and parents need and want to know that a child can't be removed from their home easily.

Some states, mainly in the east, experimented with a plan to allow foster care board payments and medical assistance to continue after a special needs adoption, until the child turned eighteen. This was not "paying people to adopt" but rather making special needs adoption affordable for average people who wanted to help but couldn't afford to feed another mouth.

These pilot programs from the seventies were hugely successful with hundreds of foster children being adopted by their foster parents. The financial roadblock was gone. This simple, successful radical idea has proved so successful that it has been copied all over the world.

The states also found that even after paying these *adoption subsidies*, as the payments came to be called, they actually saved money. Once a child is adopted, the courts' and the social workers' loads are lightened. This saves on salaries. And the family of the adopted child makes use of far fewer services than the family of a foster child. Adoptive parents assume responsibility for extraordinary expenses such as cars, college, graduate school, grandchildren, and the like. Adopted children, as studies would show, are far more likely to be productive tax-paying citizens than children who age out of the foster care system. This also saves money in the long term (Bower, 1998).

ENTER THE FEDERAL GOVERNMENT

The federal government took notice of the financial success of these early state subsidy programs and expanded them for the nation under a law called PL 96–272, Title IV-E, the Adoption Assistance and Child Welfare Act of 1980. The premise was simple: The federal government promised to reimburse states for administrative costs and anywhere from fifty cents to eighty cents on the dollar for every dollar the states paid out in adoption subsidies for children with special needs, provided the states followed the federal law as written. In other words, states could also pay state-funded subsidies to families under different rules, but they would be reimbursed only for those that fell under the terms of the federal IV-E law.

Now here was a radical idea grounded fully in the ideal of meeting the best interests of the child. Every state in the Union, no matter how poor, could encourage its foster families and other citizens to adopt by removing financial disincentives to permanency for foster children who cannot return to their families of origin.

The law was cautiously written so as not to discourage birth family reconciliation where possible. The states had to show why a child could not go home (usually because of abuse, neglect, or the ongoing drug abuse of the parents).

The new federal law was careful to allow only those children into the subsidy program who truly needed it to be adopted, children who were in foster homes with no family to return to, children deprived of the support of their parents, and children with special needs.

Since the law was complex, the federal government supplied each state with a sample "Adoption Assistance Contract," which could be modified, to a certain extent, to meet individual state rules. The response from the states varied from quick and complete compliance (some states adopted the sample contract almost word-for-word) to near total noncompliance. It would be fourteen years before all states were participating in Title IV-E.

Sadly, it took years for most states to implement the law fully and even now it is greatly misunderstood. State legislatures sometimes pass laws that make implementation of PL 96–272 more difficult, social workers are not adequately trained, and parents are not educated about the law, its intent, and their rights.

Sometimes, bureaucracies simply don't want to deal with radical solutions, no matter how effective they may be. They may see it more as a state's rights issue than as a child welfare issue. One of the authors of this book was told the following in 1986 (six years after passage) about PL 96–272 by a high-ranking DHS official in a midwestern state: "This state will come into compliance with this IV-E law when I say so—not when the feds say so."

THE FINAL ROADBLOCK?

Today, technically, all financial roadblocks to special needs adoption have been removed. If the law is applied correctly, adoptive parents should be reimbursed for their expenses relating to the special needs adoption process and legal finalization. They should be able to access a generous tax credit for those expenses not reimbursed by the state. They should receive Medicaid for their child or sibling group and extraordinary medical expenses assistance until the child is grown. They should be able to access, if they want to, monthly subsidies to help with the cost of raising the child and dealing with the extra expenses that result from the special needs. They should be able to obtain a myriad of extra service subsidies (under Title XX and various state laws) that vary from state to state, such as respite care, personal computers when medically needed, clothing allowances, residential treatment, medical mileage, and more.

But it's not happening, yet. The few families who can say they are fully aware of their rights, and the programs for which their children qualify, are few and far between. In spite of federal mandates requiring the states to "promote the program" by telling parents what is available to help their children, states do a poor job, overall, of letting families know. One state, for example, recently began distributing a pamphlet to every adopting family that offers a general outline of the assistance program. The pamphlet has far too little information and even some inaccuracies, but it is actually an improvement. For years, this same state erroneously insisted that the attorneys who finalize adoptions, not the state adoption unit, were responsible to inform parents of their rights.

The new roadblock, perhaps the final one, to achieving permanency for waiting U.S. children is the bureaucracy itself. The laws exist, but they are not fully understood even by the people charged with carrying them out. Most state politicians don't understand the problem of waiting children or the research behind the current solutions. Social workers and supervisors rarely receive adequate training or ongoing training. And ongoing training is just as important as initial training, because PL 96–272 is always being misinterpreted by bureaucratic bodies and then clarified through a series of government documents known as PIQs (Policy Interpretation Questions).

The real-life and very recent case of Jim (not his real name) is just one example of this new roadblock. It is not an uncommon scenario.

Jim was adopted in 1998 in the capital city of a central region state from the county office that places more children into adoptive homes than any other office in the state. This is the county that has access to the most up-to-date information, the best training, and the best technology in the state.

Jim is almost six years old, developmentally delayed, and has a skin condition requiring frequent attention. He came into foster care at age three after being neglected and abused. Working closely with the courts, the state terminated parental rights when it became clear there were no biological relatives willing to care or capable of caring for Jim.

The foster family could have but decided not to adopt Jim, so a suitable family was found from among a pool of homestudies in the county office. A single parent named Jean with a great deal of experience with developmental delays was chosen to adopt Jim. After a series of getting-acquainted visits, Jim moved in, and the adoption progressed well.

When the busy social worker found time to negotiate the adoption assistance contract, she brought it out to the adoptive mom's home. The social worker offered Jean the "maximum amount for Jim's needs," the same terms that Jim's foster family had been given: $320 per month in adoption assistance and a Medicaid card. The contract carried that day's date, even though Jim had actually moved into Jean's home six weeks before. Jean was told that this contract was the most the state could do, under current law.

But Jean knew better. She had belonged to a special needs adoption support group and had educated herself about what was available and about the costs she would have taking care of Jim. She had seen copies of state policy on adoption assistance contracts, the same policy social workers had access to, but which adoptive parents rarely got to see.

Jean knew she had to advocate because Jim's needs would make him an expensive child to raise, and she knew that federal law requires the states to negotiate with parents. Jean knew that Jim qualified for a higher level of payments, up to $520 a month for a child in his age range. She asked for $520 per month, a Medicaid card, and a retroactive contract dated the day Jim moved in.

The experienced worker was stunned. She'd never heard of a child in Jim's age group accessing more than $320 per month or obtaining back payments to the date of move-in. Jean provided her with copies of the state's own charts describing "specialized" rates for children with certain serious disabilities. She had circled those parts of the policy that she believed qualified Jim for the $200 additional payment (for a total of $520). She also circled the state's own policy that defined the placement date as the date the child moves into his adoptive home and out of his foster home.

The worker called twice over the next week to tell her that her request had been denied by the supervisor and the supervisor's supervisor. Jean asked for a fair hearing on her case, but that step proved unnecessary. A closer examination of state policy and Jim's documented special needs by several supervisors showed that Jim did indeed qualify for the specialized rate and that it was within policy to backdate payments to the date of the child's actual arrival in the adoptive home.

Jean received everything she asked for, and she was able to meet Jim's needs more fully with the higher payment. The social worker, who had never received training about specialized rates, was grateful for the learning experience and was able to help other families in her caseload apply for specialized funds.

It was a classic win-win situation, but it wouldn't have happened without Jean's advocacy skills. She had to be persistent, well read, and patient. She had to assume that she would need to advocate for her child, even in the most experienced DHS office in the state, and she had to assume she would be turned down—at first.

HOW CAN I TELL IF MY CHILD IS IV-E ELIGIBLE?

Only adopted children with special needs who meet the Title IV-E criteria can receive federal adoption assistance under PL 96-272. For those adopted children who do not meet all IV-E criteria, state subsidies may be available, but the rules and requirements are different from state to state.

How do you know if your child is IV-E eligible? If your social worker says so, ask for a written statement to that effect or for a copy of the child's IV-E eligibility form to be sure there is no mistake about this. More than one parent has lost benefits under a state subsidy contract that they had believed was a federal IV-E contract. A IV-E contract is more reliable than a state subsidy contract because parents have more rights and safeguards in place under the federal law. The federal laws have no control over state subsidy contracts. For example, in some states, an individual state subsidy can be lowered without the agreement of the adoptive parents, whereas a negotiated federal subsidy amount cannot be lowered without the parents' permission.

If your social worker isn't sure or says your child is not IV-E eligible, be sure this is so. Sadly, some children are erroneously denied IV-E eligibility because the person or persons who make such determinations are not well trained in an understanding of PL 96-272. In fact, erroneous determinations are so common that there is a PIQ called PIQ 92-02 that outlines how families who think their children should have been given IV-E eligibility can go back and seek such a designation, along with retroactive subsidy payments. Just as you might be advised to seek a second opinion in serious medical matters, so should you seek another opinion when your child with special needs is denied IV-E eligibility.

THREE IV-E REQUIREMENTS

The requirements for IV-E only sound complex and obtuse until the individual elements are understood. The requirements are actually very inclusive of children with special needs when the law is applied according to its word, intent, purpose, and scope. In simplest terms, a child must meet three tests in order to be IV-E eligible for adoption assistance:

- he or she must have been AFDC-(Aid to Families with Dependent Children) eligible in the birth home *or* SSI Supplemental Security Income eligible *or* IV-E foster care eligible *and*
- he or she must have special need risk factors *or* a special need *and*
- he or she must have entered the system through a voluntary placement, if the state plan allows that, *or* through a judicially determined removal from the home of a relative.

In other words, it is not enough for a child to have special needs or special needs risk factors. Let's look at each requirement more carefully.

For purposes of IV-E eligibility, there are three doors to IV-E Adoption Assistance: SSI (the disability door), AFDC (the poverty/deprived door), or IV-E foster care eligibility (the foster care door). Although children need only enter through one door, many children are IV-E adoption-assistance eligible through two or even all three doors.

The Disability Door

Supplemental Security Income (SSI) is a monthly payment made to children and adults who have serious disabilities, such as mental retardation, cerebral palsy, blindness, or mental illness. Unlike adoption assistance, SSI is means-tested assistance, tied to the income of the child before adoption finalization and to the income of the adoptive parents after finalization. For this reason, most parents switch their children at adoption from SSI to the nonmeans-tested Adoption Assistance Payments (AAP). But what matters for IV-E eligibility is SSI eligibility. The child does not have to receive SSI to be SSI-eligible. The child only needs to have an SSI "award letter."

If a child meets the SSI disability standards, then he or she is virtually certain to meet the definition of special needs. This SSI path to eligibility for Title IV-E adoption assistance does not require placement for adoption by an agency, although it may be very difficult to obtain subsidies for children who were never in agency custody. The question and answer section in Chapter 9, dealing with administrative hearings, and the appendix section, addressing PIQ 87-05, provide additional discussion of SSI, agency involvement, and federal adoption assistance.

The Poverty/Deprived Door

The second door is often used by children who, because of placement through private adoption agencies, were never eligible for IV-E foster care. Those children using this door have special needs or risk factors but do not qualify as SSI-eligible. The children come from birth homes where the birth mother or birth parents or relative caretaker were receiving public assistance such as AFDC or TANF. They also come from homes where, due to poverty, the birth parent or relative caretaker was eligible for public assistance, whether or not any assistance was ever applied for or received. This includes unemployed birth mothers, for example, and birth mothers who receive no support from the birth fathers or who cannot identify the birth father. The legal term for such children is *deprived*. A child is also considered deprived in most states as soon as the birth parents' rights have been legally relinquished or terminated. Children also are deprived when their birth parents have abandoned them, refuse to support them, or have died.

The Foster Care Door

The third door is designed to offer children who are in agency custody a continuum of care. The thinking is that if a child in state agency custody qualifies for the IV-E foster care maintenance program he or she will already have met the AFDC (or TANF) relatedness requirement and the judicial determination that the child's placement was in his or her best interest. Satisfying the special needs definition is the only remaining requirement for IV-E adoption assistance.

Sometimes, the only door for a child is the IV-E foster care door. In rare cases, a child will be erroneously denied IV-E foster care eligibility and then, as a consequence, erroneously denied IV-E adoption assistance eligibility too. In such cases, parents can use PIQ 92-02 to go back and obtain IV-E status for their child even though foster care FFP (Federal Financial Participation or federal matching funds) was never obtained by the state.

There are PIQs that support children's rights in this regard. PIQ 85-06 states that a child should not suffer for a bureaucracy's mistake. In other words, if a state fails to follow the rules for accessing foster care FFP, the state may lose some FFP funding, but the child may not be deprived of his or her IV-E eligibility. Similarly, PIQ 85-07 says that the child's eligibility may not be denied because the birth parents make a paperwork error or omission or fail to cooperate with the agency in some way.

SPECIAL NEEDS

Earlier in this chapter, we defined *special needs*. The important point to remember here is that some children will be erroneously labeled nonspecial needs when, in fact, they do qualify as children with special needs. Not all children with special needs come from sibling groups or have disabilities. Some children with special needs will qualify on race alone or on age or, especially in the case of healthy-looking infants, due to "risk factors."

Risk factors include anything that puts an otherwise normal-appearing infant or child at risk of having unseen disabilities or of developing special needs later on, such as

- genetic risk factors for mental, physical, or learning disabilities
- prenatal exposure to drugs or harsh chemicals
- lack of prenatal care
- rape conception
- unknown paternity
- maternal gestational disease
- difficult or dangerous birth
- low Apgar scores
- abuse
- neglect
- multiple foster home placements
- and more

How many risk factors or which ones will allow for a determination of the presence of special needs is a subjective decision. If at least one risk factor is present, adoptive parents can pursue a special needs determination.

In one case, a lie was used to determine a risk factor. A healthy, white adopted infant with no risk factors was later found to be HIV positive. This was near the beginning of the AIDS epidemic when screenings were not nearly as common as they are today. The HIV status was discovered accidentally during a routine blood test. The birth mother had lied about her own HIV status, fearing that her baby would not be adopted if she told the truth.

The adoptive parents requested an adoption assistance contract. In this case, the HIV status was the child's special need, but under state law, the parents needed to prove a risk factor predating the blood test in order to access reimbursement for their child's earliest medical expenses. They could have argued that, known or not, the child had always been HIV positive and, hence, had always had a special need, but this argument proved unnecessary. The risk factor in this case was the admitted deception of the birth mother, which resulted in "erroneous health information" and serious health risks for the infant.

If a parent believes his or her child qualifies as a child with special needs, but is denied this determination by the agency, that parent should seek the advice of other adoptive parents, perhaps through an adoptive parent support group. Parents may appeal agency decisions by requesting an administrative hearing. Hearings are discussed in detail in Chapters 9, 10, and 11. Parents of such children have a right to a fair hearing to try and prove that their child is a child with special needs.

LEGAL STATUS

Once the state agrees that a child has special needs, and the child can show eligibility through one of the three doors described above, all that remains is to determine the child's legal status. This will be discussed throughout the book, but put simply, a IV-E eligible child must be either voluntarily placed or have his or her legal status determined in a court of law by a judge. Although few do, all states can take the option of excluding voluntarily placed children from their state IV-E plan, but no state can opt to exclude "judicially removed children."

A voluntarily placed child is one who has been placed into foster care voluntarily by his or her birth parents under the terms of a voluntary placement agreement and with the goal of going back home eventually. When the goal cannot be reached, and the child becomes a waiting child in need of an adoptive placement, a court becomes involved. In other cases, children go into foster care without a voluntary placement agreement and the birth parents relinquish their rights immediately. If the court and a judge become involved within six months of the child going into foster care, the requirements of IV-E have been met. This rule is designed to stop "foster care drift."

FFP AND AAP: TWO IMPORTANT ACRONYMS

Keep in mind as you read further that there is a difference between foster care FFP, adoption FFP, and adoption AAP.

Federal Financial Participation or FFP is matching funds of fifty to eighty cents on the dollar given to the states by the federal government for IV-E foster care and IV-E adoption assistance. Foster care FFP helps the states but makes no financial difference in the lives of foster parents who receive board payments from the agency whether or not their foster children are IV-E eligible.

Adoption subsidy, or AAP, is available only to adoptive parents of a child with special needs. The two types of AAPs are IV-E (or federal) AAP and state AAP. IV-E AAP is subject to FFP. The states will get some of this money back, most of it in fact.

State subsidies, or state AAP, are sometimes paid to adoptive parents of a child with special needs who are not IV-E eligible. Since there is no FFP involved with state AAP, states can make their own rules about state AAP.

CONCLUSION

This is a simple overview of the IV-E requirements. The entire federal law can be found in Part III. However, it can be said in general that once a child is determined to have a special need, *and* is determined to be SSI or AFDC or IV-E foster care eligible, *and* is voluntarily placed or relinquished according to the requirements of PL 96-272, then that child is a IV-E eligible child, *and should* have an adoption assistance contract (before finalization, if possible). Any state receiving IV-E FFP must follow these rules, and all fifty states now access IV-E FFP funds.

Special needs adoption benefits society by maximizing the potential of children without families to grow up and become productive. Special needs adoption is good for children and good for the nation.

Over the last fifty years, major roadblocks to special needs adoption have been removed. Societal attitudes about the adoptability of all children have changed. Eligibility requirements have eased for adults wishing to give waiting children a home. Support groups have sprung up. Photolistings, matching parties, TV profiles, and similar tools have brought individual waiting children to the attention of the nation. Laws have been passed making special needs adoption affordable and the costs of raising the children much more manageable.

What needs to be addressed is the remaining roadblock created by a state child welfare and adoption bureaucracy that often hinders parents instead of helping them. Parents must learn to advocate for themselves, their adopted children, and their whole families. If parents know how to advocate, and what to advocate for, they can adopt children who need families and keep their financial health, too. They can participate in fair hearings and appeals without fear.

No one should be expected to sacrifice his or her standard of living or to gamble with poverty or bankruptcy to help one of society's waiting children.

RECOMMENDATIONS

In 1998, Jeanette Wiedemeier Bower, M.P.A., of NACAC, made two important recommendations in her publication entitled *Achieving Permanence for Every Child: The Effective Use of Adoption Subsidies*: "Child welfare systems need to encourage the use of subsidies in the placement of children with special needs," and "Front-line workers need to offer both prospective foster and adoptive parents more information and encouragement about subsidies."

It sounds simple enough, but it hasn't happened yet, and PL 96–272 is almost twenty years old. Until subsidies are well used and training regarding subsidies is adequate, it is up to the parents to educate themselves and empower themselves. Becoming advocates, accessing support services, and working within the system, including the use of the fair hearing process and the courts, are the best current alternatives.

2

Foster Care and Adoption Assistance Rates

Poor fellow, he suffers from files.

—Aneurin Bevan (1897–1960)

PRACTICES IN NEED OF A PHILOSOPHY

What adoption assistance rate should I or can I negotiate for my child or children? This is a common question. Basically, there is a ceiling above which most parents will not be able to negotiate because the state will be unable to access matching funds above that maximum. The key is to discover what the ceiling actually is for a child with a certain type of disability. This is easier said than done.

As will be explained in greater detail in the following chapters, a state may have several different rate structures for children with mild, moderate, and severe disabilities but may only make information available to adoptive parents about the lowest tier of rates. One of the first things prospective adoptive parents of children with special needs should know is often the last thing they learn: There is an important federal and state connection between foster care payment rates and adoption assistance rates. Understand this connection, and what the foster care rate schedules include, and you have begun to answer the question asked at the beginning of this chapter.

Adoptive parents should be aware of the family foster care payment rates for their state and county when negotiating an adoption assistance agreement with an agency, because adoption subsidy rates usually reflect the foster care rates. States are not legally required to pay adoption assistance at the same level as family foster care rates, but federal reimbursement (FFP) is available to states that do. Foster care payment schedules are based on the severity of a child's needs and the level of care required. Knowledge of foster care payment provides no gurantees, but it may help an adoptive parent to set a target figure for adoption assistance by identifying a level of foster care that fits his or her own child's situation.

Suppose that Steven, a seven-year-old, exhibits severe autism. By learning that children Steven's age with problems like his receive $900 per month in specialized foster care payments, an adoptive parent can establish $900 as a target amount in negotiating an adoption assistance agreement. Agencies may not volunteer foster care payment schedules, so adoptive parents should ask for them. If the local agency refuses, the parents should contact the legal services section in the state agency that is responsible for adoption. Foster care rates are public information and should therefore be available on request.

A survey conducted by the NACAC compared 1996 adoption assistance payment rates with average foster care rates in each state for children ages two, nine, and sixteen. The foster care data were compiled by the American Public Welfare Association (APWA).

The foster care figures represented regular rates and did not include specialized payments for children with significant medical or emotional problems. The adoption assistance payments were also taken from regular as opposed to "special" payment schedules. As such, they represented the maximum payment level that the individual states offered families adopting a child in a particular age group who was not considered to have severe or special care needs. States might attempt to negotiate a lower amount, but as a general rule, parents could expect the state to agree to the maximum regular rate if the parents requested it.

The comparison revealed an interesting, if not altogether clear picture. The most obvious feature of basic foster care payment rates and regular adoption assistance payment schedules was their variation from state to state.

Average foster care rates in the country as whole were higher than regular payment schedules for adoption assistance. (United States averages: Foster care for two-year-olds, $356; for nine-year-olds, $373; for sixteen-year-olds, $431. Adoption assistance for two-year-olds, $342; for nine-year-olds, $363; for sixteen-year-olds, $419.)

- In twenty-four states, adoption assistance payment schedules matched regular foster care rates.
- In eighteen states and the District of Columbia, foster cares rates were higher than adoption assistance payment schedules.

- Adoption assistance payment schedules appeared to be higher than regular foster care payments in seven states, even though federal funding is only available up to family foster care rate for an individual child.

- In most states, regular foster care payment rates and adoption assistance schedules lagged behind the United States Department of Agriculture's (USDA) estimated expenditures for raising a child in 1996, including those of single parents and two-parent families with modest incomes of $34,000 per year or less.

ADOPTION ASSISTANCE PAYMENTS

Foster care payment rates are set by individual states or counties. According to federal policy, adoption assistance payments are to be negotiated, but in reality they also tend to be derived from payment schedules established by individual states. Federal law states only that once a child is deemed eligible for the program, the amount of adoption assistance is to be determined by written agreement between the family and public agency based on a consideration of the child's needs and family's circumstances.

States may not employ income means tests to mandate the level of adoption assistance payments. In addition, federal policy interpretations, such as PIQ 90-02, clearly anticipate a negotiation process in which the child's background, anticipated needs, and the family's overall situation are the subject of a constructive dialogue.

Unfortunately, there are few guidelines for customizing adoption assistance agreements as individually negotiated family support plans and states generally fall back on payment categories based on such factors as the child's needs and the severity of the child's medical, emotional, or developmental problems. Many states have a "standard" or "regular" payment category with age gradations and one or two "special" payment categories for children with more serious problems.

The payment schedules usually form the context of negotiations between the parents and the agency. Let us suppose, for instance, that the state has two payment schedules, one for "regular" children with special needs and one for "severe" special needs. A family is planning to adopt a six-year-old child. The regular adoption assistance payment rate for a six-year-old child with special needs is a maximum of $385 per month. The parents present evidence that their child has been diagnosed with a reactive attachment disorder and contend that the regular rate is inadequate to meet the child's anticipated care needs. The agency agrees that the child fits into a severe special needs category and offers the adoptive family $600 per month, which is the maximum payment on the rate schedule for a child of six.

Federal funding regulations further limit the ability of parents to negotiate a completely customized plan of support. Title IV-E adoption assistance is funded by federal dollars but requires a nonfederal match. The rate of FFP in a state's IV-E program is the same as the FFP in the state's Medicaid program. The federal share ranges from lows of 50 percent to highs of 80 percent. In many states, the federal share is around 60 percent of the cost of adoption assistance payments.

Federal law specifies that FFP is available for adoption assistance payments up to the rate a child would receive were he or she in a family foster home rather than an adoptive placement. For example, suppose a child with severe emotional problems were placed in a special foster home where the caregivers were paid $1,500 per month for his care. If the child is placed in an adoptive home and qualifies for Title IV-E adoption assistance, FFP would be available for a monthly adoption assistance payment of up to $1,500. In Ohio, the FFP for a $1,500 monthly adoption assistance payment would be approximately $900. The state and county would be responsible for the remaining $600.

Federal funding limits and the absence of clear guidelines for assessing the "needs of the child and the circumstances of the family" result in states' reliance on payment schedules. Foster care rates usually function as de facto ceilings on adoption assistance payments. The maximum figure in the rate schedule is the normal payment. Suppose that the regular adoption assistance schedule in state A is as follows: $345 for ages zero to five, $370 for ages six to twelve, and $460 for ages thirteen to eighteen. A family adopting a three-year-old child might expect the agency to offer an adoption assistance payment of $345 per month, unless evidence is presented that the child meets the state's severe special needs category. The agency could offer less, but once again in the absence of clear guidelines about how to assess a child's needs or a family's circumstances, it is somewhat difficult to argue that the Smith family should be treated any differently than the Jones family.

Adoptive parents may explore service subsidies in addition to adoption assistance payments as part of an overall plan of support. Most states have some form of program that pays for services that are not covered by health insurance or Medicaid. Service subsidies are discussed in Chapter 3. By becoming well informed, families have the opportunity to help design a somewhat individualized postadoptive support plan for their child. Federal funding patterns and the difficulty of translating general terms, such as family circumstances, into amounts of monthly support make it difficult for families to negotiate payments above specified rate schedules.

Foster care rates function as payment ceilings for adoption subsidy programs in most states. The NACAC survey (see Table 2.1) found that rate schedules for regular adoption assistance payments were matched with regular foster care rates in twenty-two states. Foster care rates exceeded adoption assistance payment schedules in nineteen states and the District of Columbia (see Table 2.2).

Surprisingly, adoption assistance rate schedules (see Table 2.3) appear to

Table 2.1
States Where Regular (Not Specialized) Adoption Assistance Payment Schedules Were Matched with Regular Foster Care Rates, 1996 (Amounts are subject to change)

	Foster Care				Adoption Assistance		
State	*Age 2*	*Age 9*	*Age 16*	*State*	*Age 2*	*Age 9*	*Age 16*
Alabama	$205	$229	$241	Alabama	$205	$229	$241
California	$345	$400	$484	California	$345	$400	$484
Connecticut	$567	$586	$637	Connecticut	$567	$586	$637
Florida	$296	$296	$372	Florida	$296	$296	$372
Hawaii	$529	$529	$529	Hawaii	$529	$529	$529
Idaho	$228	$250	$358	Idaho	$228	$250	$358
Iowa	$375	$397	$460	Iowa	$375	$397	$460
Kansas	$305	$305	$386	Kansas	$305	$305	$386
Missouri	$419	$419	$531	Missouri	$419	$419	$531
Mississippi	$225	$225	$300	Mississippi	$225	$225	$300
Nevada	$304	$304	$365	Nevada	$304	$304	$365
New Mexico	$308	$341	$367	New Mexico	$308	$341	$367
North Carolina	$315	$365	$415	North Carolina	$315	$365	$415
Oklahoma	$300	$360	$420	Oklahoma	$300	$360	$420
Oregon	$315	$327	$404	Oregon	$315	$327	$404
South Carolina	$212	$239	$305	South Carolina	$212	$239	$305
Tennessee	$336	$262	$385	Tennessee	$336	$262	$385
Texas	$482	$482	$482	Texas	$482	$482	$482
Utah	$319	$319	$319	Utah	$319	$319	$319
Vermont	$416	$416	$504	Vermont	$416	$416	$504
Virginia	$262	$307	$388	Virginia	$262	$307	$388
Washington	$304	$374	$442	Washington	$304	$374	$442
West Virginia	$400	$400	$400	West Virginia	$400	$400	$400
Wisconsin	$282	$307	$365	Wisconsin	$282	$307	$365

Source: APWA.   *Source:* NACAC.

be higher than regular foster care rates in eight states. These rates represent maximum payments for "regular" children with special needs in particular age categories. States are generally reluctant to make adoption assistance payments that would not be eligible for FFP. Perhaps officials in these seven states agree to the maximum adoption assistance on certain rare occasions. It is highly unlikely that adoption assistance payment exceeds foster care rates on a routine basis.

Table 2.2
States Where Regular Foster Care Rates Exceeded Regular Adoption Assistance Payment Schedules (1996)

	Foster Care				Adoption Assistance		
State	Age 2	Age 9	Age 16	State	Age 2	Age 9	Age 16
Arizona	$403	$392	$471	Arizona	$350	$350	$406
Arkansas	$400	$425	$475	Arkansas	$300	$325	$375
Colorado	$361	$361	$430	Colorado	$293	$293	$352
Delaware	$350	$350	$450	Delaware	$342	$342	$440
D.C.	$437	$437	$526	D.C.	$431	$431	$519
Georgia	$325	$325	$325	Georgia	$240	$240	$240
Illinois	$343	$382	$415	Illinois	$297	$333	$365
Indiana	$405	$462	$518	Indiana	$304	$347	$389
Louisiana	$348	$331	$364	Louisiana	$238	$264	$291
Massachusetts	$415	$415	$493	Massachusetts	$410	$410	$486
Minnesota	$365	$365	$433	Minnesota	$247	$277	$337
Montana	$345	$345	$435	Montana	$330	$330	$419
Nebraska	$326	$393	$463	Nebraska	$222	$291	$351
New Jersey	$288	$339	$361	New Jersey	$280	$297	$350
North Dakota	$308	$349	$456	North Dakota	$295	$334	$437
Ohio	$544	$544	$544	Ohio	$250	$250	$250
Rhode Island	$274	$274	$335	Rhode Island	$252	$252	$308
South Dakota	$353	$353	$424	South Dakota	$266	$327	$393
Wyoming	$400	$400	$400	Wyoming	$399	$399	$399

Source: APWA.   *Source:* NACAC.

ADOPTION ASSISTANCE FOSTER CARE RATES AND THE COST OF RAISING A CHILD

Does adoption assistance fully reimburse the typical family for the expenses of raising a child with special needs? No, but it helps enough to make a significant and positive difference. The USDA has provided estimates on the cost of raising a child since 1960. The 1996 report divided families into four categories: three two-parent categories based on annual gross income and one single-parent category. Estimated expenditures include housing, transportation, clothing, health care, child care/education, and miscellaneous expenses. Table 2.4 replicates the USDA estimates of total annual expenditures based on six different age groups.

The USDA figures indicate that the cost of raising a child exceeds the regular foster care rates and adoption assistance payment schedules in most states. Specifically,

Table 2.3
States Where Regular Adoption Assistance Payment Schedules Exceeded Regular Foster Care Rates (1996)

	Foster Care				Adoption Assistance		
State	*Age 2*	*Age 9*	*Age 16*	*State*	*Age 2*	*Age 9*	*Age 16*
Alaska	$588	$523	$621	Alaska	$580	$700	$820
Kentucky	$300	$323	$368	Kentucky	$304	$327	$373
Maine	$325	$334	$389	Maine	$371	$379	$429
Maryland	$535	$535	$550	Maryland	$650	$650	$650
Michigan	$365	$365	$433	Michigan	$383	$383	$454
New Hampshire	$314	$342	$404	New Hampshire	$472	$514	$606
New York	$367	$441	$510	New York	$457	$494	$600
New York City	$401	$473	$547	New York City	$492	$537	$639

Source: APWA.   *Source:* NACAC.

- The 1996 USDA estimates for raising a child in families with incomes of $34,000 per year or less exceeded average foster care rates for the country as a whole in 1996. (USDA: Ages 0 to 2, $398; Ages 9 to 11, $472; Ages 15 to 17, $569. Foster Care Rates: Age 2, $356; Age 9, $372; Age 16, $431)

- The 1996 USDA estimates for raising a child in a single-parent family exceeded average foster care payment rates for the country as a whole in 1996. (USDA: Ages 0 to 2, $398; Ages 9 to 11, $472; Ages 15 to 17, $569. Foster Care Rates: Age 2, $356; Age 9, $372; Age 16, $431)

- The 1996 USDA estimates for raising a child in families with incomes of $34,000 per year or less exceeded adoption assistance payment schedules for the country as a whole in 1996. (USDA: Ages 0 to 2, $473; Ages 9 to 11, $562; Ages 15 to 17, $562. Adoption Assistance Rates: Age 2, $342; Age 9, $363; Age 16, $419)

- The 1996 USDA estimates for raising a child in a single parent family exceeded average adoption assistance payment rates for the country as a whole in 1996. (USDA: Ages 0 to 2, $398; Ages 9 to 11, $472; Ages 15 to 17, $562. Adoption Assistance Rates: Age 2, $342; Age 9, $363; Age 16, $419)

- Only a few states had foster care payment rates in any age category that exceed the USDA's estimates of the cost of raising a child for two parents or families with modest incomes or single parents.

CONCLUSIONS

In most instances, adoption assistance payments and foster care payment are quite modest and do not keep pace with the estimated expenses of raising a child for even families with relatively low incomes.

The USDA figures in Table 2.5 represent the estimated cost of raising an average child. The purpose of adoption assistance is to help parents sustain a child with special needs in a new family. It is reasonable to assume that

Table 2.4
USDA Estimated Expenditures on Children by Families, 1996 by Year and by
Month

Age of Child	2-Parent Family Income Less Than $34,700	2-Parent Family Income $34,700–$58,300	2-Parent Family Income over $58,300	Single-Parent Family
0–2	$5,670 yr. $473 month	$7,860 yr. $655 month	$11,680 yr. $973 month	$4,770 yr. $398 month
3–5	$5,780 yr. $482 month	$8,060 yr. $672 month	$11,910 yr. $993 month	$5,360 yr. $447 month
6–8	$5,900 yr. $492 month	$8,130 yr. $678 month	$11,870 yr. $989 month	$6,060 yr. $505 month
9–11	$5,940 yr. $562 month	$8,100 yr. $675 month	$11,790 yr. $983 month	$5,660 yr. $472 month
12–14	$6,740 yr. $554 month	$8,830 yr. $735 month	$12,620 yr. $1,052 month	$6,120 yr. $510 month
15–17	$6,650 yr. $554 month	$8,960 yr. $746 month	$12,930 yr. $1,078 month	$6,830 yr. $569 month

the average cost of raising children with special needs is considerably
greater than that of raising children with no significant medical or emotional problems.

Comparisons of USDA estimates with 1996 adoption assistance payment
schedules point out the financial as well as the emotional investment that
adoptive parents are willing to make. The figures strengthen the impression
of adoptive parents as community assets.

In some states, the discrepancy between foster care rates and adoption
assistance payment schedules is sizable. At a time when adoptions by foster
parents account for a clear majority of special needs adoptions, these policies place many prospective adopters in a difficult situation. Foster parents
wishing to adopt the child in their care may face a sizable drop in support
that reduces their ability to meet the child's service needs. Gaps between
foster care rates and adoption assistance payment schedules were particularly glaring in the following states:

The APWA figures were based on foster care payment rates reported by
the states themselves. APWA researchers felt that the reported foster care
rates appeared to be too high.

Foster care involves agency supervision, periodic case reviews, and judicial hearings that make it more expensive than adoption. A 1993 study
by Westat Corporation concluded that "adoption assistance clearly represents a substantial savings over foster care." The Westat report estimated
that "federal and state governments will save a total of approximately $1.6
billion in connection with a group of 40,700 children adopted with assis-

Table 2.5

Gaps Between Regular Foster Care Rates and Regular Adoption Assistance Payment Schedules (1996)

	Foster Care				Adoption Assistance		
State	*Age 2*	*Age 9*	*Age 16*	*State*	*Age 2*	*Age 9*	*Age 16*
Arizona	$403	$392	$471	Arizona	$350	$350	$406
Arkansas	$400	$425	$475	Arkansas	$300	$325	$375
Colorado	$361	$361	$430	Colorado	$293	$293	$352
Georgia	$325	$325	$325	Georgia	$240	$240	$240
Illinois	$343	$382	$415	Illinois	$297	$333	$365
Indiana	$405	$462	$518	Indiana	$304	$347	$389
Louisiana	$348	$331	$364	Louisiana	$238	$264	$291
Minnesota	$365	$365	$433	Minnesota	$247	$277	$337
Nebraska	$326	$393	$463	Nebraska	$222	$291	$351
Ohio	$544	$544	$544	Ohio	$250	$250	$250
South Dakota	$353	$353	$424	South Dakota	$266	$327	$393

Source: APWA.   *Source:* NACAC.

tance during the 1983–1987 period." The savings did not include disparities between foster care support and adoption assistance payments but considered "only the differences in administrative costs between foster care and adoption assistance up to the time the children reach age 18 and would normally be discharged from foster care" (Sedlak & Broadhurst, 1993).

A FUNDAMENTAL AND NEGLECTED ISSUE

The comparison of regular foster care and regular adoption assistance rates does not address levels of support for families who adopt children with severe medical or emotional problems, which is an issue of great concern. Foster parents can rely on support from the child welfare system if a child in their home becomes extremely disruptive or dangerous to other residents. Adoptive parents do not have the same assurances. The question of the state's commitment to an adoptive family is a crucial one precisely because parents who adopt children with histories of sexual abuse or prolonged neglect face an unknown future. Through the application of love, patience, and skill, parents are often able to mitigate the worst effects of a child's early trauma. But in cases where, despite their best efforts, the child preys on younger siblings or commits impulsive antisocial acts with no sign of remorse, the results can be catastrophic, emotionally and financially.

Beyond the obvious question of payment rates for adoption assistance lies the deeper issue of the social contract that exists between the state and the adoptive families it recruits to provide homes for its waiting children. What is the nature of the state's partnership with adoptive families? What support can adoptive families count on in times of severe crisis?

In spite of improvements in adoption assistance programs, this policy question has not been adequately addressed. Regulations that continue to require the completion of an adoption assistance agreement before the final decree of adoption place considerable pressure on families to cover every contingency that they can imagine. The state, for its part, is reluctant to make open-ended commitments to provide services for situations that might not occur. Astute parents negotiate as many provisions for future services as they are able, but in the end most families adopt with no clear understanding of the state's commitment to the success of their adoption should circumstances change for the worse.

State officials have difficulty understanding that people who are called to adopt children with serious problems are no strangers to uncertainty and personal sacrifice. If these parents wanted a smooth, uncomplicated ride, they would never consider becoming the parents of a traumatized child. What these adoptive parents want is what every family wants from their health coverage, some assurance that if things get tough and very expensive, their children will have access to necessary services. If the Adoption and Safe Families Act of 1997 is going to trigger more aggressive campaigns to recruit adoptive parents, the issue of the state's commitment to those families who raise society's homeless and mistreated children must be addressed.

RECOMMENDATIONS

The fact that so many adults experience a calling to adopt children with special needs is inspiring. It is high time that states begin to treat such families as the assets they are. At a minimum states should be required to match adoption assistance payment schedules with foster care payment rates as a condition for federal financial participation.

Given the fact that administrative costs make keeping a child in foster care more expensive than placing a child for adoption, states that are willing to raise adoption assistance payments above family foster care rates should be eligible for federal financial participation.

States should be required to keep their adoption assistance and foster care rates at or above the USDA's estimates for child rearing expenditures for two-parent families in the modest income category.

As part of their drive to secure permanent homes for waiting children, states should clarify their commitment to adoptive families over the long term. The adoption of severely traumatized children is often very rewarding, always challenging and fraught with uncertainty. The state's commitment to support the success of special needs adoptions must extend beyond the placement of the child and signing of an initial adoption assistance agreement.

SOME FINAL THOUGHTS TO BEAR IN MIND

The comparisons in this chapters are intended to provide readers with a frame of reference for assessing levels of support for adoption assistance. It is worth repeating that most states have higher specialized foster care and adoption assistance payment schedules in addition to the regular rates presented here and that rate amounts can change at any time. Parents should not hesitate to explore specialized payment rates in applying for adoption assistance.

The 1996 adoption assistance figures were used in this chapter because of the availability of foster care rates and USDA cost figures for the same year. NACAC has updated its state-by-state adoption assistance (subsidy) profiles to include 1998 payment rates in both regular and specialized categories. NACAC can be reached by phone at (800) 470–6665 or (651) 644-3036. Adoption subsidy profiles are also published on the organization's Web site at http://www.cyfc.umn.edu/Adoptinfo/nacac.html. Jeanette Wiedemeier Bower, NACAC's adoption assistance specialist, also can be contacted by E-mail at Wiedemeier@aol.com.

Table 2.6 shows the first or lowest tier of rates, usually called basic or regular rates.

Table 2.6
1996 Regular Foster Care and Adoption Assistance Payment Schedules, State by State

	Foster Care				Adoption Assistance		
State	*Age 2*	*Age 9*	*Age 16*	*State*	*Age 2*	*Age 9*	*Age 16*
Alabama	$205	$229	$241	Alabama	$205	$229	$241
Alaska	$588	$523	$621	Alaska	$580	$700	$820
Arizona	$403	$392	$471	Arizona	$350	$350	$406
Arkansas	$400	$425	$475	Arkansas	$300	$325	$375
California	$345	$400	$484	California	$345	$400	$484
Colorado	$361	$361	$430	Colorado	$293	$293	$352
Connecticut	$567	$486	$637	Connecticut	$567	$586	$637
Delaware	$350	$350	$450	Delaware	$342	$342	$440
D.C.	$437	$437	$526	D.C.	$431	$431	$519
Florida	$296	$296	$372	Florida	$296	$296	$372
Georgia	$325	$325	$325	Georgia	$240	$240	$240
Hawaii	$529	$529	$529	Hawaii	$529	$529	$529

Table 2.6 (continued)

	Foster Care				Adoption Assistance		
State	Age 2	Age 9	Age 16	State	Age 2	Age 9	Age 16
Idaho	$228	$250	$358	Idaho	$228	$250	$358
Illinois	$343	$382	$415	Illinois	$297	$333	$365
Indiana	$405	$462	$518	Indiana	$304	$347	$389
Iowa	$375	$397	$460	Iowa	$375	$397	$460
Kansas	$305	$305	$386	Kansas	$305	$305	$386
Kentucky	$300	$323	$368	Kentucky	$304	$327	$373
Louisiana	$348	$331	$364	Louisiana	$238	$264	$291
Maine	$325	$334	$389	Maine	$371	$379	$429
Maryland	$535	$535	$550	Maryland	$650	$650	$650
Massachusetts	$415	$415	$493	Massachusetts	$410	$410	$486
Michigan	$365	$365	$433	Michigan	$383	$383	$454
Minnesota	$365	$365	$433	Minnesota	$247	$277	$337
Missouri	$419	$419	$531	Missouri	$419	$419	$531
Mississippi	$225	$225	$300	Mississippi	$225	$225	$300
Montana	$345	$345	$435	Montana	$330	$330	$419
Nebraska	$326	$393	$463	Nebraska	$222	$291	$351
Nevada	$304	$304	$365	Nevada	$304	$304	$365
New Hampshire	$314	$342	$404	New Hampshire	$472	$514	$606
New Jersey	$288	$339	$361	New Jersey	$280	$297	$350
New Mexico	$308	$341	$367	New Mexico	$308	$341	$367
New York	$367	$441	$510	New York	$457	$494	$600
New York City	$401	$473	$547	New York City	$492	$537	$639
North Carolina	$315	$365	$415	North Carolina	$315	$365	$415
North Dakota	$308	$349	$456	North Dakota	$295	$334	$437
Ohio	$544	$544	$544	Ohio	$250	$250	$250
Oklahoma	$300	$360	$420	Oklahoma	$300	$360	$420
Oregon	$315	$327	$404	Oregon	$315	$327	$404
Pennsylvania	$321	$375	$482	Pennsylvania	N/A	N/A	N/A
Rhode Island	$274	$274	$335	Rhode Island	$252	$252	$308
South Carolina	$212	$239	$305	South Carolina	$212	$239	$305
South Dakota	$353	$353	$424	South Dakota	$266	$327	$393
Tennessee	$336	$262	$385	Tennessee	$336	$262	$385
Texas	$482	$482	$482	Texas	$482	$482	$482
Utah	$319	$319	$319	Utah	$319	$319	$319

Foster Care				Adoption Assistance			
State	*Age 2*	*Age 9*	*Age 16*	*State*	*Age 2*	*Age 9*	*Age 16*
Vermont	$416	$416	$504	Vermont	$416	$416	$504
Virginia	$262	$307	$388	Virginia	$262	$307	$388
Washington	$304	$374	$442	Washington	$304	$374	$442
West Virginia	$400	$400	$400	West Virginia	$400	$400	$400
Wisconsin	$282	$307	$365	Wisconsin	$282	$307	$365
Wyoming	$400	$400	$400	Wyoming	$400	$400	$400
Averages	$356	$373	$431	**Averages**	$342	$363	$419

Source: APWA.

Source: NACAC.

3

Special Service Subsidies:
Important Extras

God gives every bird his worm, but He does not throw it into the nest.
—P. D. James (b. 1920)

SERVICE SUBSIDIES

Adoption assistance is much more than a monthly check. It also includes service subsidies, financial assistance to pay for the cost of the adoption process, income tax breaks, and medical assistance. The last three types of assistance are discussed in Chapter 7. This chapter is devoted to service subsidies, an important resource for keeping families formed through adoption intact and functioning well.

Service subsidies include services such as respite care, day care, residential treatment, dental braces, counseling, medical mileage, extraordinary medical expenses, tutoring, speech and occupational therapy, clothing allowances, personal computers, and even items such as vitamins and software.

State subsidy profiles compiled by the NACAC indicate that forty-four states and the District of Columbia operate some form of state-funded service subsidy program. Instead of regular monthly payments, service subsidy programs generally pay for mental health, medical, and other services that are not covered by Medicaid or a family's private health insurance. Service subsidies can be combined with Title IV-E adoption assistance or a state-funded monthly payment subsidy to provide a more comprehensive plan of support.

In principle, service subsidies can be customized to fit the particular circumstances of the adoptive family. While service subsidies can be very helpful, adoptive parents should be aware of possible limitations.

Funding

Unlike IV-E and other entitlement programs, funding for service subsidies is finite. In short, when the money is spent, it's usually gone for the remainder of the state's fiscal year. Programs may cover a wide variety of services, but the state may restrict the amount of funding to individual families. Children, as a result, may be eligible for more services than the state is willing to pay for.

Adjusting Subsidy Agreements

Some states, such as Ohio and Minnesota, have postfinalization service subsidies that can be accessed as the need arises. Others apparently require that service needs be identified in the initial subsidy agreement in order to receive consideration. Predicting future problems, of course, is hardly an exact science in any family. It is particularly difficult in situations involving the adoption of an infant or very young child with a family history of mental illness, drug exposure, or other medical problems. Health insurance coverage for mental health is slowly improving but is still woefully inadequate to meet the needs of a child who develops truly serious problems.

Let us take the Glover family as an example. The Glovers adopted Eddie at the age of four. Because the birth mother used cocaine and alcohol during her pregnancy and left her infant son alone for long hours at a time, Eddie was considered at risk for possible emotional and developmental problems and on that basis was defined as a child with special needs. After conducting an eligibility review, the state agency determined that Eddie was eligible for Title IV-E adoption assistance. In addition to a monthly payment and Medicaid coverage, the Glovers also negotiated a service subsidy with the agency. The service subsidy agreement called for mental health services and respite care.

Eddie was not affectionate toward his parents and was given to bouts of rage expressed in violent tantrums. As he grew older, Eddie engaged in compulsive acts of stealing and destruction of the neighbors' property. When confronted with his misdeeds, he would tell blatant lies and show no signs of remorse. Eddie was a handsome child and the Glovers' pastor and adult friends found him charming in their brief encounters with him. The Glovers worried about Eddie and blamed themselves for their inability to overcome his traumatic infancy.

Things got progressively worse after Eddie entered school. He assaulted a younger child and stole constantly from the other students in the classroom. At home, he attempted and failed three times to kill the family dog and attacked his younger brother Billy with a knife.

The Glovers took Eddie to a psychotherapist. When additional records of Eddie's medical and social history were retrieved, the Glovers discovered that he had been in and out of five foster homes prior to his placement with them. Abuse was substantiated in one of the homes.

Because of Eddie's potential for violence, the Glovers feared for the safety of their youngest child. They hesitated to leave him alone and were becoming emotionally and physically exhausted. The therapist recommended an eight to ten week program of out-of-home care in a facility specializing in the treatment of children with emotional problems like Eddie's. After completing the residential phase, a treatment team would work intensively with the Glovers, the school, and other local agencies to ease Eddie's transition back into the community.

The program prescribed by the therapist was not covered by Medicaid. The Glovers' insurance policy covered only a small portion of the cost. The Glovers applied to the state for an increase in Eddie's adoption assistance payment. Federal reimbursement was available at sixty cents for an increase in the payment up to rate of support that would be available for Eddie in a family foster care setting. Raising the adoption assistance payment would help, but still leave several thousand dollars in bills, along with the task of paying for any psychotherapy that Eddie might need in the future.

The Glovers also sought assistance through Eddie's special service subsidy. The subsidy agreement, as noted earlier, called for mental health services and respite care. The agreement did not specify if mental health services included residential care and, more important, how much support the Glovers were entitled to receive.

Happily, a relatively small percentage of adoptive families face the kind of serious and expensive emotional problems encountered by the Glovers. When they do, however, they often encounter the same kind of uncertainty.

As a point of illustration, a surprising twenty-eight states in the NACAC survey reported that adoptive parents had some access to residential treatment. A closer look, however, reveals the obstacles and uncertainties that families often face in accessing these services.

Some states require that a public agency assume temporary legal custody as a condition for residential care. While providing some financial relief, this strategy often discourages parents from playing an active role in their children's treatment.

Other states rely on Medicaid to cover residential treatment cost. Medicaid reimbursement rates are relatively low and facilities with the most expertise in treating serious emotional problems afflicting adopted children may not be Medicaid providers.

Some states set dollar limits on service subsidies that fall far short of the cost of residential care. Some states appear to require that the special needs condition or service be specified in the initial adoption assistance agreement. This condition is particularly burdensome to families adopting infants or very young children whose future problems are very hard to predict.

A number of states indicate the possibility of covering residential care through their special service subsidy programs but do not reveal what applicants can count on in terms of the amount of support or the type of care that the state is willing to fund.

See Table 3.1 for a more detailed breakdown of states indicating that coverage for residential care is available to adoptive families.

Funding limits will continue to be an issue in special service subsidies, but parents can take some steps to become more effective advocates for their children. Think of state or federally funded payment subsidies and service subsidies as components of a good postadoption support plan. In some cases, higher payments can be negotiated in place of some funding for services or vice versa. The goal of the parents is to establish an adoption assistance agreement that best anticipates and covers their children's needs.

A Service Subsidy Checklist

The following are a few suggestions for parents to consider when exploring a special service subsidy:

- Find out if service subsidies can be initiated after finalization and what services can be obtained if an agreement was not signed before the final decree of adoption.

- Find out if it is advantageous to complete an agreement for a special service subsidy before a final decree of adoption.

- Even though subsidies can be amended at any time with the mutual consent of the parties, there is no guarantee that parents will receive the support that they need if it is not already specified. Try to define the service provisions as explicitly as possible in negotiating the initial agreement. If residential care, outpatient psychotherapy, or respite care are covered, try to list them on the agreement.

- Find out if the amount of support is open-ended. If it is, try to insert a clause to the effect that "X service will be provided as needed, as determined by a qualified provider in consultation with the adoptive parents." If the commitment is not open-ended, try to arrive at some agreement about how much support will be provided. A clause such as the following helps adoptive families know what they can count on: "X service will be provided up to X amount per year. Additional services will be covered if funding is available."

- In the initial agreement, try to address services that may be needed in the future based on risk factors in the child's background. Once again try to establish the level of support that will become available should certain needs arise.

- Hearing rights apply to state as well as to federal subsidies in most states. Find out how they apply to service subsidies.

Table 3.1
State Coverage of Residential Case As of September 1996

State	Possible Limitations/Conditions
Arizona	IV-E children covered by Medicaid; Mental health need should be identified in the initial agreement.
Colorado	The agency must assume custody as a condition for receiving services.
Connecticut	Parents apply to the state for "noncommitted treatment services"
Delaware	Parents may apply to the state's Division of Mental Health. Medical/psychological subsidy also provides up to $3,000 per year and may be used for residential care
D.C.	The special service subsidy can be used to pay for residential care. Parents must obtain a recommendation from a mental health provider and should look for a facility that accepts Medicaid or their health insurance.
Georgia	Families apply to a local social service agency that will work with local mental health providers. Parents apply for services through a postadoption "policy waiver."
Hawaii	Residential treatment is covered by federal Title XX funds, which may be limited.
Illinois	The state must assume custody as a condition for receiving services.
Indiana	Court intervention is required for parents to receive services
Kansas	Services are accessed through Medicaid. Residential care facilities are certified as Medicaid providers.
Kentucky	Families with adoption assistance agreements may be able to access "private care funds" to pay for residential treatment.
Massachusetts	Families contact the local department of social services to apply for regional treatment (RT). Medicaid pays for the placement.
Michigan	Residential treatment is covered by a separate Medical Subsidy agreement. Payment must be authorized prior to treatment, and authorization is time-limited.
Minnesota	The adoption assistance program does not reimburse for the cost of residential treatment. The local social service agency may not assess a parental fee based on the family's income. Monthly maintenance payments may be assessed to meet out home placement expenses.
New Mexico	Medicaid is used to cover costs for IV-E children. Non–IV-E children are covered by state subsidy funds at Medicaid rates.

Table 3.1 (continued)

State	Possible Limitations/Conditions
New York	In order to receive residential treatment, the child must be placed in the custody of the local child welfare agency by the family court.
North Dakota	Families must use facilities that are Medicaid providers.
Ohio	Families may receive a maximum of $20,000 per year to cover the cost of services including residential care.
Oregon	Residential care must be provided in a facility licensed by the mental health division in order for the costs to be covered under state's medical assistance (Medicaid) program.
Rhode Island	The state child welfare agency may pay for residential treatment after other sources of funding, such as private health insurance, has been utilized.
South Carolina	Most residential treatment is funded by Medicaid with the match provided by one of several state agencies with potential involvement in the case.
Tennessee	Residential treatment must be covered in the adoption assistance agreement.
Vermont	Adoption subsidy can be used to pay room and board costs. The Department of Mental Health pays therapeutic costs through Medicaid. The Department of Education covers the educational component of residential care. Families fill out an application to obtain a referral to the case review committee.
Virginia	"Special Service Payments" may be used to cover residential care if less restrictive alternatives have been considered.
Washington	The state provides funding to local offices of children and family services. State funds also fund services that facilitate the child's transition back home. Questions may be addressed to the state adoption office.
Wisconsin	There is no state special service subsidy program. Residential treatment is handled at the local level by county social service agencies.
Wyoming	In order to receive residential treatment, the child must be placed in the custody of the state department of family services by the court. In cases where a foster or group home is considered appropriate, families may enter into an agreement with DFS for a "voluntary placement agreement" with the Department of Family Services for 6 to 120 days. Not all counties will agree to voluntary placements. Some may insist on going through the court.

Source: NACAC.

THE QUALITY OF TREATMENT

Not all residential treatment programs and therapists are effective in treating reactive attachment disorder and other severe emotional problems that afflict some adopted children. Parents should carefully explore treatment options before deciding to place their child. One good starting point is ATTACh, a nonprofit organization committed to education, training, and advocacy for all parties interested in the attachment and bonding process. ATTACh can be reached at (703)914-3928 or fax (703)914–3929, P.O. Box 665, Annandale, VA 22003–0665.

There is much more information in Chapter 7 about negotiating all the types of adoption assistance, including monthly rates, service subsidies, adoption process expenses, tax breaks, medical assistance, and extraordinary medical assistance. Chapter 11 offers a detailed example of one family's negotiation process.

NACAC has updated its state subsidy profiles. Please consult the organization's Web site at http://www.cyfc.umn.edu/Adoptinfo/nacac.htm/ or contact the agency by telephone at (651) 644–3036. As noted in Chapter 2, subsidy specialist Jeanette Wiedemeier Bower may also be contacted by E-mail at Wiedemeier@aol.com.

4

Welcome to the Bureaucracy: Adoptive Parents and Agencies

> If you're going to sin, sin against God, not the bureaucracy; God will forgive you but the bureaucracy won't.
> —Hyman G. Rickover (1900–1986)

NEGATIVE EXPERIENCES

Many families report negative experiences with state and county agencies. Foster parents often live in fear that the public agency will place their foster child for adoption with another family, regardless of how long the child has lived in their home or the degree of emotional attachment that has been formed. Instead of looking for ways to assist adoptive families in crisis, agencies often direct their energies toward resisting the family's request for services.

THE ORGANIZATIONAL CULTURE OF CHILD WELFARE AGENCIES

The most plausible explanation for these frustrating situations appears to reside in a bureaucratic organizational culture that treats all families as dependent "clients" and emphasizes the agency's gatekeeper responsibilities above all else. In the traditional bureaucratic paradigm, the experiences of adoptive and foster parents are devalued in favor of the "expertise" of agency professionals. Parents' observations about their children's problems or service needs are not taken at face value but often viewed with skepticism. Instead of being afforded the benefit of the doubt, parents must often go to great lengths to demonstrate that their observations are valid. Some medical schools have begun training future doctors to view their patients as partners and to listen more effectively to them. This attitude is not yet prevalent in children services agencies.

Bureaucratic agencies are geared to provide standard packages of services and benefits to members of target client groups who meet specific sets of eligibility criteria such as age, income limits, or type of health condition. Foster children, children with special needs, elderly, families with annual earnings below a certain figure are all examples of client categories. Case workers traditionally are trained to offer only the services associated with a particular program.

Bureaucracies place an enormous emphasis on adherence to uniform processes as a means of maintaining control and exercising authority within the organization with some of the following consequences.

- Clients are treated the same instead of as unique individuals.
- Initiative by staff is discouraged.
- If a family's situation does not fit well into the agency's standard procedures, the staff person is paralyzed and the agency is unable to respond.
- A family's contact with the agency is limited to service providers who have virtually no authority over policy or budget decisions. Families have little access to persons or bodies that make crucial policy and budget decisions.

The organizational culture of agencies often appears designed to thwart the concerns of families rather than to address them as the following list illustrates:

What Parents Want	What Parents Get
To be treated as responsible adults who know the needs of their families	Treated as dependent "clients"
An information resource, a guide to help, them solve a problem	A "gatekeeper" whose primary concern is that the family meets eligibility requirements for a standard package of services and benefits
A partner and collaborator	A surrogate parent and "expert"
A consultant that will take an interest in them as distinct individuals and address their specific situation	A "gatekeeper" whose definition of professional responsibility is to follow procedures so that no one will be given favorable treatment or receive assistance they don't deserve

| A timely, flexible creative response to the family's situation | A cautious response, with little incentive to take action beyond well established procedures |
| A sense of urgency | No sense of urgency |

THE GATEKEEPER MENTALITY

What happens when an adoptive family, feeling the stress of its child's special needs, applies for adoption assistance to an agency with a gatekeeper mentality? Although the two parties may agree on the basic issue before them, namely, whether the child will be able to receive postadoption services, different ways of addressing the problem often lead to frustration. The adoptive parents, driven by the immediacy of their child's medical or emotional condition, expect the agency representative to listen and to take their predicament seriously. They want the agency to respond quickly and to aggressively look for resources to help them obtain the services their child needs.

An agency worker in a bureaucratic culture is inclined to respond cautiously to requests for assistance. Medical and psychological services are often expensive. Approval of adoption assistance may not only involve a significant commitment of funds to one family but also signal a precedent to support other families in similar circumstances. Accordingly, the agency representative feels institutional pressure to carefully scrutinize the child's eligibility for the assistance.

Adoptive parents often interpret the agency worker's dispassionate response as indifference to their child's problems. To the family, the agency's focus on eligibility requirements signifies a determined attempt to find a pretext for denying assistance. The agency worker, for her part, is often frustrated by organizational obstacles that hinder her ability to assume a more supportive role on behalf of the family. She often has very limited control over the amount of funding that may be committed to an individual family. Moreover, there is little support for family advocates in gatekeeper agencies where dispassionate professionals are the norm.

In such a situation, there is an enormous temptation to identify the parents as the problem in order to avoid the risks of confronting agency policy. If the primary issue is unreasonable or greedy parents instead of inadequate services for a child with special needs, then there is no responsibility to take on the system. This is one reason why parents find their motives being questioned when they press the issue of adoption assistance or postadoption services with an agency. What the parents regard as a straightforward problem of identifying sufficient resources for their children becomes translated into a complicated screening process to ensure that families don't get more than they deserve.

Conflict escalates as the parties talk past one another. The adoptive parents appeal to the broad purposes of adoption assistance, contending that the program was expressly designed to help families such as theirs. In response, the agency ignores the goals and purposes of adoption assistance, concentrating instead on the literal language of the eligibility regulations.

CITIZEN POWER

Adoptive and foster families need to establish an independent power base because the organizational culture of public agencies generates priorities that are different from their own. Parents and agencies may share an allegiance to long-term goals but often have quite different perceptions of how to get there. Agencies are also subject to pressures that place them at odds with families on budget matters. For these reasons, bureaucratic agencies cannot be counted on to represent the interests of families. Families must represent themselves.

Some agency employees, for example, may fully realize that investing in permanent families through adequate postadoption assistance is sound policy, but the organization itself has much more incentive to save money than to spend it, even if the spending of an additional dollar brings in $1.60 in federal matching funds. Resources are limited and several programs may be competing for the same pool of funds. Persons with the authority over funding decisions usually are not directly engaged with families and are therefore removed from their concerns. From a distance, those concerns take on a certain abstract quality, making it easier to reject a subsidy request or budget proposal. As noted earlier, workers who are most familiar with, and committed to, addressing the issues raised by families, usually have no authority to make decisions that fall outside the realm of established agency policy.

Adoptive families can work constructively with public agencies on a variety of adoption and foster care projects as long as they are aware that when controversy arises, agencies will tend to take the path of least resistance whether that path is the one that adoptive and foster parents want to travel. In order to exert an influence on policy and budget decisions, families must develop capacities in at least four areas:

1. Information and Information Resources: Families must gain access to policy- and budget-related information and assume responsibility for its organization and dissemination. Although federal regulations require states to "actively promote" the adoption assistance program, foster and adoptive parents cannot afford to rely entirely on the commitment of whatever administration is in power. Ask your next door neighbors if they are familiar with adoption assistance programs for children with special needs.

2. Audiences: Families must identify the proper audiences for their information. Important policy- and budget-related information must reach individuals and organizations that are in a position to affect agency decisions.

3. Relationships: With so much information competing for people's attention, adoptive and foster parents cannot be content to appear once a year with information pertaining to their concerns. Parents must establish ongoing relationships with individuals and organizations that have influence over agencies so they can assume a regular place at the table when important issues arise. In areas of the country where adoption groups have formed working coalitions with other types of family support organizations, the partnership has benefited both sides.

4. Service Coordination: Adoptive and foster parents will need to articulate where they fit in the continuum of support for children, including what they have in common with all families and what distinctive assets and needs they bring to the table.

The legislature is one potential audience for information pertaining to foster care and adoption. Participating in the legislative process presents an opportunity to influence the direction of agency policies.

Terra Incognita: The World of Bureauspeak

Advocates quickly learn that providing information to embattled parents about the finer points of adoption assistance policy is only one part of their role. Parents often call or dispatch a frantic E-mail message to advocates after a bewildering encounter with the strange bureaucratic customs of a state or local child welfare agency. They typically emerge from these contacts like stunned victims of an alien abduction and have an intense need to tell some sympathetic listener what they have just experienced. The narrative of their adventures usually careens back and forth between outrage ("Do you know what she said to me!?") and incredulity ("Am I crazy? Can they do that?").

The advocate's job is to function as a guide through the bureaucratic wilderness, a jungle filled with unpredictable obstacles. Like all good guides, the advocate must help point the way while encouraging the people in the party to trust their own instincts, which in the case of adoptive families are usually quite sound. Even well-informed, confident adults can become confused or riddled with self-doubt, however, when their requests for adoption assistance are met with responses such as the following: "When you adopt, you are expected to be responsible for your child's care. No one helps me when my child gets sick."

The Lira family have exhausted their health insurance and are $50,000 in debt after discovering that their adopted son suffers from a severe reactive attachment disorder. The agency never disclosed the fact that their child's mother was a heavy drug user and during his early infancy left him alone for hours. The Liras just discovered that he had been in and out of five foster homes before being placed with them.

Mr. and Mrs. Lira believe that adoption assistance was designed to help adults adopt and raise children with severe problems. They are shocked at the agency worker's suggestion that they are not acting like responsible parents.

Ann Miller has been exploring the various services and support programs that might be available to Sarah, the child she intends to adopt. She has been acting on the belief that she has a duty to advocate on behalf of the child whose family history placed her at risk for some serious medical conditions. "If you need all of that assistance, maybe you're not prepared to adopt this child. Maybe we should find another home for Sarah." The agency worker responded to Ms. Miller's attempt to negotiate a plan of support for her daughter with a veiled threat to place the child with another family if she continued to be so demanding.

"What if everyone requested that amount of subsidy?" The Bradys are trying to secure some commitment for payment of out-of-home care for their son should it become necessary. The boy has a history of impulsive, self-destructive behavior and the family's insurance policy offers only limited coverage. The question posed by the agency worker implies that the Bradys are making an outrageous request and that if the commitment to cover the cost of out-of-home care can't be made to every child then no child should receive it. Since the Bradys are not the parents of every adopted child in the state, they are a bit unsure how to respond to such logic. Should they give up trying to care for their child because some other children might not be able to receive the same level of care?

"We don't care what the federal policy interpretations say. We go by our state regulations" The Nielsons have been told that Title IV-E adoption assistance is a federal entitlement program. They assume that state adoption assistance programs must conform to federal law. The agency representative seems to be telling them otherwise.

Of course, not all agency representatives are out of touch with the realities of special needs adoption. Many are very knowledgeable and extend themselves to provide quality service. Adoption assistance is a strange program in that it affords states considerable flexibility to help families or to confound them with literal interpretations of specific sections in the federal and state law. Thanks to the persistent efforts of adoptive parents, the long-term trend has been a positive one. Over the past decade, more and more agencies have come to recognize the importance of adoption assistance. Despite obvious gains, however, inexperienced adoptive parents and would-be parents are still subject to the disturbing language and practices of bureaucracy.

The adoptive parents in each of the above scenarios needed more than the just the facts. They needed someone to help them examine the distance between their own concerns and those expressed by the agency. A threat to remove a child if the prospective parent persists in trying to secure particular postadoption services or levels of adoption assistance is always frightening. Advocates can help parents sort through disconcerting encounters with agency workers. The more familiar parents become with bureaucratic culture, the more confidence they develop in their abilities to negotiate the system. The last section of this volume lists advocacy resources that can help parents map their journeys through the terra incognito of agency bureaucracies.

SOME ADVICE FOR AGENCIES

The following letter (An Open Letter to State Adoption Administrators Who Are Trying to Save Money, from a Couple of Concerned Advocates) was published by NACAC recently in their newsletter, *Adoptalk*:

October 1998
Dear State Administrators:

May we tell you a true* story? It's about the kind of family you are looking for to adopt children who are languishing in foster care, the kind of family that Congress envisioned when it passed the Adoption and Safe Families Act in November 1997.

John Austin and his wife, Jan, adopted four daughters from different states. The children all have special needs and the Austins managed to negotiate adoption assistance on behalf of each one. Jan Austin quit her job as a nurse after the second child. Without assistance, the couple would have hesitated to expand their family given their modest income and less than optimum insurance benefits.

Over time, the Austins came to view adoption assistance agreements as social contracts with the states. The states had hundreds of children in foster care without families. They needed people like the Austins to make a lifelong commitment to adoption. John and Jan discovered that they had a powerful calling and the right blend of skills to serve as parents for traumatized children. They committed their personal and economic assets to building a family for four children. The states agreed to invest in the adoptions by providing financial support and services to help the Austins meet the ordinary and special needs of their daughters until they reached adulthood. But now, in the wake of a national campaign to find permanent homes for foster children, the Austins find that four states are rolling back their commitments to them.

It started with the southwestern state from which ten-year-old Debbie had been adopted. Debbie uses a wheelchair to get around because of cerebral palsy. SW state had said it would pay for a wheelchair lift for their van by the time Debbie was too big to lift easily. When they applied for that lift, they were told that funds are no longer available. Sorry.

Then things got worse. Six-year-old Maria, adopted from a northeastern state, has very severe Attention Deficit Hyperactivity Disorder (ADHD) and is destructive and excitable. NE state had been providing the family with five hours a month of respite care so that they could get a break from the constant stress and renew their energies. NE state recently sent John and Jan a letter stating that the respite care program has not received enough funding this year and has been discontinued. Sorry.

But worse setbacks were yet to come. Sherry, their oldest, is a college freshman, a miraculous accomplishment considering her background. No one from her birth family has even graduated from junior high school for the last three generations. Sherry overcame serious emotional disorders to achieve her level of success. But her ongoing therapy and medications are expensive. The Austins would not have been able to manage her college expenses if it wasn't for the rules in the southern state from where Sherry had been adopted a decade earlier. The state told them that Sherry could continue to receive her full monthly subsidy and Medicaid coverage up to age twenty-one as long as she was a full-time college student. This benefit was made available to adopted children based on its enormous success with

---

*Names have been changed to protect privacy. The Austin family is a compilation of actual families, and the circumstances are real.

foster children. The program has been shown to greatly encourage college atten-
dance.

The blow came in September when a letter arrived from the southern state instead
of a check. It informed the Austins that subsidies had been rolled back to the
eighteenth birthday on all adopted (not foster) children as a means to save money.
Sorry.

Sherry immediately dropped a couple of college courses and looked for a job.
Her parents are unsure if her delicate emotional balance can withstand the strain
of working and college simultaneously.

As bad as all of this is, the Austins were not terribly discouraged because of a
bright star on the horizon called "retroactive IV-E subsidy." For those of you who
may not have heard of it yet, this is a federal ruling (called PIQ 92-02) on PL-96-
272, Title IV-E, that allows parents in some cases to go back and access retroactive
subsidy payments when they can prove their child was wrongfully denied them. (As
you know, many families were erroneously denied IV-E eligibility, especially during
the eighties.) The Austins heard about this PIQ from their NACAC representative
and had been vigorously pursuing it for months for their twelve-year-old daughter,
Teresa.

Teresa, adopted from a midwestern state in the early eighties, was the first child
they adopted. She came to them shortly after birth and was addicted to cocaine.
At that time, no one ever mentioned a subsidy or Medicaid or IV-E. The Austins
didn't know about that stuff until they adopted Sherry later on.

Teresa was a delightful baby, but she was sickly. Eventually, she would be diagnosed with a partial permanent hearing loss and with mild mental retardation.
Meeting her needs has been expensive because of her difficulties in school and need
for extra help.

When Jan and John Austin first read PIQ 92-02 cover to cover, they were very
excited. It described their situation perfectly. It said that there were several "extenuating circumstances" under which a family could ask for back payments. One, the
state's failure to inform the family of adoption subsidy programs, applied to them.
Could they be on the verge of getting justice for Teresa?

They couldn't afford legal help so John did the research for their case on the
Internet and Jan called every child advocate she knew for advice. With liberal support from their NACAC representative and some technical information from their
DHHS regional office, they put together what looked to them to be an airtight case
for Teresa's qualification. The beauty of it is that it was a win-win situation from
the start. The state stood to profit financially from the "retro" action, too, because
Teresa had eventually qualified for a state subsidy. Because state subsidies receive
no reimbursement from the federal government, but IV-E subsidies and retroactive
payments are reimbursed 50 percent to 80 percent state subsidies cost the state
more real dollars than IV-E subsidies do

Therefore, John told the state administrator of the midwestern state, if we can
agree to this retro action in a stress-free "nonevidentiary" fair hearing as described
in PIQ 92-02, my daughter will receive the back payments that she is due, and the
state will show a net increase of thousands of dollars over what they would have
paid if the subsidy were not converted to a IV-E contract.

The administrator, however, had other ideas. She wanted to stop this retro thing
dead in its tracks because in those cases where a nonsubsidized child qualified for

retroactive IV-E assistance the state wouldn't save any money at all. She denied the retro request even though the family had proved that Teresa qualified for IV-E on every single point of law, and a decidedly stressful retro administrative hearing took place. The Austins lost the hearing on a technicality, but after buckets of tears, decided to appeal the decision.

The decision is being appealed, but they face another battle even if they win. The midwestern state has a new policy severely limiting IV-E retroactive subsidy payment amounts. Now the Austins must continue their research to discover if the Code of Federal Regulations (CFR) on administrative hearings allows states to limit retro payments. They may even have to go through another administrative hearing on the issue of whether the state that is ordered to pay retro as the result of a hearing or a hearing review must actually do so.

Additionally, the family is trying to decide if they should ask for fair hearings on the wheelchair lift denial from SW state and on the respite care cancellation from NE state. It's a tough call because they are emotionally exhausted advocating for their children. The southern state did eventually reverse itself on the denial of subsidy to their college-age child. When several families threatened a class-action lawsuit, the state decided to "grandfather" in all children who were already in college when the new regulations went into effect.

The Austin family, like thousands of other American families who have been through similar situations, are still reeling from the stress of this year. Their faith in a system that had promised to help them help kids has been shattered. And their ability to help other kids has been compromised. Just last week, the NE state called to tell them that Maria's younger biological sister, Marta, is available for adoption now and that the Austins can adopt her if they wish. Marta is also very hyperactive.

In any other year, the Austins would have jumped at the chance to adopt again, and especially to give permanency to the biological sibling of one of their beloved children. But the decision is not as easy now. There will be no respite care for Marta or Maria. How well can they cope? What if NE state erodes other benefits in the future? How can the family swim headlong into such dangerous financial waters with no lifeboat in sight?

This is what you need to be made aware of, my dear state administrators. This kind of human cost is what you don't see when you make budget-tightening decisions. Not only are you hurting adopted kids and their families when you cut off services and fight retro applications, you may also be costing the state federal dollars, and you are actively discouraging future adoptions. And in case you haven't noticed, this last point is especially serious because foster care populations are growing. In my state, we've recently broken all records for the number of children in foster care whose goal is adoption.

Studies show that adopted adults tend to be more productive citizens that foster children who age out of the system. Every adoption saves every taxpayer money in the long run by saving in administrative costs, among other things. And you must remember that adoptive families of special needs kids are not only a state's most precious resource when it comes to waiting children, they are the state's volunteer adoption ambassadors. If they feel wronged or victimized, they are not likely to encourage other families to consider adoption.

So what's the answer? After all, your state IV-E budgets are growing at alarming rates and you must find ways to cut costs and increase funding. Well, we're glad you asked. Here are a few suggestions:

1. Take advantage of the commitment that Congress and President Clinton have made to special needs adoption and to waiting children. Squeeze every penny out of current programs and then press Washington and ask us to help you press them for adequate future funding. We'll also help convince state legislatures that these programs need support. Waiting kids are the most defenseless of the defenseless, so the politicians will at least listen. Communicate your needs and let's lobby for the kids together!

2. Before cutting programs, ask the real experts for advice and for their volunteer help. We are the real experts. We are the advocates, the adoptees, the birth parents, the foster parents, the adoptive parents, the grandparents, the aunts and uncles of adopted children. We are the citizenry. Ask us for input. Put us to work. Seek our wisdom. Hold a town meeting. Contact the local foster and adoptive support groups. Call NACAC and NAC and AFA and AASK and the other national groups who study the needs of kids and ask for advice.

3. Send out a survey to everyone who has adopted in your state in the last decade. Tell us how much you need to cut and show us what you are spending. We're smart enough to comprehend it. We'll tell you what can go and what is essential from our perspective. Then you can make an informed decision from your perspective.

4. Don't be penny wise and pound foolish. Avoid blanket take-backs. If you block all retro payments, for example, you block the ones that can make the state money as well as the ones that can cost the state money. If you cancel a badly needed service, like respite care, you risk expensive legal battles with large groups of angry families.

5. When services have to be cut, reduce them gradually and as painlessly as possible. Seek advance input from the people who will be hurt the most by the cuts.

6. Deal with adoptive parents as the federal law tells you to, on a case-by-case basis. Negotiate with us as individuals who parent children with individual needs. Some families can afford to accept some cuts while other families are struggling to maintain their families with maximum benefits in place. Work with us instead of against us. Together, we are powerful allies for children!

7. I saved the most important suggestion for last, so that it's the last thing you read here. Try to maintain a child-centered attitude. Put kids first. Can I say that again? Won't you put kids first, please?

Sincerely,
R. Laws and T. O'Hanlon,
NACAC State Representatives,
Oklahoma and Ohio

SUMMARY

Children services agencies could benefit from a keener sense of irony. Agency officials appear to have little awareness of the degree of pain that bureaucratic procedures inflict on the very persons they have carefully studied and certified as suitable parents for children in their custody. Even if none of the current flaws in the adoption assistance program were addressed, it would nonetheless make a world of differences to adoptive families if states simply defined their mission in terms of a simple question: "How can we help empower these parents who have dedicated their lives to this child with special needs?"

Parents don't want the state to raise their adopted children. Rather, they want the state to invest in their commitment to those children when their own resources fall short. Adoptive parents are no strangers to the problem of limited resources. They can be remarkably patient as long as they are reasonably convinced that the agency is committed to helping their children. Much of the frustration and anger exhibited by parents at support group meetings and adoption conferences could be avoided if agencies observed the following principles:

- Recognize that adoption assistance programs exist to help sustain families for children with special needs. As a point of departure, agencies should look for ways to say yes to requests for help rather than search for reasons to deny assistance. This change in agency culture alone would dramatically improve adoption assistance programs.

- Recognize that adoptive parents are forced to become advocates for their child with special needs. Applying for adoption assistance is not a particularly pleasant experience. It is a mark of parental responsibility, not greed.

- Remember that requests for assistance are made by the very families that have been studied extensively and approved as adoptive parents. If you placed the well-being of a traumatized child in their hands, they are entitled to a large measure of credibility when they tell you that their child needs a particular service or services.

5

Adoption Assistance: Progress and Obstacles for Adoptive Families

So many signatures for such a small heart.
— Mother Teresa, on filling out forms

SPECIAL NEEDS ADOPTION: THE ULTIMATE VOLUNTEER PROGRAM

Amy Glenn is a single parent with three adoptive children. The family lives on a quiet street near a park in Princeton, New Jersey. Amy originally became involved in adoption while serving as a nurse in Harlem. She moved to Princeton to pursue graduate studies in Public Health at the university. Before Amy completed her Ph.D. dissertation, however, she succumbed to the call of adoption once again.

Although she was not looking to become a parent of children with problems, she eventually adopted Joseph, the survivor of a third-trimester abortion attempt, and Elizabeth, a child with a mysterious immune disorder that caused severe arthritic pains in her joints. The Glenns are truly a multicultural family: Joseph is of Indian heritage, Amy is Jewish, and Elizabeth and the latest addition, Sarah, are African-American.

Joseph, despite some learning disabilities, is growing into a bright, pleasant young man. Elizabeth, though subject to spells of recurring weakness and pain, is an outstanding student who manages to play soccer and ride her bike. The Glenns are a loving family that could well serve as a model for the benefits of adoption.

The family situation also reflects some typical obstacles encountered by parents who adopt children with special needs. Amy Glenn turned her back on a lucrative professional income to provide a home for children who needed one. Guided by her love and knowledge, they have the potential to become happy, productive adults. The family lives modestly, and Amy must constantly be concerned about the children's access to needed educational services to address Joseph's learning problems and medical services for Elizabeth. She worries about the consequences to the children's future if they cannot secure the support they need.

Adoptive parents, such as Amy Glenn, invest so much of themselves and their limited resources to provide permanent families for children who would otherwise spend their days in state-supported foster care. There can be no more radical intervention than offering a legally homeless child a family. Adoption is the ultimate volunteer program. Federal and state adoption assistance programs were established to enable suitable adults to incorporate a new child into their homes and to help to support and sustain the family. Since the Adoption Assistance and Child Welfare Act of 1980 (PL 96–272) established the federal Title IV-E adoption assistance program, thousands of families have benefited from its monthly financial support and medical coverage.

Yet, even in the midst of the recent push to secure permanent homes for foster children launched with the Clinton administration's "Adoption 2002" initiative and passage of the Adoption and Safe Families Act in November 1997, dedicated, skilled parents like Amy Glenn often run into obstacle after obstacle in their attempts to obtain needed services, when their own resources are inadequate or exhausted.

FUNDING

Ideally, adoption assistance (subsidy) programs should be designed to respond to children's needs as they arise. Funding will always be an issue because the requirements of an adopted child with special needs are harder to predict than those of other children and the service needs of adopted children with severe disabilities are very expensive. They may run into hundreds of thousands of dollars.

The funding controversy in adoption assistance is a familiar one. Foster care is more expensive because of its related administrative costs, but public agencies are required to support foster children in their care. Adoption assistance, on the other hand, is negotiable.

Advocates for adoption assistance also encounter the difficulty of making a case for early intervention shared by other children's programs. Although the benefits of intervention in the life of a traumatized child appear obvious on one level, it is hard to demonstrate the direct consequences of opportunities not taken. What might have happened if such and such adoptive placement had not taken place?

Proponents can point to such figures as the high proportion of ex-foster children in prisons but, like all prevention programs, it is difficult to show how a child might have turned out had he or she not been adopted by a particular family and provided with needed services. Furthermore, although the social and economic costs resulting from the failure to provide adequate medical, psychological, and educational services to children with special needs are borne by society as a whole, the burdens fall on different public agencies. The argument that support for adopted children with special needs will reduce the social and economic costs of substance abuse, unemployment, and crime may not sway the state's child welfare agency because the responsibility for addressing those adult problems falls on the criminal justice system or some other public entity.

Advocates need to become more effective in pointing out the opportunity costs associated with adoption assistance to legislatures and governors. Pointing out the comparative advantages of adoption assistance over foster care maintenance is a start. More effort also needs to be made to document the very real differences that adoptive families make in the lives of children who have experienced horrors that many people can only imagine.

In addition to the ongoing struggle to secure adequate funding levels for adoption assistance, the programs also suffer from a basic structural defect. One primary problem with existing state and federal subsidy programs is that they still concentrate on the wrong end of the adoption time line. Federal and state programs both require that the adopting parents and state agency complete a written agreement as the final step in activating adoption assistance. While the negotiation of a postadoption service plan before legalization is a sound policy, the insistence that agreements can only be executed before the final decree of adoption has plagued the program from its inception.

A FUNDAMENTAL WEAKNESS OF ADOPTION ASSISTANCE PROGRAMS

From a certain naive perspective, the requirement that adoption assistance agreements must be executed prior to finalization made sense when the various laws were first enacted. Adoption assistance was primarily viewed as a tool for increasing the number of adoptive placements. Monthly payments, Medicaid, and various postadoption services would remove financial obstacles that prevented suitable parents of modest means from providing families for waiting children. By completing assistance agreement prior to finalization, the parents would know exactly what kind of support would be available to them.

Experience soon exposed the flaws in this outlook. Many of the most devastating problems facing adoptive families originated in their children's prenatal exposure to drugs or in the abuse or neglect they suffered during infancy. Years often passed before the adoptive parents fully realized that they were raising a son or daughter without a normal conscience who lied, stole, and committed acts of violence without remorse.

When adoptive families confronting emotional and financial exhaustion approached public agencies for support, the inadequate design of the adoption assistance programs became all too apparent. Although in the vast majority of cases, the embattled parents were desperately seeking to hold their families together and wanted nothing more than adequate services for their troubled children, the adoption support system was not constructed to respond to the dynamics of special needs adoptions. Agency representatives informed the parents that there was nothing they could do to help, thereby reinforcing the view that the state's responsibility for sustaining adoptions ended at finalization.

The requirement that adoption assistance agreements must be completed before a final decree of adoption discriminated particularly against families adopting younger children. Prospective parents, particularly those who had not adopted before, were extremely dependent on the agency for information about their future child's medical history and family background. Even if the parents received complete background information and a thorough explanation of adoption subsidy programs, future problems were very difficult to predict. From a developmental standpoint, a child was often simply not old enough to express certain behaviors or disabilities.

In fact, many agencies did not disclose sufficient information about a child's family history. Others simply decided that the prospective parents did not need adoption assistance and never mentioned it. Large numbers of families reported that they were uncomfortable with the idea of receiving assistance, as if it tainted their commitment to the child. Still others remembered feeling intimidated by the agency's power to place the child with another family if they pushed too hard for adoption subsidy benefits. For all of these reasons, families who ended up facing the most stressful situations and severest challenges often had the least access to support, either because they had not specified certain service provisions in their adoption assistance agreements or never completed an agreement at all.

ADJUSTMENTS IN ADOPTION ASSISTANCE PROGRAMS

Several policy changes have succeeded in making adoption assistance programs more flexible, but the basic structural problem remains.

Appeals for Adoption Assistance after Finalization

Federal Policy Interpretation Question ACYF-PIQ 92–02 set forth guidelines through which adoptive families could obtain Title IV-E adoption assistance after finalization through an administrative fair hearing. Although some states have responded to this major policy reform by aggressively contesting appeals, families who adopted children with special needs with no assistance have access to the federal program that was formerly denied.

An "At Risk" Category of Special Needs

In many states, children may be considered to have special needs on the basis of factors in their family history such as drug exposure, abuse, or hereditary medical conditions that are commonly associated with the development of future problems. The recognition of "at risk" as a special needs condition enables a state to make support available to adopted children who are simply too young to have developed certain full-blown medical or behavioral problems.

Postadoption Service Subsidies

As we discussed in Chapter 3, a number of states supplement federal adoption assistance with a subsidy program that pays for certain types of medical and psychological services that are not covered by the family's health insurance or by Medicaid. A few of these programs allow agreements for service subsidies to be initiated after finalization.

A BASIC PROBLEM REMAINS

Adoptive families have clearly benefited from these policy revisions. Formidable obstacles remain, however, and ironically serve to illuminate the basic structural defect of adoption assistance programs. In spite of all we have learned, subsidy programs still maintain an artificial distinction between pre- and postfinalization which is ill-suited to the needs of adoptive families.

PIQ 92–02, for example, requires that in order to obtain a review of their child's eligibility for the IV-E program, adoptive families need to show that extenuating circumstances prevented them from applying for or receiving adoption assistance prior to finalization. Extenuating circumstances will be discussed in Chapter 10, but in most cases they ought to be fairly easy to establish. Most adoptive families explore the appeals process after a prolonged encounter with the escalating cost of services for their children. In nearly every instance, the parents are obviously struggling with problems that originated in their child's preadoptive history. Had the parents been remotely aware of the challenges they would eventually confront, they surely would have pursued adoption assistance at the time the child was placed with them.

The federal Children's Bureau published PIQ 92–02 in response to the overwhelming evidence that regulations preventing adoption assistance from being initiated after finalization were undermining the primary goal of the Title IV-E program, to support permanent families for children. The policy interpretation offers guidelines to the states rather than a prescription for defining what constitutes an extenuating circumstance. Yet, many states have not embraced PIQ 92–02 as a flexible tool to empower adoptive families.

Public agencies often spend inordinate amounts of time aggressively contesting appeals for adoption assistance. Instead of assuming that serious medical or emotional problems are nearly always rooted in a child's preadoptive experiences; any rational parents would have welcomed adoption assistance had they known how serious their children's problems would become; and many of the most disruptive conditions such as reactive attachment disorders and attention deficit/hyperactivity disorder may not be diagnosed for years after the adoption, agency representatives demand that applicants assume an unreasonable burden of proof. Not only must the parents document their adopted child's special needs, but they are asked to establish that their child should have been considered a candidate for assistance when he or she was initially placed for adoption.

Arguments against the applicant's eligibility for adoption assistance finalization often take sharp turns toward the surreal. A number of families have been confronted by a bizarre syllogism. Children with special needs are by definition difficult to place for adoption without adoption assistance. Your child was not only placed but also legally adopted without assistance. Therefore, your child was obviously not difficult to place and is not eligible for adoption assistance.

State-funded service subsidy programs often pose the same obstacles as IV-E adoption assistance. While some state regulations permit postadoption service subsidies, many limit services to those detailed in subsidy agreements completed before finalization.

One state designed a state subsidy program for children with special needs who could not qualify for a IV-E subsidy. However, over a period of years, the state tightened the requirements for a state subsidy until they mirrored the requirements for a federal subsidy. Thus, the state had a program in place for children who could not qualify federally but the children could only access it if they could qualify federally.

Adoptive families with agreements in place may request an increase in adoption assistance as their situations change. State and federal regulations permit existing agreements to be modified at any time by mutual consent of the adoptive family and agency. Agencies must respond in writing to requests for higher amounts of adoption assistance and inform applicants of their right to appeal adverse decisions. Unfortunately, federal law does not specify much in the way of criteria for settling disagreements when agencies refuse a request to amend an existing adoption assistance agreement. Therefore, adoptive families who experience a dramatic change in circumstances may still encounter an unresponsive service system even if they are fortunate enough to have an adoption assistance agreements in place.

A MODEST PROPOSAL

Adoption assistance programs should be organized to respond to the needs of adopted children as those needs present themselves. Prospective parents and agencies should design postadoptive plans of support based on the best knowledge at hand, but the unreasonable boundary between the pre- and postadoption period should be eliminated. Regulations requiring adoption assistance agreements to be completed before finalization should be changed. Adoption assistance agreements should be flexible instruments initiated and amended at any time as circumstances dictate. Parents might want some kind of agreement in place before the final decree of adoption, but they should have the right to either defer or amend the agreement as determined by the progress of their children and their individual family circumstances.

The section of federal law that addresses the adoption assistance program, 42 USC 673, does not specify when subsidy agreements must be put into effect. The source of the problem lies in Chapter 42 of the Code of Federal Regulations at 1356.40. Paragraph (b) (1) stipulates that the adoption assistance agreement must "be signed and in effect at the time of or prior to the final decree of adoption." As an administrative rule, this provision does not require congressional action, but could be amended or simply rescinded by the U.S. Department of Health and Human Services. Now that the Title IV-E program appears safe from block grant fever, advocates should seriously consider a campaign to modify the rule in two respects: (1) Adoption assistance agreements can be completed either before or after the final decree of adoption, and (2) existing adoption agreements must be modified to reflect documented changes that adversely affect the family's ability to meet the service needs of the child.

The issue of cost will surely surface along with any proposal to eliminate time limits for completing adoption assistance agreements. There is nothing inherently more cost effective about the current regulations, except that they afford more opportunities for errors and omissions. States currently save money when eligible children fail to receive adoption assistance before finalization because their parents do not receive adequate information or encouragement to apply for the program. If states actively promoted adoption assistance as required by the Code of Federal Regulations at 42 CFR 1356.40 (f) and assumed a supportive attitude toward adoptive families, there is no particular reason why the ability to initiate adoption assistance agreements after finalization should be more expensive than limiting agreements to the period before the final decree of adoption.

The cost of adoption assistance has more to do with the state's sense of responsibility to children with special needs and their adoptive families than with regulations governing time frames for agreements. Families would be much more willing to defer adoption assistance benefits if they could be assured that future support would be available in time of need. As things now stand, knowledgeable parents are under tremendous pressure to write every conceivable service that their child might need into the initial adoption assistance agreement because the future is so unpredictable, and if the service provision is not listed, it might later be denied. Prospective adoptive parents have a serious responsibility as advocates for their children to craft the best postadoption support plan possible; but it is a difficult task, often placing them in direct conflict with the public agency. The agency does not want to make an unconditional commitment to cover any service need that might arise, while the parents seek to have some idea of what they can count on in a time of crisis.

In addition to conflicts over finances, agencies often pressure parents to finalize the adoption, making negotiations for adoption assistance even more difficult. Parents find themselves on the horns of a terrible dilemma. If they continue to push for services and financial support their child might need, the agency may threaten to place the child with another family. Allowing parents to negotiate adoption assistance agreements after finalization and requiring the state to renegotiate when things take a turn for the worse would not solve the perennial problem of funding, but it would allow questions of support for children with special needs to be addressed in terms of families' actual situations. At present, when a family runs into unexpected problems and contacts an agency, the issue of how to meet the child's needs gets lost amid legalistic discussions about the content of the initial adoption assistance agreement, which may have little relevance to existing problems and circumstances.

It is time to consider the question of cost effectiveness in a larger context and begin paying more attention to the positive effects of adoption on the lives of children with chronic medical conditions, attachment disorders, and other serious problems stemming from early abuse and neglect. The public policy alternative to investing in adoptive families for children with special needs is supporting foster care with its higher administrative costs. When children grow up without the normal bonds of trust and love, society pays an enormous price. When we look a bit closer, we might find that adoptive families are one of the best investments that society can make.

PART II

TOOLS FOR ADVOCACY

6

Why Adoption Support Groups?

> She discovered with great delight that one does not love one's children just because they are one's children but because of the friendship formed while raising them.
>
> —Gabriel García Márquez (b. 1928)

ELEMENTS OF ADOPTION SUCCESS

There has been a great deal of research about what elements go into a successful special needs adoption. Certain elements show up again and again in these studies and can be grouped in seven categories, including:

- adequate financial assistance
- full disclosure about the child's history, behavior, and needs
- preparation of the child to live in the new family
- ongoing and frequent contact with the adoption agency
- parent advocacy skills (financial, educational, medical, and others)
- training and information about adoption issues, behavior management, and parenting
- a support network of relatives, friends, and other adoptive families

THE IMPORTANCE OF FINANCIAL ASSISTANCE

This book deals primarily with the first category, adequate financial assistance, which not only benefits children by encouraging adoption, but saves tax dollars in the long-term by shortening foster care stays

(O'Hanlon, 1995). PL 96–272 has proved to be an extremely cost-effective federal program.

Just how important is financial aid in special needs adoption? Dr. L. Anne Babb, author of *Ethics in American Adoption*, considers financial assistance important enough to list it under Principle Number Seven in her "Recommended Model for Ethical Standards in Adoption":

> Adoption professionals should tell adoptive parents about the expenses they are likely to incur as a result of adopting a certain child and disclose accurate and complete information about Adoption Assistance Payments, Difficulty-of-Care payments, Medicaid, Crippled Children's Services, SSI availability, and other resources available to help the child and the adoptive family after the adoption is finalized.

James Rosenthal and Victor Groze make these comments about the need to advocate for adoption subsidies, and the importance of subsidies in adoption outcome in their book entitled *Special Needs Adoption: A Study of Intact Families*:

> Financial subsidies provide tremendous benefits to families and children. . . . Several problems may be encountered in the delivery of subsidies. Bureaucratic red tape may slow the process. As is clear in parent comments, both parents and workers need to advocate to ensure the child's subsidy. . . .The provision of adequate subsidies is essential in recruiting these families and in enabling these families to effectively meet the children's needs.

Finally, Richard Barth and Marianne Berry sum up some of the studies that have been done on the impact of financial assistance and adoption success in their oft-quoted book, *Adoption and Disruption: Rates, Risks, and Responses*:

> Finances are stressors in adoption. Zwimpher (1983) found that the families with the fewest financial resources had a higher rate of disruption. The special medical and psychological needs of the child may strain the financial resources of the family, one of the most difficult strains with which any family must cope (Olsen et al., 1983). Subsidies for special needs adoptions are granted in the majority of cases and are federally funded in recognition of these stressors and their effect on the ability to make and keep adoptive placements. Yet, . . . subsidies . . . hardly approximate the actual costs of adoption.

THE OTHER SIX CATEGORIES

The next two categories containing elements of successful adoption are the responsibility of the agency. The agency must give the family full disclosure about the child's history, behavior, and needs, or the parents can't prepare themselves to meet the needs of the child. As one mom put it, "I want to know everything about the children I'm adopting—from their pre-natal care to what they had for breakfast yesterday."

As unbelievable as it may sound to people who have never adopted, full disclosure can be difficult to obtain. Whether well-meaning and intentional or simply a matter of overlooking information in a file, a lack of infor-mation about a child can result in terrible stress for the parents. Commonly, when parents realize they have not received full disclosure, it involves issues like the child's background of sexual abuse, part of the medical history, mental health problems, behavioral problems, and learning difficulties.

If parents are given full disclosure, no matter how painful the informa-tion, the placement is far more likely to be successful. Withholding anything or relating inaccurate information puts the parents at a disadvantage and makes adjustment tougher. Lack of full disclosure also makes adequate financial assistance negotiation impossible. Without complete information about the child, the parents cannot plan intelligently for her future service needs or determine how much and what kind of financial assistance the family will need to raise her.

The agency also must adequately prepare the child for adoption. Prep-aration of the child to live in the new family is more important than many people realize. The child must be informed about his or her new family, but more important, the child must be emotionally disengaged from the birth family. If the newly arrived child does not want to be adopted, or is still hopeful of reunification with a birth parent whose rights have been terminated, the chances of adoption success are greatly diminished.

The fourth category, ongoing and frequent contact with the adoption agency, places particular emphasis on a continuing involvement with the social worker originally assigned to work with the parents. Several studies have shown the benefits derived from a relationship between the adoptive family and social worker that extends beyond finalization of the adoption. Building a trusting relationship with an agency worker gives the family a better opportunity to access crisis intervention services, residential treat-ment, and to find support, legal, educational, and medical resources when needed.

The importance of parent advocacy skills (financial, educational, medi-cal, and others), category number five, has received a lot of attention from adoption researchers in recent years. Parents must become advocates, and not only in the financial sense. They need training from their agencies and support groups in advocating for their children medically within the com-plex Medicaid bureaucracy with insurance companies and with doctors, therapists, counselors, and pharmacists. For example, counselors who have little experience helping adopted children may overemphasize or under-emphasize the importance of adoption in the treatment process.

Parents also need training in educational advocacy. This comes hard to many Americans because we are brought up to respect and obey teachers, not to disagree with them. Parents of adopted children with educational, physical, and behavioral problems need to learn about important tools such as Section 504 contracts, remedial classes, the best testing instruments, retention success studies, special classes for emotionally disturbed students, special transportation, and educational fair hearings. This kind of advocacy training can come from the agency and from the parents of children in special education in the same school district as the adoptive family. However, adoption support groups may be the best classroom for this type of training. More on that later in the chapter.

Category six, training and information about adoption issues, behavior management, and parenting, includes transracial adoption, open adoption, search and reunion, nature-nurture research, adoption ethics, and the most common special needs, among others. Many people, for example, have never heard about Fetal Alcohol Syndrome (FAS) or Attention Deficit Hyperactivity Disorder (ADHD) or Oppositional-Defiant Disorder (ODD), yet these conditions are not uncommon among waiting children. One study found that as many as 32 percent of all adopted boys exhibit symptoms of Attention Deficit Disorder (ADD) (Brodzinsky). This contrasts with an overall incidence of ADD in the general population of only 10 percent.

Four valuable phone numbers for parents wishing to learn more about adoption issues, parenting, and behavior management are included here and, happily, they are all toll-free. The first is the NACAC Help Line (800-470-6665) for questions about adoption support groups and adoption assistance contracts. This resource can save a family from bankruptcy and can save and has saved many a placement from disruption.

The second phone number is for all parents, not just foster and adoptive parents. It's the Boys Town Hotline (800-448-3000). The expert counselors who staff this information line offer free help based on more than 100 years experience dealing with youth and troubled youth.

Third, check out NAIC, the National Adoption Information Clearinghouse. Their free catalog is a must-have for all adoptive parents and the phone number is 888-251-0075. Finally, there is a wonderful reprint from AFA called "Guide to Adoption" that is carefully updated on a regular basis. AFA's phone number is 800-372-3300.

Because many people adopting child with special needs are first-time parents, it is important to make available to parents training in behavior management for children with behavior and emotional problems, information about adoption issues, and parenting classes. With children who have been abused, neglected, and moved around a lot, parents will need training in dealing with problems like lying, stealing, attachment disorders, cheating, aggression, defiance, sexual acting out, fire-starting, eating problems, drug abuse, gangs, vandalism, and suicide, among others. Many agencies now require all prospective parents to complete this training during the homestudy or assessment process. Again, this is an area in which many special needs adoption support groups choose to become active.

The final category of elements that tend to predict adoption success concerns the support network of the adoptive family. This network is the relatives, friends, coworkers, church members, neighbors, and support group members who offer the family help, friendship, and encouragement. The special needs adoption support group is a crucial element in this category because involvement in such groups has been shown again and again to be of help to adopting parents.

The Many Benefits of Support Group Membership

In 1979, a woman named Ruth was given the phone number of a local special needs adoption support group by a neighbor who had read about the group in the newspaper. The group's president, Debbie, answered the phone and Ruth's questions.

Ruth wanted to know how to get started. She wanted to adopt a child who "really needs me" and she didn't relish the idea of wading through the red tape. Debbie told her about some shortcuts, such as the name of a local adoption agency that usually completed homestudies in under three months. Debbie also gave Ruth some real hope that an adoption was possible. "After all," Debbie said, "I'm working on my second adoption. If I can do it, so can you. Call me anytime."

A friendship grew as the two women exchanged information and ideas. When Debbie's oldest adopted son, Jesse, needed extra help in school due to a hyperactivity disorder, Ruth was able to recommend another adoptive parent, Joe, who had successfully advocated for his son under similar circumstances.

Since Jesse could not sit still in class and concentrate, even with medication, Joe recommended that Debbie ask for a Section 504 contract. Section 504 is federal legislation designed to help children who are experiencing educational difficulties, but who do not qualify for other special programs. Joe's son, very hyperactive and very bright, could not benefit from remedial classes, but he wasn't successful in regular classes either. He needed customized modifications of his learning environment, and that is what a Section 504 contract provides.

Joe told Debbie to make a list of everything the school could do to help her son learn more effectively. Debbie spoke to Jesse and they made the following list:

- A smaller, quieter bus with seat belts, so Jesse stays in his seat

- A smaller class for reading, with extra one-on-one help with phonics

- Frequent breaks, every twenty minutes, to release energy and walk up and down the hall or visit the water fountain

- Weekly progress reports that list grades and any missing assignments

Next, Debbie gave the list to the school counselor along with a letter from the family doctor verifying Jesse's ADHD. The counselor had never heard of Section 504 but promised to look into it. Eventually, a contract was written and Debbie's son showed immediate improvement after the contract was implemented. Jesse rode to school on the Special Education bus, visited a lab class only for reading, and took frequent breaks. The progress reports helped him develop a better homework habit. The support group made all of it happen.

Twenty years after the first phone call, Ruth and Debbie remain close friends and speak together on the phone nearly every day. Together, they weathered the storms of parenting, and enjoyed the rainbows, too. Debbie, never married, is the proud mother of six grown adopted children and is a happy grandma as well. Ruth, divorced, adopted four times during and after her marriage and is also a grandmother. Ruth passed the support group torch years ago to her friend Katy, just as Debbie's mentor, Charlie, had passed it to her. Katy and her husband, Bobby, have biological and adopted children. Katy and Ruth are also very close friends.

The adoption support group has had several different names since Charlie founded it in the mid-seventies, but it's still going strong. New families join every year and infuse the small organization with enthusiasm and fresh ideas. Recently, they affiliated with a national support organization. The older leaders often go on to serve on statewide and national committees that influence adoption law and state policy. Both Debbie and Ruth have attended a couple of adoption bill signings in the governor's office over the years.

People like Ruth will tell you that support groups not only offer special needs adopters information, they also offer rare and valuable understanding and, sometimes, priceless friendship.

WHAT DO SUPPORT GROUPS OFFER?

Joining a support group, as tens of thousands of Americans and more than a few researchers will attest, is one of the single best ways to ensure adoption success (Barth & Berry, 1988; Tremitiere, 1992; Ross, 1986; Laws, 1998; Meaker, 1990). Being active in an adoption support group helps minimize costs in the areas of money, time, and frustration.

Money is saved because the experienced families can point to the highest quality special needs agencies with the lowest fees and the best adoption lawyers for the lowest cost. Members can share information about government programs and state policies that are designed to lower the cost of adopting and raising children with special needs.

Time and frustration also can be saved as the members of a support group trade short-cuts, strategies for dealing with red tape, information about waiting children, and the realities of various disabilities common among waiting children. Old-timers can also explain complex state and federal laws and DHS policies regarding financial issues.

Special needs adoptive parent support groups offer fellowship and information at meetings and get-togethers. Adopted children get to meet and socialize with other adopted children. Meetings may be local, statewide, regional, or national in scope, such as the annual conferences held by NACAC and AFA.

The support group services that save prospective parents money, time, and frustration may include:

- buddy families (pairing experienced parents with inexperienced ones)
- respite care (specialized child care designed to give parents a break)
- warmlines (telephone and on-line support)
- lending libraries
- photolisting books (catalogs featuring profiles of waiting children)
- conference calendars
- newsletters
- guest speakers
- social activities for parents and for children

Finally, support groups offer intangibles such as fellowship, understanding, compassion, encouragement, laughter, socialization, and friendship.

The Ultimate Adoption Support: Society's Attitude

Experienced special needs adoptive parents are often told they are saints or are asked if they are crazy because they have adopted children who face challenges (Babb & Laws, 1997). A few such parents of large families have been accused of "collecting" children or of running "institutions" instead of heading families.

The truth is that parents are parents. Infertility sparks the initial interest in adoption in many cases, but the most common motivation to adopt a waiting child is the universal desire to parent. People who adopt children with disabilities are not saints. They simply see the child first and the disability second. The lack of genetic ties is unimportant. The lifelong emotional bond is what matters. The disability is something to deal with, compensate for, incorporate into everyday life, and then forget about. Families built through special needs adoption feel and love like any other family, regardless of how they look to society.

This lack of understanding of the adoptive family speaks to an underlying attitude in American society that adoption, especially special needs adoption, is a second-rate path to parenthood. This attitude is the main reason why tens of thousands of American children are waiting right now for a permanent family. Ironically, it was not always so.

Take, for example, the ancient Indian attitude toward adoption that was found among many tribes prior to Columbus, including the Choctaws of Oklahoma and Mississippi. Adoption was an everyday fact of life (Oklahoma Choctaws Council [OCC], 1983) among the Choctaws, one of the largest agricultural tribes. Newly married couples expected to become parents through adoption and birth. This was especially true after the new European diseases swept through and created an even larger number of orphans. J. F. H. Claiborne, a nineteenth-century explorer, commented on Choctaw adoption customs in his writings. Claiborne wrote that the adoption of orphans was common, even among families that already had children. Further, the adopted child shared equally in any inheritance and was sometimes allotted the best share (OCC, 1983).

The Choctaw attitude toward the *alla toba*, or adopted child, mirrored the tribe's attitude toward family ties. Children were cherished and encouraged to play instead of work (OCC, 1983). The tribe was not seen as a collection of families but as one large family living in many different homes. In the Choctaw culture, all men were uncles to all children, all women were aunts, and all adults shared in the responsibility for all children. Therefore, even adoption by a stranger was, culturally, an adoption by close relatives. Since parentless children were immediately and permanently placed within the tribe, there was no need for foster care or for orphanages.

This attitude of community as family, and of adoption as a culturally normal response to an orphan, defines adoption support at its best. Adoption support helps create and keep families together and functioning well. Full cultural acceptance is a type of silent but highly effective adoption support.

When adoption is seen as an inferior way to build a family, it is more difficult for the adoptive family to function within a society. When adoption is a cultural norm, families feel supported because of the widespread acceptance. America has a way to go before it is as supportive of adoption as it once was.

SUMMARY

Drug abuse, poverty, crime, AIDS, neglect, child abuse, teen pregnancy, and the disintegration of the family have all combined to create a high number of children in America's foster care system. And with passage of the ASFA, the numbers are expected to swell further in the short term. This is because this innovative new law makes safety a national top priority and makes it less likely that children will be returned to dangerous birth homes.

Some states currently have a record number of children in foster care. For instance, half of the nation's foster children reside in California. And in 1998, Oklahoma newspapers carried the DHS statistic that 1,000 of the state's 5,000 children in foster care were waiting to be adopted. Just a few years prior to this, one-third as many children were said to be waiting.

At the same time, social services budgets throughout the country are inadequate (Cohen & Westhues, 1990). Some families do not turn to their adoption agencies when they need adoption support services because such services are too difficult to obtain (Barth & Berry, 1988; NACAC, 1989). Previous studies have shown adoption support services to be waning, sporadic, inadequate, and difficult to locate, access, and keep (Barth & Berry, 1988; Cohen & Westhues, 1990; Groze, Young, & Corcran-Rumppe, n.d.; Nelson, 1985).

RECOMMENDATIONS

Children need permanent homes in order to be productive members of society, and the families who adopt them need adequate adoption support services in order to be able to raise them. Studies tell us that adequate adoption support minimizes adoption failures, known as disruptions (Rosenthal & Groze, 1992; Barth & Berry, 1988).

Adoption agencies and support groups are the major providers of support services that include training in financial advocacy. Prospective parents should choose an agency with an eye toward what services are offered. They should ask "Will the agency be there for us even after the adoption is finalized?" Parents should locate, join, and become active in local and national support groups for the sake of their own children and the adoptive families who will come after them.

A book entitled *Adoption Subsidy: A Guide for Adoptive Parents*, (O'Hanlon, 1998) puts it succinctly: "As adoptive parents, you are eloquent voices for the welfare of your children. Fortified with sufficient information and confidence, you are formidable advocates. Although much still needs to be accomplished, you are changing the system for the better."

7

Adoption Assistance and the Crucial Adoption Assistance Contract

You take a number of small steps which you believe are right, thinking maybe tomorrow somebody will treat this as a dangerous provocation. And then you wait. If there is no reaction, you take another step: courage is only an accumulation of small steps.

—George Konrád (b. 1933)

NEGOTIATING AN ADOPTION SUBSIDY CONTRACT

Once you or the agency have determined that your child qualifies as IV-E-eligible, it is time to negotiate. Title IV-E is very clear that all adoption assistance contracts should be negotiated, not just assigned. (See Chapter 1 and Part III for more information on IV-E eligibility and for the text of PL 96-272, Title IV-E.)

When it comes to adoption assistance negotiation, the old adage applies: "An ounce of prevention is worth a pound of cure." You can avoid problems and possibly save a great deal of money by doing some advance homework on local policy and federal and state subsidy law.

A PARENTS RIGHTS MODEL?

This homework may not be as much of a challenge in the future as it is now. PL 96-272, signed in 1980, is not yet twenty years old. As important new federal legislation goes, it is a young law, barely a teenager, and nowhere near mature. For example, all states do not routinely inform parents about their rights under PL 96-272 even though this has been a mandate since the law's inception. But, overall, more states are doing a better job of this than they were one decade ago. As states do a better job of promoting the act, educating parents and workers, and fully implementing all provisions, parents won't have to work so hard to find this information on their own.

Perhaps, someday, parents will be informed of their PL 96-272 rights as thoroughly they are currently informed of their special education rights. Parents of children who receive specialized education services are very familiar with a federally mandated document called "Procedural Safeguards Notice: Parents Rights In Special Education." By law, a parent must receive a copy of this and acknowledge the receipt of it for every educational evaluation referral, reevaluation, request for due process, and on notification of a meeting to write or amend an Individualized Education Plan (IEP).

The helpful four-page Special Education Procedural Safeguards Notice is divided into many clearly worded sections, among them: Prior Notice Requirements for Parents, Parent Consent, Parent Participation in Meetings, Access to Records, Evaluations, Impartial Due Process Hearings, Rights, Civil Action and, my favorite section, Resources for Parents and Schools. If a parent had no other educational resource other than this document, he or she would have an excellent tool for educational advocacy.

The closest thing to a document like this that special needs adoptive parents are given is the Adoption Subsidy brochure, which may or may not be printed and distributed by any given state and for which there are no rules governing the contents. Until there is a federally mandated informational document, parents will need to read books like this one and contact organizations like NACAC, AFA, NAIC, NAC (see Part IV), and their local adoptive parent support groups. All of these organizations print well-balanced documents about PL 96-272 that are of enormous value to adoptive families.

PRICELESS PHONE NUMBER

First, you will need this phone number: 800–470–6665. This is the help line of the National Adoption Assistance Training, Resource, and Information Network (NAATRIN), which is a program of the NACAC, 651–644–3036. The NAATRIN help line will provide you with preliminary information you need to answer your most immediate questions about adoption subsidies and other kinds of assistance. On request, NAATRIN will follow up by sending you important printed material that is specific to the state you are dealing with.

The NAATRIN hotline can also tell you how to reach your state's NAATRIN expert. This volunteer will have a copy of the NAATRIN subsidy profiles for all fifty states and may have a copy of NACAC's helpful user's guide to PL 96-272: *A Summarization and Codification of Administrative*

Ruling by Tom Gilles and Joe Kroll. This book is an invaluable resource if your negotiations have ground to a halt or if you are seeking legal interpretations of the law to prepare for a fair hearing. If you need copies of other PIQs and laws, see Part IV of this book for some terrific Web sites where you can download whatever you need at no cost.

OBTAIN COPIES OF FEDERAL AND STATE LAW AND POLICIES

Detailed information about adoption subsidies is usually found in the state administrative code or the equivalent document. Copies of the portion of the administrative code covering adoption assistance should be available on request from the state agency that has responsibility for adoption. If detailed information about adoption assistance is not contained in state regulations, the agency usually has some form of policy manual. In the event the agency does not act on your request, contact the legal section of the state child welfare agency. The documents should be considered public information.

You also will find it necessary to have a copy of your state's general adoption laws, federal laws, and those laws of the state the child is coming from. There are several ways to obtain this vital information.

A free copy of federal and state laws, along with many other useful documents, is available at low or no cost from a very useful and user-friendly government agency called The National Adoption Information Clearinghouse (NAIC). The toll free number is 888–251–0075, voice-mail, 703–352–3488, and the address is 330 C Street, SW, Washington DC 20447.

Any legal library or large university library will also have copies of state laws and policies regarding adoption. The librarians are a priceless resource for parents and will be happy to show you how to access the needed information and how to make copies of it.

If visiting a library is difficult, you may first try asking the state adoption department for this information. It is not uncommon for parents to be told that information is not available to parents when in fact it is perfectly legal for parents to have a copy of the laws and policies that will govern their own adoption. Another way to sidetrack this problem is to seek out your state archives department and ask for a copy of these policies under the Freedom of Information Act. The archives keep copies of all past and current state laws, policies, and regulations. Citing the Freedom of Information Act requires the archives to get your requested information to you in a timely manner.

NEGOTIATION IS ABOUT ADVOCACY

Ideally, then, before you begin the negotiation process, you will have obtained a determination of IV-E eligibility for your child or children, and a list of national and local support group resources, (see Chapter 6), and a nice, thick stack of adoption-related state and federal laws and policies.

Advocacy is the key to successful negotiation. Your goal is to negotiate the best contract possible to meet your child's or children's needs. Don't assume that your social worker is infallible or that everything you are told is correct. He or she may not even understand PL 96-272 as well as you do. Negotiation is a question of advocating for our children, not one of faith or trust in the system.

As we have seen in previous chapters, the adoption bureaucracy does not necessarily share the adoptive parent's agenda. Adoption assistance law and policy are based on the assumption that parents will engage in ongoing negotiations with the state for their children until those children are grown. Don't take anything for granted. No one can or will even try to read your mind. When it comes to adoption assistance for special children, if you don't ask, if you don't negotiate, you probably won't receive.

WHEN SOMEONE ELSE NEGOTIATES FOR YOU

Sometimes the private adoption agency or a social worker will handle the negotiation at no extra charge on behalf of the adoptive parents and do an adequate job. However, in most cases, the adoptive family's input is crucial. When the agency's or social worker's experience is combined with the family's knowledge of their child, their own lifestyle, and how the child will impact on that lifestyle, the result is better and more realistic.

A few lawyers and child advocates will help parents negotiate a contract for a fee. They may charge by the hour, or by the job, at a set rate, or on a sliding scale. Some of them will advise parents about fair hearings and retroactive payment hearings and act as expert witnesses if a case goes to court. These professionals may charge a contingency fee based on the outcome, or charge by the hour.

When these professional services are available, they can be enormously helpful and financially beneficial for the special needs adopted child. Some parents are simply too busy, too shy, or both to negotiate their own contracts.

When hiring a professional advocate or lawyer-advocate, don't hesitate to ask for references. The individual should be experienced and knowledgeable of both federal and state law. They should have experience with administrative hearings in the state in question. Use the same caution you might use when hiring any company. For example, you can check with the Better Business Bureau, you can ask your fellow adoption support group members about the advocate's reputation, and you can ask if any former clients of the professional advocate would be willing to talk to you.

NEGOTIATION IN THREE STAGES

Adoption assistance negotiation takes place in three stages: previsitation, preplacement and ongoing postlegal negotiation. All three stages contribute to a contract that can serve the needs of the child without causing financial hardship to the adoptive family

The Previsitation Stage

The previsitation process is not negotiation but a fact-finding mission. The prospective adoptive parent or parents investigate a particular state's subsidy rates to determine if the rates are adequate to make adoption possible within their family. Such an investigation is necessary because of the great variance in IV-E AAP across the country.

Rates vary from lows like Alabama's starting rate of $205 per month to Connecticut's basic rate of $567 per month. The national IV-E AAP basic rate average in 1996 was $356 per month, according to NACAC. Some states have only a basic rate, which increases slightly with the child's age, but most have higher specialized rates, too, for children with more severe disabilities. This is complicated by the fact that some higher tiers of rates may not even be published information that an adoptive parent can easily lay hands on.

Basic Versus Specialized Rates

Margie and her husband, Scott, recently wanted to add to their family a sibling group of two sisters that they found in the photolisting book of a southern state. Since they already had a large family, they were afraid their straining budget could not handle a low subsidy. One of the children in the sibling group is blind, and raising her will require expensive modifications to their home and the purchase of specialized equipment. Before asking for a visit with the children, Margie sought help by calling NACAC and asking about NAATRIN.

Margie's NAATRIN representative looked up the state where the children live in the NAATRIN book and found a below average basic rate of $250 per month. Margie had already been told by the children's social worker that this basic rate was probably the amount each child would qualify to receive.

However, the NAATRIN book also indicted a more realistic specialized rate of $600 per month when certain criteria are met. The children's social worker had not even known about this rate. This family was able to apply for the specialized rate on the vision-disabled sibling. When they received it, they continued with the adoption of both children. Without their previsitation investigation, this adoption would not have happened and the children might still be waiting.

Purchase of Services

Purchase of Services, or POS, is a benefit that should be negotiated during the previsitation stage. Although this negotiation often takes place between two agencies without involving parents, it is a good idea for prospective adopters to know what POS is and how it can affect their ability to adopt and their finances.

The POS contract is made between a private adoption agency and a state or public adoption agency in a special needs adoption situation. The two agencies can be in the same state or in two different states. This contract dictates how much the state agency will pay the private agency in the way of fees and costs for their work on the adoption. This is both a finder's fee, because the private agency has found an adoptive family for a waiting child with special needs, and a "purchase of the private agency's services" to the family and to the state agency.

The POS contract impacts families because the higher POS the state agency will pay, the lower the fees charged to the adopting family. For example, if a private agency charges $2,500 for a special needs adoption, start to finish, and the state agency is willing to pay a POS of $2,000, the family will only be responsible for paying the remaining $500 of that bill. Furthermore, using nonrecurring and adoption tax credits, as we shall see later in this chapter, this same family can easily be reimbursed this expenditure and other personal one-time adoption costs after the finalization of the placement. This results in a free adoption. And we know that when the special needs adoption process is free or very low cost, many more adoptions and repeat adoptions will take place as a result.

The POS contract is the definition of a win-win proposition. The state agency, which may not have the manpower to recruit enough adoptive homes, finds adoptive families, waiting children find permanency, private agencies recoup costs so they can stay in business, and adoptive families pay lower fees to open their homes to waiting children.

Sometimes, states, counties, and cities will refuse to negotiate or pay POS to any private agency other than those local private agencies they have previously negotiated annual POS contracts with. They may adopt this rule thinking it will save money. While this is probably a "penny wise and pound foolish" philosophy in the long term, there is no law that says state agencies must pay a POS if they don't want to.

But that is not the worst problem. Sometimes, state agencies will automatically set aside the homestudies that come in from private agencies so that they do not have to deal with paying POS. This is unfortunate both because it makes adoptive matches more difficult and because some private agencies don't try to or no longer negotiate POS contracts. Since 1986 when the federal nonrecurring program was developed, and especially since federal and state adoption tax credits came into existence, the special needs adoption process has become a great deal more affordable for most families. In many cases, all fees paid can be eventually reimbursed to the adoptive family without the need for a POS contract.

In one case we know about, a certain state agency would not accept any private agency studies on younger child with special needs who they felt could be placed without POS. One family working with a private agency had so much trouble getting their homestudy looked at, their worker eventually wrote "NO PURCHASE OF SERVICES NEEDED" on the top of every page of the homestudy in big red letters. After that, the study was accepted, read, and a child was eventually placed with the family. Happily, the nonrecurring program and the state's policy of paying all visitation costs made the adoption a free one for the family without POS.

For families who are adopting through a private agency, and who do not necessarily need a POS contract, it is a good idea to feature this information prominently on page one of the adoption homestudy. In this way, the study will not be set aside before it is read. For instance, the top of page one might read: "This adoption agency will not necessarily (or does not) need to negotiate a Purchase of Services contract for this placement. Please contact the agency director for more information."

As you prepare to negotiate, look to the future. This is the time to anticipate and plan. One-time help and miscellaneous assistance may be available even if there is nothing official in the policy. It doesn't hurt to inquire. Ask yourself and your social worker questions such as:

- Will my child arrive with sufficient clothing, shoes, winter clothing, any necessary specialized education materials, medical apparatus or machinery, enough prescription medications and food supplements for at least one full month, a car seat, eyeglasses, limb braces, and other necessary items?

- If not, are there funds to supply these missing items? Which items can you afford to supply, and which ones must be supplied by the state?

- Does the child need, or might he or she need, specialized tutoring, counseling, physical therapy, dental work, operations, medical procedures, or other expensive extras?

- Does the contract address these present and future needs? This is the time to ask about dental braces. (One parent we know of had sacrificed her savings account to purchase her son's braces only to discover that the state from where she had adopted him would have paid for the braces if she had requested it. She is currently trying to negotiate a refund from the state, but it is easier to obtain payment for a service than it is to get reimbursement for a bill you have already paid.)

- Think ahead to home modifications. You may not need a wheelchair ramp while your child weighs twenty pounds, but you will need one, and an electric wheelchair lift for your van, when that child is older. These are expensive items and should be written into the contract.

- Will your child need bathroom modifications in order to achieve hygiene independence? Ask now that this need be written and paid for as it comes up.
- Some children will eventually need computers to succeed in school. Whether because of speech or fine motor disabilities, some children will need a home computer and/or a laptop computer to use away from home or to keep at school. Request funds for these computers at the time of adoption. Usually you will need a doctor's statement about the child's need or a prescription in order to negotiate this.
- Are extras like medical appointment mileage reimbursement, baby-sitting, and respite care available? Some states pay for these helpful programs with Title XX funds. Some states won't use Title XX funds for these purposes. Again, ask.

Adoption Tax Credits

This is a good time, before you have spent money, to start thinking about the adoption tax credit. Federal tax credits are available to all people who adopt children, but this credit will expire in the year 2001 for some adopted children. A phone call to the IRS should be on the to-do list of every prospective special needs adoptive parent because the tax rules are always changing. As of this writing, IRS Publication 968 says: "After 2001, the adoption credit applies only to an adoption of a child with special needs and does not apply to an adoption of a foreign child."

When you contact the IRS, ask for Publication 968, Tax Benefits for Adoption, and for Form 8839, Qualified Adoption Expenses, and for any other tax-related publications that are currently available. Get the latest information the IRS has to offer and save those adoption-related receipts. You can download forms from the IRS Web site at http://www.irs.ustreas.gov.

Also, ask about state adoption tax credits. Many states now offer special needs adoption tax incentive programs of their own. For special needs adoption, the federal tax credit depends on several different factors and can go as high as $6,000 but you can only receive a credit against taxes you actually pay. In other words, if you paid $7,000 in income taxes, you can get as much as $6,000 of that back in a credit. But if you only paid $3,000 in income taxes and had adoption expenses of $4,000, you will only be able to receive a tax credit of $3,000. Happily, the nonrecurring program can pick up where the tax credit leaves off. Find out more about nonrecurring later in this chapter.

Preplacement Negotiation

The second stage of contract negotiation is preplacement negotiation, because it happens after the child's first visit but before the child is officially placed into the home for purposes of an adoption.

In older child and sibling group adoption, there are often one to five visits before adoption papers are signed and the child or children move out of the foster home into the adoptive home. In the case of infant special needs adoption, when no preplacement visits usually occur, this stage and the third stage will combine into one.

Preplacement negotiation is the first—not the only—negotiation of an assistance agreement. It may happen prior to the first visit, but is more likely to occur after one or more visits and just before the placement of the child or children. Full disclosure of records helps, but most parents cannot accurately begin to gauge the present cost of raising a particular child until one or more visits have occurred.

The foster parents are an important resource during this time. Ask them about the costs of raising this child or sibling group. Discuss every aspect of the day from breakfast to bedtime. If possible, ask the foster parents about the foster care rate they believe the child qualifies for and why. The foster parents may know about specialized rates that you do not know about.

During the first visit or visits, take notes. Look at the child's eating habits. Is a special diet required? Are there food allergies? Are dietary supplements needed? Look at how the child treats his belongings. Is he or she unusually tough on clothing, shoes, or toys? Is the child destructive or impulsive? Look at the child's educational records. Will you need to supplement his education with the purchase of learning devices, workbooks, computer software, or other specialized learning materials? Will this child have medical costs not covered by IV-E Medicaid or your private health insurance? For example, will there be frequent trips to doctors, dentists, and therapists and over-the-counter medications that must be purchased regularly? Does the child wet the bed? This is an added expense. Are special skin creams or lotions needed for dry skin? If the child has asthma, is there a breathing treatment machine? This is the time to make a list of all of these special considerations because they all contribute to the cost of raising the child above and beyond what is considered to be ordinary.

Study the child's records. Look up any conditions the child has been diagnosed with in a good medical encyclopedia. Read, read, read. This is your chance to make an accurate assessment of the costs of raising this child. You can always negotiate again in the future, the law gives you that right, but doing your homework now assures your child of a better contract from the start. One new adoptive dad had no idea that his young son was supposed to wear eyeglasses at all times, take daily iron for anemia, or that the boy had been diagnosed with ADHD until he looked at old records. The current foster parents had not been aware of any of this either.

A Healthy Typical Four Year Old

Mike is adopting Jerry, described by his social worker as a healthy typical four-year-old. Jerry is a delightful child, pleasant, calm, sweet-natured, and cooperative.

He eats whatever Mike cooks, except for beets and asparagus, which is definitely typical for four-year-olds. Since Jerry's only disability is mild asthma, the agency is pressing Mike to sign a IV-E AAP contract at the basic rate for children in Jerry's age bracket.

But before he signs, Mike interviews the foster parents about Jerry's needs, and he reads and re-reads Jerry's file. What he learns is that Jerry was an expensive child to take care of, according to the foster parents. They confirmed what was buried in the thick file of papers that had arrived in Mike's home with his new son. Jerry has been diagnosed with developmental delays, speech impairment, speech delay, learning disabilities, asthma, sleepwalking, keloid scarring tendencies, bed-wetting, severe skin allergies, and is at–risk for attachment disorders.

None of these problems discouraged Mike from adopting his son, but they gave him pause about signing the first contract he was offered. Based on Jerry's many needs, he was able to negotiate a much more realistic specialized AAP rate. And it was a good thing, too. The skin creams and over-the-counter allergy medications alone became a substantial cost just two months into the adoptive placement.

Which Rate Do I Request?

Every parent must decide what to negotiate. In general, however, adoption advocates recommend that parents who live on a tight budget initially request and negotiate for the maximum amount of subsidy their child qualifies for. Under federal law, you can easily have the rate lowered or eliminated if you don't need that much subsidy later. One state administrator told us that it is rare, but occasionally a family will call and ask that the subsidy be discontinued because the family can now afford to pay all costs associated with the raising of their adopted child or children.

Another reason to pursue the maximum rate from the start is that parents generally have more leverage before the adoption than after the adoption is finalized because they want to place the child in an adoptive home. After finalization, there is no longer any question about whether the adoption will happen, so there is less motivation for the state, which puts adoptive parents at a psychological disadvantage.

Know All the Available Rates

The challenge is in making sure that you know what the maximum is. Foster care rates are public information and should be available on request from the state. If rates vary by county, a state official should be able to provide the information or tell you who to talk to at the appropriate county agency. Ask about the basic rate, the specialized rate (which may go under names like Level of Care or Difficulty of Care), and the highest rate reserved for specialized homes that care for children with severe developmental disabilities and life-threatening conditions.

Under federal law, any rate that is received by any foster family home is also theoretically negotiable in an AAP contract. This is true even if the foster family home rate is associated with a state department other than the one that handles adoptions and foster care. For example, the state department of mental health may have its own rate schedules for specialized foster homes that care for children who are mentally ill or mentally retarded. There is no law against adoptive parents of children with those conditions negotiating with the state foster care and adoption department using foster care rates from the department of mental health.

Institutional Rates

Federal funding regulations restrict the ability of parents to negotiate a Title IV-E adoption assistance payment that is equivalent to a foster care rate for institutional care. Federal law specifies that FFP is available for adoption assistance payments up to the rate a child would receive were he or she in a family foster home rather than an adoptive placement. Adoption assistance payments at the level of therapeutic or other types of specialized foster homes are eligible for FFP. States may raise adoption assistance beyond the child's appropriate family foster care payment level, but they generally refuse to do so because they must shoulder the entire financial burden for such an increase. Maximum family foster rates, therefore, function as de facto ceilings for adoption assistance.

Parents can negotiate any institutional rate that can also be paid to a qualifying family foster home under state law. Again, don't take anything for granted here. One family we know barely survived financial disaster caring for a multiply handicapped child who required twenty-four-hour supervision and round-the-clock medical intervention. For years they accepted the specialized foster care rate because their worker told them that the next highest rate was only for institutions. By chance, the adoptive mother came across the actual law and found that the institutionalized rate can also be paid to foster family homes that are equipped to deal with medically needy children.

The mother of this family asked for a fair hearing and was not only granted the new highest rate, she also was afforded several years of retroactive payments to make up the difference between what her child had been receiving, and what her child should have been receiving. The most important document in her hearing was a copy of a letter she had written soon after the adoption in which she requested the institutionalized rate if it was open to foster homes and, hence, to adoptive homes. This letter proved that she had been erroneously denied.

Can I Negotiate a Rate Higher Than What the Foster Parents Were Receiving?

Yes, as long as it is a rate that applies to the child's disabilities and can be paid to foster family homes now. In other words, it doesn't matter what your child was actually receiving in foster care; what matters is the amount the child could receive in foster care right now if he or she had not been adopted. This "what the child could receive in foster care today" rate is the true maximum an adoptive parent can usually negotiate for.

If the foster parents who cared for your child were receiving less than what the child's needs qualified him or her for, this does not mean that you must continue to receive this lesser amount. Each adoptive family is free to negotiate up to the maximum the child would receive if the child were in foster care right now. So, for example, if the maximum Jill could receive is $200 per month in 1990 when she was adopted, but foster children like her can get $350 per month in 1998, the adoptive parents can reopen negotiations anytime and ask for up to $350.

To this day, we hear about families who are denied increases because some states continue to insist that parents can negotiate only the rates that were in place when the child was adopted. This is simply not so, and it violates the whole intent of PL 96-272. Congress recognized that the needs of children change. Special needs that were not apparent at age one may become apparent after the child begins school. Children are more expensive as they grow, especially children with special needs. Negotiating increases is always the right of the parents, up to the maximum current amount payable to a similar child in a foster family home setting. And any state that tries to limit increases in more ways than PL 96-272 does is in danger of losing FFP funding. In other words, if states want federal dollars, they cannot put additional limitations on PL 96-272. PIQ 87-05 puts it this way: "State statutes which limit access to the Title IV-E Adoption Assistance Program by the addition of eligibility requirements . . . are not in conformance with Title IV-E."

What the PIQs Say about the "Current Rate"

The federal portion of adoption assistance may not exceed what the child would have received in a family foster home suitable to his or her needs. If the family foster care rate serves as a reference point, does it change as the child grows older or encounters more serious problems or is it limited to the foster care rate that the child would have received prior to the adoption?

As a reference point for federal funding of adoption assistance, the family foster care rate is a flexible standard that changes as the child's situation changes. The question is not what foster care rate did the child receive before the adoption, but what family foster care rate would be appropriate if the child were placed in an appropriate family foster home today.

The exact wording of the federal law is as follows:

. . . in no case may the amount of the adoption assistance payment exceed the foster care maintenance payment which would have been paid during the period if the child with respect to whom the adoption assistance is made had been in a foster family home (section 473[a][2] of the Social Security Act).

The "payment" refers to federal funding limits. States are free to spend more if they choose. The key phrase is *which would have been paid during the period.*

What does this mean? PIQ 86-05 notes that states may make across-the-board adjustments for such items as clothing. A number of states raise adoption assistance rates automatically when a child moves from one age group into another. The federal law permits the adoption assistance to be modified at any time as a result of changes in the child's needs or family's circumstances.

If federal financial participation were limited to foster care rates that were in effect before the adoption, none of the adjustments cited above would be allowable under federal law. As a point of reference for determining the limits of federal funding, the foster care rate means the rate that the child would receive if he or she were removed from the adoptive home today and placed in an appropriate family foster care setting. Although federal funding does not include institutional rates, adoption assistance rates could be raised to the highest family therapeutic foster care levels and still be eligible for federal participation if a child's emotional problems escalated and such a placement were warranted. The agency and parents would need to obtain sufficient documentation from qualified providers verifying the child's situation and the types of services he or she needed.

But My Child Came from a Private Adoption Agency

May states categorically deny access to the Title IV-E adoption assistance program to children who are not in the care (custody, responsibility) of the state if such children meet the eligibility requirements? No! See the hearing chapters and the discussion of PIQ 87-05 in Part III for more information.

Paying Legal Costs

Between POS, nonrecurring, and tax credits, many families end up with free or very low-cost special needs adoptions. When costs run higher than reimbursements, they will typically be related to the final major adoption process expense, paying the attorney for finalizing the adoption in court. Finalization legal costs run anywhere from $250 to $1,000 or more, plus court costs. Some lawyers set a flat fee and others charge by the hour.

But there is an alternative. It is possible in some states to finalize your own special needs adoptions and not hire a lawyer at all. Finalizing a special needs adoption can be pretty simple because these types of adoptions are not contested and because the adoption agencies do the vast majority of the legal paperwork prior to the involvement of an attorney.

We know of a recent case in the Midwest where a family finalized on an older child adoption, a child who came from overseas, and did all the legal work themselves. The experienced adoptive mother, who does not have a law degree, described the process as surprisingly easy.

However, the involvement of an attorney in the finalization of adoptions affords maximum protection to the child, the birthparents, the adoptive family, and the adoption agency. If money is the issue, shop around. Experienced adoption attorneys understand how much less time a special needs adoption typically requires of them and may negotiate discounts on noncontested special needs adoptions. Ask about legal aid. Ask your social worker, adoption support group and local disability law center about low-cost legal alternatives. If you still want to do your own legal work, make sure you have the advance cooperation and approval of your social worker, the child's Court Appointed Special Advocate (CASA) or Guardian ad litum and the judge who grants the adoption.

On-going Postlegal Negotiation

The third and last stage of negotiation occurs after the adoption is finalized. This is an ongoing process that may occur any number of times. When parents see a change in their child's needs, or a reason to renegotiate anything in the contract, they have a right to do so. States may not lower a subsidy without the parent's agreement.

RECERTIFICATION

This right and process of renegotiation should not be confused with a different process called "recertification" (sometimes called annual recertification.) Parents in some states will be asked to resign a IV-E AAP contract every one or two years or more. However, question number 7 in a recent PIQ, called 98-02, declares that states are not required to have a recertification process at all.

This recertification process should not be confused with postfinalization negotiation. The recertification process does not limit parental rights in any way. In other words, if you sign a new contract on May 1 and find that you need to renegotiate part of the subsidy contract on May 2, you can do so.

Remaining eligible for IV-E should be easy. PIQ 98-02 speaks to this in great detail. The following three questions speak to ongoing eligibility:

• Is the child under age 18 or 21 or mentally or physically disabled?
• Are the adoptive parents legally responsible for the child?
• Are the adoptive parents continuing to support the child?

The continuing eligibility process should not be intrusive. The parents' income cannot be considered since adoption assistance is not means-tested. Families should not be subjected to time consuming investigations into their finances. If a state requires annual recertification, it should be a painless process for families that satisfy the minimum requirements listed above.

Tax Returns, Receipts, and Family Budgets

Dr. Maria Ramirez, a podiatrist, admits to being something of a privacy nut. She guards her personal information closely. Perhaps the long and detailed adoption homestudy process and the home visits by so many social workers and the legal questions and the personal questions total strangers ask about her transracially adopted child have contributed to this attitude. Whatever the reason, now that her adoption is finalized and the IV-E contract negotiated, she wants to recapture a sense of privacy that she feels she has lost.

When a recertification letter arrived in the mail demanding a copy of her last tax return and a detailed family budget, she balked. She knew PL 96-272 is not a means-tested assistance program. Why did the state want so much financial information from her, and what right did they have to ask for it? As she read further, she grew angrier. The same letter demanded copies of receipts for medical expenses not covered by health insurance or Medicaid. Now she had to keep receipts, too?

Dr. Ramirez contacted a child advocate and was told that such requirements are not part of PL 96-272, nor can the information legally be used to lower a subsidy amount. However, such information can be required of people with state subsidy contracts because state subsidies have no connection with federal law. Since hers was a federal IV-E contract, Dr. Ramirez decided to try a little passive resistance. She wrote a cheery note across the top of the recertification letter that said: "This request is illegal. My adopted daughter remains my responsibility and I am supporting her. This is all you need to know under federal law. But I will also be happy to inform you that she is a joyful child who is making new friends, and she is the light of my life. Thank-you."

A few weeks later, she received a phone call from a state administrator informing her that her child's subsidy check would be immediately discontinued if she did not supply the requested tax return, family budget, and receipts. It did no good to recite the law to the administrator who said he was only "doing my job."

Dr. Ramirez faced a choice of giving them this information or asking for an administrative hearing. She chose the latter and eventually prevailed in her assertion that the state's request was illegal. She had lost three months subsidy in the process but was given full retroactive payments by the hearing officer. And she may not stop there. She has plans to go see the director of the state's adoption unit and ask for a review of the state's recertification policy for IV-E contracts. After all, there's no reason why a bad policy should go unchallenged and unchanged.

HOW TO RENEGOTIATE

When a child's needs change, renegotiating changes to a contract involves the same steps as the initial negotiation. Talk to your support group or NACAC representative, gather copies of the latest state laws and policies, and document the need. Letters from doctors and teachers, test results, psychological summaries, and the like are all examples of documentation that is required for renegotiation.

Negotiation: A Give and Take

Jenny has ADHD and she is not responding well to medication. Her inattentiveness is the least of the problem. It is her impulsivity and hyperactivity that cause most of the problems. Her mother, Anne, has kept a list of all of the toys and furniture and knick-knacks that Jenny has destroyed in the last six months. The list is three pages long. Jenny is on her third bed in four years because of the way she jumps on it, kicks it when she is angry, and because of her habit of gouging holes in her mattress at night using toys. Jenny has also destroyed a desk at school, two calculators, and a computer keyboard.

In the initial negotiation process, Anne had negotiated a first-level specialized rate for Jenny because of the ADHD. Now, armed with a letter from Jenny's doctor, a letter from Jenny's teacher, and Anne's own list of items Jenny has destroyed, Anne is negotiating a third-level specialized rate. She writes a letter making the request, quotes the state requirements of the third-level specialized rate (that is "child is destructive at home and away from home"), and encloses her letters of documentation.

Two weeks later, she is phoned by her worker and told that they find only enough evidence for a level-two rate. Anne now faces a choice. She can accept level two and sign a new contract and receive that increase, or she can try again for a level three and eventually receive a fair hearing on the matter. She has nothing to lose from a fair hearing, but she decides that a level two is adequate for now and agrees. In the future, should she feel Jenny's needs warrant it, she will go back again and try for a level three.

This is negotiation. It is a give and take, a two-way discourse. Some parents will negotiate more strenuously than others. But what matters is that parents have the information they need to negotiate from a position of knowledge. Knowledge is strength.

EVERY CONTRACT HAS FOUR PARTS TO BE NEGOTIATED

AAP is not the only item to be negotiated in a IV-E AAP contract. There are three other parts to the contract: Nonrecurring expenses reimbursement, Medicaid, and Service Subsidies.

Nonrecurring Expenses Reimbursement

Nonrecurring is short for Nonrecurring Adoption Expenses Reimbursement, an important federal program with an unfortunately cumbersome name. Nonrecurring was initiated in 1986 to help parents defray the one-time (nonrecurring) cost of adopting children with special needs.

One time costs include items like legal fees, adoption agency fees, the cost of the homestudy, medical exams for the homestudy, long-distance phone calls, and other adoption-related expenses. States have an option to set the dollar amount on this singular benefit, but the federal government will offer only the highest rate of FFP up to the first $2,000.

Part of the previsitation investigation should include the question, "How much does this state pay in nonrecurring?" If the amount is set low, at $1,000, for example, this is something parents should know up front.

Happily, there are two big positives that every parent should know about nonrecurring. First of all, at this time, it is available to all children with special needs, regardless of IV-E eligibility. Many states routinely give non-recurring to people who adopt children with special needs born overseas and secondly, if the nonrecurring is insufficient to reimburse parents for all of their adoption process expenses, generous tax breaks and POS also may be available. See the Tax Credit and POS sections in this chapter for more information.

To apply for nonrecurring, ask your social worker, because every state has its own way of handling this program. Usually, at finalization, the parents are given a form to fill out listing their one-time adoption expenses. These include things like legal fees, adoption agency fees, the cost of the homestudy, medical exams for the homestudy, long distance phone calls, and other adoption-related expenses. Make a copy of the completed form and receipts for your records, attach your receipts to the form, and send them to the address indicated on the form. Keep the copy for your records. A few weeks later, a check will arrive. Be careful not to claim a tax credit for any expenses that were reimbursed to you under this program. Double-dipping in this way is illegal.

Recently, a parent called one of the authors asking for help with his nonrecurring claim. He had saved every receipt from the numerous pre-placement visits with his son, but his social worker was now refusing to accept them. She told him that nonrecurring only reimbursed adoptive parents for attorney fees. He didn't think this sounded right.

It isn't. The authors knew of other families in that same state who had been reimbursed for several different kinds of nonrecurring adoption-related expenses in recent years. The new dad is going to go back to his state adoption office and ask again. He is going to take with him a copy of a flyer from NAIC describing all the expenses nonrecurring can legally be used for. The flyer also explains how this federal program reimburses the states half of every dollar they reimburse to adoptive parents. With a little patience and persistence, he is very likely to see of all of his receipts accepted and reimbursed.

Medicaid

Basic medical coverage is a cornerstone of PL 96-272. Congress realized early on that children with special needs have many, varied, and expensive medical needs. Making Medicaid a part of IV-E removed a major financial disincentive to special needs adoption.

Medical assistance is not called Medicaid in every state, but medical assistance (MA) of some type must be made available to every IV-E eligible child, under federal law. To keep things simple, we refer to medical assistance as Medicaid throughout this book.

Medicaid has always been a part of IV-E contracts and, since 1997, Medicaid must also be provided to all children who receive state or non-IV-E subsidies, too. The 1997 Adoption and Safe Families Act requires that children with non-IV-E adoption subsidies receive Medicaid or equivalent coverage through an alternative state-funded health care plan if they are determined to have "special needs for medical or rehabilitative care." If your child has medically or psychologically related special needs or is "at risk" for medical, emotional, or developmental problems, he or she may meet the definition of a child in need of medical or rehabilitative care.

Parental experience and satisfaction with Medicaid varies from state to state. In states where parents are not happy with the system, dealing with the Medicaid bureaucracy is not easy, but with patience and determination it is possible. One adoptive parent said of her Medicaid experience, "Every single year since 1986, one or more of my adopted children has been dropped by Medicaid at least once due to "computer glitches" and other unexplained reasons. I always manage to get the coverage reinstated but there is a new case worker each time I call. I'm used to this hassle now, but I wish I knew when I could stop worrying about whether or not all of the children will be in the computer each month."

Remember first that you can only use Medicaid for those medical services not covered by your private health insurance or by other free sources, such as the public schools. For example, if the school offers free speech therapy, you can not use the Medicaid card to pay for speech therapy. Medicaid is your "court of last resort."

Secondly, remember that IV-E-related Medicaid is unique. You will need to explain this again and again to health care providers and to Medicaid workers. In some states, children with income-based Medicaid are assigned to HMOs (Health Maintenance Organizations) while children with IV-E-based Medicaid are not. You may need to explain repeatedly that your child receives IV-E Medicaid, or "traditional Medicaid," and not income-based Medicaid.

The advantage to having traditional Medicaid in some states is that you can choose your own health care providers (as long as the ones you choose accept Medicaid). By contrast, with HMO Medicaid, you are restricted to

certain health care providers who may or may not be geographically con-
venient. IV-E Medicaid will also transfer as you move from state to state.
For example, if you move from Rhode Island to Florida, your child's Rhode
Island Medicaid will be transferred to Florida Medicaid.

IV-E Medicaid is based on special needs and IV-E factors and is not
parental or child income-based. IV-E Medicaid's eligibility cannot be
means-tested against parental or child assets, and it is not something that
can be canceled before the child is grown. Eligibility for this type of Medicaid is permanently tied to the eligibility factors present at the time the
child originally received his or her IV-E status.

Even in 1998, Medicaid Remains Misunderstood

Some states continue to ask for financial information about the parents and child
that gives the impression that IV-E Medicaid is income based. As recently as 1998,
one state we know of was canceling the Medicaid coverage of adopted teens who
held jobs that earned them in excess of $1,000 total for the year. When a single
parent complained to her support group about the loss of her daughter's Medicaid
card under such circumstances, the support group leader found the case worker
especially intractable on the subject. It took several weeks and a phone call from
the state's highest-ranking Medicaid administrator to the child welfare worker explaining how and why IV-E Medicaid is different before the Medicaid card was
restored.

Across the country in a western state, a family therapist contacted Tim O'Hanlon
about a Medicaid problem in her state. This state has given Medicaid administration duties to the counties in 1998. Adopted children with Medicaid were being
told that their cards are good only in the county where the card originated. And
the card is no good if the family moves to a different county. Some of the therapist's
clients live outside her county and she could no longer obtain Medicaid payment
for her services to those children. She asked how to help these families advocate
for their children's Medicaid rights.

Tim's response helped her change the illegal policies. He told her that children
who qualify for Title IV-E adoption assistance are categorically (automatically) eligible for Medicaid. Medicaid transfers with the child, when the child moves.
County boundaries within a state have no bearing on Medicaid eligibility for Title
IV-E eligible children. In fact, Federal Adoption Assistance regulations stipulate that
Title IV-E adoption assistance agreements must stipulate that the child is eligible
for Medicaid and that the agreement remains in effect regardless of the state in
which the child resides: "(b) The adoption assistance agreement for payments pursuant to section 473(a)(2) must meet the requirements of section 475(3) of the Act
and must: (3) Specify the nature and amount of any payment, services and assistance to be provided under such agreement and, for purposes of eligibility under
title XIX of the Act, specify that the child is eligible for Medicaid services; and (4)
Specify, with respect to agreements entered into, on, or after October 1, 1983, that
the agreement shall remain in effect regardless of the State of which the adoptive
parents are residents at any given time."

On August 8, 1983, the federal Children's Bureau issued Policy Interpretation

(PI) ACYF-PI-83-08 to amplify the federal regulations. The PI made it clear that if a child who was eligible for Title IV-E adoption assistance moved from one state to another, he or she was eligible for Medicaid in the new state of residence. It reaffirms that "the written adoption assistance agreement shall contain provisions for the protection of the interests of the child in cases where the child is placed with adoptive parents living in another State and in cases where the adoptive parents and the child move to another State while the agreement is in effect. 45 CFR 1356.40(b) outlines what must be contained in the adoption assistance agreement."

The policy interpretation notes that in order to remain eligible for federal funds, states "which enter into adoption assistance agreements must take measures to assure that the terms of the agreements are met." This includes provisions for medical care inasmuch as "children eligible for title IV-E adoption assistance payments are deemed eligible for title XIX (Medicaid) regardless of their residence within the nation . . ." PI 83-08 announced the formation of the Interstate Compact on Medical Assistance, which was created specifically as a vehicle to transfer a IV-E child's Medicaid coverage to his or her state of residence.

Furthermore, non-IV-E eligible children who qualify for the state-funded adoption subsidy plan are eligible for Medicaid coverage if they are determined to have a "special need for medical or rehabilitative care." The Adoption and Safe Families Act of 1997 requires that states cover children in this category under the state health plan. Clearly the children's county of residence has no bearing on a child's eligibility under this federal law.

Section 306 of the law "provides for health insurance coverage (including, at State option, through the program under the State plan approved under title XIX) for any child who has been determined to be a child with special needs" and on whose behalf a non-IV-E adoption assistance agreement has been completed. In order to be eligible for Medicaid or an alternative state health care plan, the child must be determined to have "special needs for medical, mental health, or rehabilitative care. . . ."

The law also specifies that if the state provides coverage under a health plan other than Medicaid, it shall ensure that "the medical benefits, including mental health benefits, provided are of the same type and kind as those that would be provided for children by the State under title XIX" (Medicaid). Should the health care funds become depleted, the child will be deemed eligible for Medicaid.

If any children described above are being denied Medicaid coverage, the state is in violation of federal law. There may be question of which county pays the bills, but there is no question of the child's eligibility.

Families with children who are eligible for Title IV-E adoption assistance and families with children who are eligible for non-IV-E state adoption subsidies have hearing rights. They should immediately apply for an administrative fair hearing if they are denied Medicaid coverage. The hearing is free and they can consult advocates to help them present their arguments."

Not all Medicaid is adoption-related, of course. Some Medicaid cards are temporary, are based on income, and can be legally means-tested. This describes the type of Medicaid coverage that come with TANF benefits, for example. These Medicaid rules are different from the ones that apply to adoption-related Medicaid.

Since there are different rules for different kinds of Medicaid, it is likely that some states will continue to erroneously discontinue Medicaid coverage for adopted children. If this happens to you, make sure that when coverage is reinstated, it is retroactive so that recent medical bills will be paid and not forwarded on to you.

Erroneous Medicaid cancellations can be and are reversed, but if a parent can avoid the problem, all the better. Parents can sidestep possible problems by taking a few simple steps when it comes to their children's assets. For example, if a college savings account in a child's name could trigger problems for Medicaid coverage, parents could put their child's college savings into their own savings account or into a college IRA instead. And when a case worker calls with the annual Medicaid recertification, make sure you explain that your child's Medicaid coverage is adoption-related and not subject to means-testing.

For this reason, it is important for adoptive parents to be aware of Medicaid rules and laws in their own state and in the state from which the child was adopted. Keep the phone number of your state's highest-ranking Medicaid expert handy and the number of your local Medicaid case worker, because you will probably need these sooner or later.

Service Subsidies

Service subsidies is the term for a miscellaneous group of important benefits and programs that are available to both children with IV-E and with state AAP contracts, depending on state laws and policies. The funding for service subsidies comes from FFP, Medicaid, Title XX, state budgets, county and city funds, and other federal programs. Unlike AAP funding, the availability and funding of service subsidies are something that is always changing, so it is a good idea to ask about these on a regular basis.

Service subsidies include services like respite care, day care, residential treatment, dental braces, counseling, medical mileage, extraordinary medical expenses, tutoring, clothing allowances, personal computers, and even items like vitamins and software. For more information about service subsidies, see Chapter 3.

THE LITTLE KNOWN COLLEGE CLAUSE

Title IV-E adoption subsidies don't have to end at age eighteen. PIQ 85-05 states: ". . . title IV-E adoption assistance, at State option, may be continued to age 21 with respect to a child with a mental or physical handicap."

In some states subsidies are extended to the end of the senior year in high school, even if this is past the child's eighteenth birthday. In other states, the subsidy ends on the child's eighteenth birthday, no matter what grade the child is in. Ask in advance about this and try to negotiate an end in subsidy that coincides with graduation, at least.

Many adoptive parents don't know this, but in some states, subsidies can continue until age twenty-two under certain conditions, such as the child's full-time college, community college, or vocational-technical student status. In some places, a IV-E subsidy becomes a state subsidy after the child's eighteenth birthday and during the college years, ending right before the twenty-second birthday.

It's been said many times, but rules do vary from state to state, so each parent must check this important benefit out carefully. For example, in some states, the student must live at home while in college for the subsidy to continue after the eighteenth birthday, while in other places, the student may live at home or in a college dorm. In some states, this age extension is open to all IV-E children who are full time students, and in other states, it is only open to those children who have more serious disabilities.

At least one state has recently eliminated this extension, so be sure that it is available before you plan the financial details of your child's freshman year in college.

WHAT IF THEY SAY NO?

Happily, well-informed negotiations that are in the best interest of the child often go well. When they do break down, remember that you are entitled to a fair hearing under the law. Chapters 9, 10, and 11 have more on that process.

CAN MY CHILD'S SUBSIDY BE ARBITRARILY LOWERED OR CANCELED?

No, not without your permission. Unlike some temporarily funded service subsidies, IV-E AAP payments cannot be lowered or eliminated and Medicaid cannot be canceled because, for example, the state decides a particular family should receive a smaller check. But this does not necessarily mean that some states won't try. A few years ago, a southwestern state sent letters to adoptive families telling them their subsidy amounts were being rolled back to save state funds. (This letter made no mention of the fact that more than half of the IV-E subsidy funds are federal in origin!) The letter did not ask for anyone's permission, it simply stated that this would happen across the board.

Some families wrote back protesting that such a rollback was illegal under PL 96-272. One of these parents told us that her subsidy amount did not drop "by one penny" as a result of her protest. How many other families lost badly needed funds for their children because they did not know that this arbitrary rollback action is illegal or because they did not know they could protest the decision? See Chapter 9 on administrative hearings for a further discussion of this issue.

SIDE EFFECT

The adoption assistance contract negotiation process carries a side effect worth noting. It often makes true advocates out of parents. Parents can use their newly acquired negotiation skills to advocate for their children medically and educationally. You might say that raising children with special needs is a long-term negotiation process on several fronts. However, the end result, a successful and self-assured young adult, makes it all worthwhile.

8

Adoptive Families As Community Assets

> Bureaucracy, the rule of no one, has become the modern form of despotism.
>
> —Mary McCarthy (1912–1989)

CAPACITY INVENTORIES: TOOLS FOR EMPOWERMENT

Adoptive and foster parents have a curious relationship with child welfare agencies. They are recruited as valuable resources for children needing homes. Then, once in the fold, their skills and experiences are often devalued. Agencies study, train, and certify families, yet rarely treat them as full partners. The considerable knowledge of adoptive and foster parents rarely plays an influential role in shaping major policy decisions or informing standards of practice.

A capacity inventory is a tool that family support groups can use to identify and mobilize the wealth of individual skills and talents that they possess. In addition to their years of experience in caring for children from all types of backgrounds, members of adoptive and foster family support groups routinely construct budgets, publish newsletters, organize events, counsel troubled parents, make referrals, and contribute a wide variety of other skills to their communities. A capacity inventory offers a more systematic approach to what most support groups are already doing, sharing their knowledge and skills.

At heart, a capacity inventory is a process for building relationships and partnerships by listing the skills and talents that individuals have and are willing to contribute and harnessing those skills in service of goals identified by the group.

SOCIAL SERVICE AGENCIES AND THE DEFICIT PRINCIPLE

The cataloguing of individual skills in capacity inventories reflects a new approach to family services, one that emphasizes people's strengths and as well as their needs. The child welfare and social services systems have traditionally operated on a deficit principle. Agencies typically identify deficiencies and attempt to address them in certain characteristic ways.

• Deficits such as poverty, illness, child abuse, unemployment, and inadequate housing are identified and translated into corresponding needs such as jobs, food, health care, rent assistance, child protection, counseling, foster care, or a permanent family.

• Public and private agencies specialize in providing services to address particular needs of children and families.

• Individual agencies often specialize in providing services to a particular category of needy individuals or "clients" such as the elderly, welfare mothers, at risk children, foster children, adopted children, and the disabled.

• Client categories are determined by eligibility standards such as age, income, or diagnosed disability. Individual clients must meet a particular set of eligibility requirements in order to receive a particular service from a specialized agency.

AN ASSET-BASED APPROACH

Agencies provide essential assistance to children, families and the elderly, but as commentators such as John Kretzmann and John McKnight of the Institute for Policy Research at Northwestern University in Evanston, Illinois, have observed, the social services system came to view clients exclusively in terms of their problems and needs rather than their strengths and skills. After studying dozens of communities, Kretzmann and McKnight became convinced that even the most deprived neighborhoods had unrecognized assets in the form of individual talents and voluntary associations of citizens. In one particularly deprived Chicago neighborhood, for example, investigators identified 319 churches, business organizations, block clubs, advocacy organizations, support groups, and other viable voluntary associations operating in the community.

The deficit model in Kretzmann and McKnight's view was not incorrect so much as limited and one-sided. Communities that were becoming revitalized were aware of their deficiencies, but made a conspicuous effort to identify and build on their own individual gifts and capacities. Kretzmann and McKnight outlined general principles and strategies for mobilizing the gifts of individuals and the assets of voluntary citizen associations in their 1993 book, *Building Communities from the Inside Out*. Since that time they have formed the Asset-Based Community Development (ABCD) Institute, an informal faculty of people around the country engaged in the application of community capacity building principles. A variety of workbooks, a videotape, and other materials explaining asset mapping and individual capacity inventories are also available through the ABCD Institute.

McKnight and his colleagues make an interesting distinction between the domain of social services and that of community associations. The former domain is dominated by the professional client role in which the primary focus is determining what kinds of services are needed and available. The primary questions in the service context are what do you need and do you meet the eligibility requirements?

The community domain is focused on building relationships. It is the domain of the citizen in which questions predominate such as: "What are your interests? What gifts and talents do you have to contribute?" Many of us belong to networks of friends and associations to which we contribute our time and talents and receive various kinds of support in return in the form of information, emotional resources, and even financial assistance.

ADOPTIVE AND FOSTER PARENTS AS CLIENTS AND ASSETS

Historically, adoptive and foster parents have been treated principally as social service clients based on the identified needs of their children. What has not been recognized is how strikingly they embody the kinds of citizen assets discussed by Kretzmann and McKnight. Adoptive and foster parents often bring an array of gifts to the table. Many acquire a sophisticated knowledge of child development and childhood health issues. Even more impressive is the mysterious calling to provide a family for an abused or neglected child, a decision that often transforms their lives in profound ways. The willingness of thousands of single adults and couples to knowingly assume the risks and challenges of special needs adoption as well as the joys is an awe-inspiring phenomenon.

In addition to the individual gifts and skills possessed by adoptive and foster parents, their support groups are fine examples of the assets possessed by voluntary community associations. Parents join family support groups, not to receive services, but to form relationships. In doing so, they contribute their time and experiences to other families and receive much in return.

To say that adoptive and foster families have unrecognized gifts and assets does not imply that the service domain should be reduced. As the child welfare system gears up to find more permanent homes for children in foster care, there is a greater need than ever before to invest in the success of individuals who step forward to adopt children with medical and emotional problems. Recognizing adoptive and foster parents as people with individual gifts and collective assets, however, has the potential to change the way services are provided and to mobilize the resources of these citizens more effectively.

THE CONSTRUCTION AND USES OF CAPACITY INVENTORIES

As long as parents are treated exclusively as clients, their ability to contribute to improving adoption and foster care policy will remain quite limited. Alternatively, if support groups begin conducting individual capacity inventories among their members and other adoptive and foster parents in the community, they will undoubtedly document an impressive array of experience and knowledge that could be put to use on behalf of the state's children.

A collection of capacity inventories representing major foster and adoption support organizations in the state would be an impressive document to present to key legislators and state and local agencies. A skills database could help adoptive parents communicate more effectively with one another and help generate creative ideas about the ways that parents could participate in policy decisions and shape adoption and foster care practice.

The information collected in a capacity inventory depends on the purpose of the group. For example, an adoptive or foster parent group interested in affecting child welfare policy and practice might inventory interest and skills in communication and advocacy such as setting up Web pages, dealing with legislators, or experience in desktop publishing.

One organization in Kansas City asked its members to list connections with associations and organizations in the larger community. A support group could use the capacity inventory as a tool for building community partnerships by surveying individuals' connections to various individuals and institutions such as local politicians and business leaders, churches, and foundations. Adoptive and foster parent organizations might also include a section that asks what individuals could contribute to other families such as respite care, mentoring, advocacy, information and referral, or participation in a car pool or cooperative child care.

Depending on their concerns, support groups can select any one of several areas to conduct an individual capacity inventory. The information can then be organized into a database and used to create a skills and services exchange as a basis for more effective organization and communication around policy issues or for a variety of other purposes.

Kretzmann and McKnight offer some tips for citizen groups who undertake individual capacity inventories.

- Before constructing an individual capacity inventory form, take some time to consider what you want to achieve and what the information will be used for. Return to these questions throughout the process.

- Collect the data with a purpose in mind. The process of discussing individual skills and gifts should stimulate new ideas and relationships. You can begin forging new connections and partnerships as the information is being collected. You don't need to wait until all the information has been accumulated.

- Members of the group or organization should conduct the individual capacity inventory because it is a tool for building community. It is not a survey conducted by an outside researcher but a means of forging a dialogue with friends and neighbors.

- Try to strike a reasonable balance between comprehensiveness and trying to collect too much information at one time. A group might begin with skills and capacities in one area and then expand to other areas.

- Concentrate on people's gifts and skills even though you are often painfully aware of unmet needs.

- Think about ways to be inconclusive. The adopted and foster children have gifts and skills as well as the adults.

- For further information on individual capacity inventories and asset mapping, readers may contact Eliza Earle at the Asset-Based Community Development Institute at (847) 491–8711 or by E-mail at earlee@nwu.edu. Readers also might want to visit the ABCD Institute's Web site at http://www.nwu.edu/IPR/abcd.html.

Below, we offer an example of a capacity inventory. It is not presented as a prescription, but a means of stimulating discussion. Capacity inventories should always be customized to reflect the goals of the community.

SAMPLE CAPACITY INVENTORY

We are trying to identify the gifts, strengths, abilities and interests that you are willing to share with the community of foster and adoptive parents. The information you provide will be used to build relationships and connect people and resources in a way that will benefit our children. The inventory will take about 20 minutes per person to complete. Your participation and time are greatly appreciated!

Personal Information

Name
Address
Phone
Fax

SAMPLE CAPACITY INVENTORY

Communication and Advocacy

Experiences and Skills	Have Experience	Interested
Setting up web sites		
Doing research on the internet		
Setting up e-mail loops		
Testifying before legislative committees		
Legal skills		
Specialized knowledge in an area of public policy		
Desktop publishing skills such as producing a newsletter		
Contacting and organizing people		
Writing skills		

Connections and Relationships I Have in My Community

Please indicate organizations in which you actively participate or individuals within those organizations with whom you have a personal or professional relationship.

Type of Organization	Name of Organization or Individual and Title	Nature of Relationship
Church		
Legislator		
Local political leader		
Corporation		
Foundation		
Advocacy group		
Professional Association		
Law firms or lawyer		
Community groups		

Personal Inventory

Gifts and Skills	Am Doing	Am Willing to Do
Organizing social events		
Providing respite care		
Serving as a mentor for a foster or adoptive family		
Serving as an advocate for a family needing services		

Gifts and Skills	Am Doing	Am Willing to Do
Serving as telephone pal		
Participating in a car pool		
Participating in cooperative child care		
Serving as a referral or information source in a particular area of child development or disability.		
Serving as an officer in a family support group		

Other skills that you are willing to share:

_____

_____

Priority Skills: When you think of your gifts and skills, what three things do you do best?

1. _____

2. _____

3. _____

Which skills are you most likely to volunteer?

1. _____

2. _____

3. _____

The Green Valley Adoptive and Foster Care Support Group

The Green Valley Adoptive and Foster Care Support Group had grown to 150 families. Members relied on one another for respite care, moral support, and information about doctors and other medical providers. The monthly meetings of the support group were well attended.

Several concerns arose at the group's October meeting. The new administration was taking a harder line on adoption assistance, demanding that families settle for the most minimal payments and services and refusing to amend existing agreements. One member heard that a number of children had recently been determined ineligible for adoption assistance. As the members exchanged stories, they suspected that many of the state's actions were based in questionable information.

The parents were angry, but also somewhat uncertain about how to proceed. Taking on the state bureaucracy was an intimidating experience because it was hard to know how to respond when a bureaucrat began flinging rule numbers and policy claims at an anxious family. Finally, Matt Mahaney spoke up and suggested that the support group conduct an inventory of the skills possessed by its members. "We have a lot of capable people," he argued. "I'll bet that we will be surprised by the resources within our group."

Matt was appointed to lead a subcommittee to construct a capacity inventory. The subcommittee decided to place particular attention on skills and experiences that would be useful in advocacy for adoption assistance. The instrument was drafted and approved at the next support group meeting. Members of the subcommittee and a dozen volunteers began calling on families to administer the inventory. In some cases, the instrument was completed and returned by mail.

Within six weeks, seventy capacity inventories were completed and the results were complied in a database. As Matt Mahaney had predicted, the results were impressive. A lawyer in the support group agreed to work with two parents with backgrounds in research to collect federal and state laws and policies pertaining to adoption assistance. Three parents volunteered to serve as a policy team to families who were negotiating adoption assistance agreements or going through administrative hearings.

Four persons in the group were particularly skilled in computer technology. They constructed a Web site and published the policy team's materials on the Internet. The technical group also organized an E-mail system to facilitate rapid communication.

The inventory identified several parents with writing ability and teaching experience. Six of these people got together and devised a curriculum to assist families in negotiating subsidy agreements and pursuing administrative hearings.

Two executives in the group knew prominent republican state legislators. The father of one adoptive family was a retired union official and had strong ties to the Democratic Party. Another member served as director of a nonprofit organization and had some lobbying experience. These four individuals formed a lobbying team to keep track of pending legislation and to communicate policy concerns to leaders in the House and Senate.

After small teams with common interests and abilities began to form, the resulting dialogue at monthly support group meetings began to generate ideas for new projects. The policy team and the training curriculum groups, for example, decided to develop a program for advocates to work with individual families and accompany them to subsidy negotiations and hearings. The attorney lined up some colleagues to serve as consultants on a limited basis free of charge.

The research group identified a dozen parents from the capacity inventory who had extensive experience with mental health providers and with negotiating special education plans. Two of these parents were recruited to compile a list of therapists and other service providers. Four agreed to serve as advocates for families in negotiating special education plans with the schools. The technical team published the list of providers and their areas of specialization on the Web site as well as list of attorneys that could represent families on adopted related issues.

The lobby group identified a list of key legislative leaders and the technical group set up a system for generating faxes and E-mail messages on important topics to the support group.

9

Administrative Hearings: Appealing Agency Decisions

Latin phrases [for administrative hearings]:

- "Heu, modo itera omnia quae mihi nunc nuper narravisti, sed nunc Anglice." (Listen, would you repeat everything you just told me, only this time say it in English.)
- "Cuae mihi non est quod alii parentes faciant." (I don't care what the other parents are doing.)
- "Non sum iniquus." (I am not being unreasonable.)
- "Haud fiet, et clavo fixum est." (Nothing doing, and that's final.)
  —Henry Beard, from his book *Latin for All Occasions*

THE FAIR HEARING

When adoption assistance negotiation or renegotiation does not go well, parents can opt to request an administrative hearing, or a fair hearing, to air their grievances. As veterans of this process will attest, fair hearings are not always fair, but they are a powerful tool in any advocate's toolbox.

Applicants and participants in federal assistance programs have the right to appeal agency decisions that affect subsidy benefits. Federal regulations at 45 CFR CH.II 205.10, (a) (5) provides that "An opportunity for a hearing shall be granted to any applicant who requests a hearing because his or her claim for financial assistance (including a request for supplemental payments under 233.23 and 233.27) is denied, or is not acted upon with reasonable promptness, and to any recipient who is aggrieved by any agency action resulting in suspension, reduction, discontinuance or termination of assistance, or determination that a protective, vendor, or two-party payment should be made or continued."

Paragraph (a) (3) specifies that "every applicant or recipient shall be informed in writing at the time of application and at the time of any action affecting his claim: (i) Of his right to a hearing as provided in paragraph (a) (5) of this section: (ii) Of the method by which he may obtain a hearing: (iii) That he may be represented by an authorized representative, such as legal counsel, relative friend, or other spokesman, or he may represent himself."

Each state, in accordance with federal law, has established an administrative fair hearing process to handle such appeals. A denial of the child's eligibility for Title IV-E adoption assistance or reimbursement of nonrecurring adoption expenses or the denial of a request for a higher amount of federal adoption assistance must be communicated to the applicant in writing along with information about how to request a hearing.

Administrative fair hearings are relatively informal proceedings in which you as adoptive parents have the opportunity to present your case in your own words. You are permitted to be represented by counsel, but depending on the issue, may choose to represent yourself and reserve the option of enlisting the services of an attorney if you decide to pursue the appeal to the final stage of the hearing process. Lack of resources to hire an attorney should never prevent you from requesting a hearing. Adoptive parents are often quite successful in representing themselves. When making a decision about whether to seek representation or go it alone, it is usually a good idea to consult with an experienced adoptive family or advocacy group.

ADDITIONAL STEPS IN THE HEARING PROCESS

Hearing decisions must be communicated in writing. If the initial hearing decision goes against you, the notification letter must also provide information about the next level of appeal. The second step in the appeals process in a number of states is an *administrative review* of the hearing, usually by a section in the state department of human services. The administrative review is not another hearing but a reconsideration of the hearing decision based on the hearing record and relevant state regulations. Once again, the administrative review decision must be communicated to the adoptive parent in writing along with information about the next level of appeal. Some states do not have the equivalent of an interim administrative review step in the appeal process. In those states, the appeal proceeds directly from the hearing decision to a local court.

An appeal to a local court for a *judicial review* of the hearing decision is the final step in the administrative hearing process itself, although families have the option of pursuing their case through the state appellate court system. Some parents have taken their appeals to the state supreme court. Two such cases are discussed at the end of Chapter 10.

The judicial review involves a judge's consideration of the issues and arguments that arose from the hearing. Because judicial reviews and administrative reviews are not separate hearings, it is important to present all the essential arguments and documentation at the original hearing so that they will become part of the record that is reviewed. Parents or their representatives are usually permitted to file depositions with the court outlining their argument for assistance.

The hearing itself and the administrative review are available to the appellants at no cost. Judicial reviews generally require modest filing fees. Adoptive families often secure legal counsel to file for the judicial review and to represent them before the court if they decide to carry their appeal to the final step in the administrative hearing process or take further legal action through the state's appellate court system.

SOME BASIC SUGGESTIONS

When faced with an adverse agency decision pertaining to adoption assistance, you should seriously consider an appeal. The following are some practical steps to take when faced with the prospect of pursuing an administrative hearing:

- *Follow the time frames for requesting an administrative hearing.* That information should be contained in the agency's written denial of your request for adoption assistance. If it is not, contact the state office of administrative hearings in the state agency that administers the adoption assistance program and ask them about the deadlines for appeal.

- *Federal hearing regulations require that families be given "adequate notice,"* which, among other things, includes the specific reason for the proposed action by the agency and the relevant laws or regulations on which it is based. Adequate notice tells you what issues you must be prepared to address at the hearing. If a hearing is scheduled without the agency providing you with a written statement of its decision on your child's eligibility and the reasons for its determination, contact the hearing section of the state children services agency. Tell the hearings official that you have not received adequate notice and cannot prepare your case because you do not know what the agency's position will be. Ask the official to contact the agency and ask the relevant parties to provide you with a list of all of its reasons the agency will cite as grounds for denying adoption assistance. Try to obtain some assurance from the hearings official that the agency will be limited to presenting issues cited in its written denial. Then, ask that a date for the hearing be postponed until after the agency complies so that you have adequate time to prepare. After you receive notice from the agency, don't be shy about asking the hearings section to allow you several weeks to put your case together if you need the time to obtain statements supporting your position or lining up witnesses.

- *Contact the state agency with responsibility for adoption and request a copy of the state adoption subsidy regulations.* If detailed information about adoption assistance is not contained in state regulations, the agency usually has some form of policy manual. The portions of that document pertaining to adoption subsidy should be available on request from the state agency.

- *Contact the legal section of the state child welfare agency and the unit that conducts administrative fair hearings if the agency refuses to send you a copy of the subsidy regulations or policy manual.* The documents should be considered public information. Remind them that federal regulations entitle you to adequate notice and that you cannot present adequate testimony on behalf of your child without access to the regulations cited by the agency to deny adoption assistance benefits.

- *Contact the agency to make arrangements to see and acquire relevant documents and to determine the basis for the agency's proposed denial of benefits.* Federal hearing regulations stipulate that the family or its representative shall have "adequate opportunity" to "examine the contents of his case file and all documents and records to be used by the agency at the hearing at a reasonable time before the date of the hearing as well as during the hearing. . . ." If the agency will not comply, contact the hearing and legal sections of the state child welfare agency. Arrangements can be made to subpoena the records if necessary.

- *Insist on sufficient time to present your case and to refute testimony presented by the agency.* Federal hearing regulations afford you the right to "(v) advance any arguments without undue interference, and (vi) to question or refute any testimony or evidence, including opportunity to confront and cross-examine adverse witnesses."

- *If the hearing officer considers an independent medical assessment necessary to reach a decision, the cost of obtaining the assessment must be borne by the state agency.*

- *If you have difficulty meeting expenses associated with the hearing, request help from the state.* Federal reimbursement is available to states that: (a) cover the cost of transportation to and from the hearing for the parent, his or her representative or witnesses, (b) incur costs associated with conducting the hearing, including additional medical assessments, and (c) pay other expenses incurred by the parent in connection with the hearing.

- *If the agency is making confusing claims about groups that are excluded from its IV-E adoption assistance program, you can obtain a copy of the state's IV-E plan.* Contact the state's agency's legal section or the regional office of the U.S. Department of Health and Human Services, Administration for Children and Families. The regional offices are listed in the "Information Resources" section in Part IV of this book.

Once the basis of the agency's objection is identified, you can begin to prepare an argument against the agency's position. At this point, it is a good idea to contact an advocacy group to consult with your case. A person or group with experience in administrative appeals can help you to determine what kind of evidence you need to gather. Some national advocacy groups are listed under "Information Resources" in Part IV of this book.

Taking steps to contest an agency decision often invests families with a sense of empowerment whether they ultimately win or lose. Launching an administrative appeal is not confusing if you take it a step at a time, particularly if you walk through the process with a more experienced family or advocate. Other practical realities of the fair-hearing process that may affect your decision to pursue an appeal will be addressed below in the next section on retroactive adoption assistance payments.

EXAMPLES OF POLICY ISSUES IN ADMINISTRATIVE HEARINGS

Are Children with special needs who are not in the care of the state potentially eligible for adoption assistance? Does this include children adopted from abroad? Federal Policy Interpretation (PIQ) 87–05 addressed the question of whether states could "limit eligibility under Title IV-E to children who are committed or relinquished to the State agency." The PIQ made it clear that such restrictions were not "in conformance with Title IV-E."

The policy interpretation proceeds to list three types of situations in which a child who is not in the care of the state may be eligible for adoption assistance: I. Children who are being adopted by a relative, II. Children who meet the eligibility requirements for the SSI program, and III. Children who are placed for adoption by private agencies.

In situations 1 and 2, children may meet the eligibility requirements for IV-E adoption assistance even if they are not placed for adoption by an agency. A child adopted from abroad should be regarded as candidate for adoption assistance if the child meets the eligibility requirements for SSI. A copy of PIQ 87-05 appears in the appendix.

How can a family respond if an agency denies its request for Title IV-E adoption assistance on the grounds that there was no "reasonable effort" made to place the child without provision for assistance? Agencies that use the phrase "reasonable effort" as grounds for denying adoption assistance are referring to Part Three of the federal special needs definition, which reads as follows:

Except where it would be against the best interest of the child to place the child because of such factors as the existence of significant emotional ties with prospective adoptive parents while in the care of such parents as a foster child, a reasonable but unsuccessful effort has been made to place the child with appropriate adoptive parents without providing adoption assistance under this section or medical assistance under subchapter XIX of this chapter.

For a number of years, adoption professionals were frustrated by this section of federal law that appeared to require agencies to make a "reasonable effort" to place a child without adoption assistance. When interpreted literally, the effort to place children without subsidy seemed to undermine the very purposes of the federal adoption assistance program, namely to expedite and to sustain adoptions. To make matters worse, the "reasonable efforts" to place without subsidy portion of the law was often cited without reference to the words that immediately preceded it, ". . . except that where it would be against the best interests of the child."

For years, the standard method of complying with this provision of federal law was to list the child on the state's adoption resource exchange to show that the child was waiting for a permanent home. Although this approach still meets the letter of the law, it has some serious limitations. What if suitable parents are located for a child with special needs right away without listing a child on the resource exchange? This is presumably a desirable situation. But, what if the parents need adoption assistance to provide services for the child or to incorporate the child into a new family? Is the agency obliged to either talk the parents out of the adoption assistance, placing the child's needs at risk, or to look for another family, thereby delaying the child's incorporation into a permanent family?

In the first place, either action would seem to be clearly contrary to the child's best interest. Secondly, in 1992, federal officials formally recognized that a focus on "shopping" a child until adoptive parents could be found who did not need the subsidy was contrary not only to sound adoption practice but to the very intent of the adoption assistance program.

Federal PIQ 92-02 essentially leaves the decision as to whether adoption assistance is needed to the adopting parents. The PIQ notes that "once the agency has determined that placement with a certain family would be the most suitable for the child, then full disclosure should be made of the child's background, as well as known and potential problems. If the child meets the state's definition of special needs with regard to specific factors or conditions, then the agency can pose the question as to whether the prospective adoptive parents are willing to adopt without a subsidy." If the parents say they cannot or will not, then the requirement is met.

Asking the prospective parents if they are willing to adopt the child without assistance is not intended to put the placement at risk by forcing the parents to choose between the subsidy and the child. The federal policy interpretation makes the adoptive parents active participants in the subsidy program by posing the following question: "As the chosen parents, having considered the child's background, do you need federal adoption assistance to incorporate the child into your family and to meet the child's future needs?"

By extension, this argument would also apply to parents who adopt an SSI eligible child or to relative adoptions without benefit of an agency. As long as it is reasonable to assume that the prospective parents represent a suitable placement, there is no obligation to try and place the child without adoption assistance. A copy of PIQ 92-02 appears in the appendix.

May an agency reduce a child's Title IV-E adoption assistance benefits on the basis of changes in family income without the adoptive parents' consent? No, federal PIQ 90-02 observes that some states have used the reference to family circumstances in the law to "justify extensive investigation of the financial circumstances of the potential adoption parents and at yearly recertification periods subsequent to the adoption." It is certainly reasonable for an agency to inquire about the adopted child's needs and the family's circumstances periodically as part of an ongoing dialogue, but federal law and policy interpretations provide no basis for an agency to propose a reduction in the amount of adoption assistance based on the income and financial resources of the adoptive family.

1. The intent of federal law and policy is to subject adoptive families to minimal amounts of scrutiny once an adoption assistance agreement is in place. Federal law and PIQ 90-02 make it quite clear that adjustments in the amount of adoption assistance specified in the agreement may only be made with the consent of the adoptive parents.

2. PIQ 90-02 affirms that an income means test cannot be used by the state to regulate the amount of adoption assistance after an adoption assistance agreement is in place. (A copy of PIQ 90-02 appears in the appendix.)

3. PIQ 86-05 affirms that once the adoptive parents and the agency have established an amount of payment in an adoption assistance agreement, the family has virtually complete discretion as to how they use the assistance on behalf of the child. (A copy of PIQ 86-05 appears in the appendix.)

In light of federal policy, annual or semiannual investigations of adoptive families' finances are not only demeaning, but are wasteful as well, squandering significant amounts of time and tax dollars on unnecessary administrative procedures. An adoption assistance agreement is an integral part of a family's commitment to a special needs adoption. Federal law recognizes this commitment by establishing only the most minimal requirements for continuing eligibility. In order to remain eligible for Title IV-E adoption assistance, the adoptive families must remain legally responsible for the child's care and continue their financial support for the child. There are not even any federal provisions specifying how often individual states must conduct reviews of ongoing eligibility for assistance, and PIQ 90-02 confirms that there is no federal "statutory requirement" for annual financial recertification of individual adoptive families. Many states have established annual reviews of continuing eligibility, but federal officials expect them be rather quick checks on the situations of families, not lengthy inquisitions.

Federal law at 42 USC 673 (a) (2) (c) (3) notes that adoption assistance payments may be "readjusted periodically, with the concurrence of the adopting parents. . . ." PIQ 90-02 concludes that once a child is found eligible for adoption assistance "the child's adoptive parents may not be rejected for adoption assistance or have payments reduced without their agreement because of the level of their income or resources. The purpose of the adoption assistance program is to provide incentives for families of any economic stratum and to remove barriers to the adoption of child with special needs."

An adoptive family may request a modification of its adoption assistance agreement at any time. If the agency denies the request, the parents have a right to an administrative hearing. In challenging the agency's decision, the parents should attempt to establish that the child's medical or emotional condition is the equivalent of children receiving specialized levels of assistance and/or the family's circumstances have changed reducing its ability to provide needed services.

Does the fact that a child never received foster care payments adversely affect his or her eligibility to receive a particular level of adoption assistance? No, many children placed through private agencies never receive foster care payments of any kind and in fact are not eligible for the federal Title IV-E foster care maintenance program. Since private agency children are eligible for the federal adoption assistance program, they are obviously qualified to receive adoption assistance. Some states have argued that because a child has not received foster care payments, they have no criteria for determining a level of payment because adoption assistance is tied to foster care rates.

States, however, do have payments schedules for adoption assistance based on age and severity of special needs. When a child has no record of foster care payments, negotiation of adoption assistance can begin by considering what payment schedule is most consistent with his or her circumstances.

Federal law specifies that federal financial participation in Title IV-E adoption assistance is available up to the "foster care maintenance payment which would have been paid during the period if the child with respect to whom the adoption assistance payment is made had been in a foster family home." Does this standard refer exclusively to the foster care payment rate prior to the adoption? No, federal financial participation is available up to the rate of support that a child would receive if he or she were placed that day in a family foster home appropriate to the child's needs. As a point of reference, the "foster care maintenance payment" is a changing standard. The phrase "during the period if the child with respect to whom the adoption assistance payment is made had been in a foster family home" poses the following questions: "If my adopted child were in a family foster home suitable to his or her care needs right now, what level of support would he or she receive?"

As noted in Chapter 2, a number of states derive their adoption assis-

Table 9.1
State A's Basic Monthly Schedule for Adoption Assistance

	Regular	Special	Severe
Ages 0 to 4	$350	$450	$650
Ages 4 to 11	$375	$575	$675
Ages 12 to 16	$400	$600	$700
Ages 17 to 18	$425	$625	$725

tance payment rates from their family foster care payment schedules. Foster care rate schedules are based on age ranges as well as other factors such as the severity of special needs and the difficulty of care. Table 9.1 State A's Basic Monthly Schedule for Adoption Assistance

In Table 9.1, adoption assistance rates are based on the state's foster care rates. When a child being paid at the regular rate reaches the age of four, state A automatically proposes to change the adoption assistance agreement and raise the adoption assistance payment from $350 to $375 per month. Such raises would not be eligible for federal financial participation if the family foster care rate referred only to the level of support that the child would have received prior to the adoption. One can be sure that states would be much more reluctant to allow increases if they had to assume the entire burden instead of relying on federal funding that covers from 50 percent to 80 percent of the cost.

Federal law envisions the adoption assistance agreement as a flexible plan of support by providing that it "may be readjusted periodically, with the concurrence of the adopting parents (which may be specified in the adoption assistance agreement), depending upon changes in such circumstances." PIQ 90-02 explains that the section of the law pertaining to the adoption assistance agreement is "interpreted to pertain to the parents' ability to incorporate the child into their household in relation to their lifestyle, standard of living, and future plans and to their overall capacity to meet the immediate and future needs (including educational needs) of the child." It is common knowledge that adopted children's emotional and medical problems often become more severe and costly to treat as they grow older. The capacity to adjust the adoption assistance agreement to meet the changing circumstances of a family would be seriously hampered if federal funding were tied to the child's preadoptive foster care payment rate. Such an inflexible policy would discriminate against families who adopted infants and young children.

Finally, adoptive families may request a modification of their adoption assistance agreement at any time as needs dictate. If the agency denies the request, the parents have a right to an administrative hearing. The guarantee of a hearing, of course, does not assure that an adoptive family will gain an increase in adoption assistance, but it does anticipate that the circumstances of adoptive families and their children change and should be given due consideration. The opportunity to appeal rates of adoption assistance would be dealt a crippling blow if federal funding for adoption assistance were based solely on a child's preadoptive foster care rate.

Parents who wish to modify an existing adoption assistance agreement should obtain copies of the state's adoption assistance and foster care rate schedules along with the regulations that define the various levels of care. This information should be available on request. If the agency refuses to send the information, contact the hearing section at the state agency with jurisdiction over child welfare.

After parents receive the rate schedules and definitions that define levels of special needs, they can begin to document the level of support that best fits their child's situation. The object is to show as clearly as possible how the child's condition fits a particular foster care or adoption assistance payment category. It is usually a good idea to ask a therapist or other provider to submit written or oral testimony explaining how the child's problems fit a particular level of care and payment schedule as defined by the state.

May an agency set restrictions on how adoptive parents may spend adoption assistance in support of their child as a condition for providing or increasing benefits? No, unlike foster care, adoption assistance does not impose restrictions on how adoptive families may use the payments to support their children. A state, for example, may establish exceptional adoption assistance payment rates for children with severe medical or emotional problems, but once an agreement calling for such payments has been completed, the state does not have the authority to impose a requirement that additional funds may only be used in support of particular services. As PIQ 86-05 puts it, "the payment which is agreed upon will be expected to combine with the parents resources to cover the ordinary and special needs of the child projected over an extended period of time. Anticipation and discussion of those needs are part of the negotiation of the amount of the adoption assistance payment and the adoptive parents are free to make decisions about expenditures for the child, once adopted, without further agency approval."

ADMINISTRATIVE HEARING CHECKLIST

Adequate Notice Provisions

- Has the agency informed you in writing of its determination to deny your child eligibility or benefits?

- Does the written notice contain reasons for the denial and references to relevant rules or statutes?

- Does the written notice inform you of your appeals rights, how to obtain an administrative hearing, and the time limits for requesting a hearing?

- Have you requested a copy of the state's adoption subsidy regulations and policies from the state agency in charge of adoption assistance? If you run into difficulty, have you checked with the agency's legal action or office of administrative hearings. Have you made this official aware that you are seeking public information and that the adequate notice provisions of federal hearing regulations entitle you to be informed about policies that pertain to appeal?

Preparation

- Have you consulted experienced adoptive families or advocates about your situation?

- Do you understand the basic eligibility requirements for the adoption assistance program in question?

- Are you reasonably well informed about the basis for the agency's denial and specific issues that will need to be addressed at the hearing?

- Are you aware that you may obtain a copy of the state's IV-E plan from the state agency's legal section or the regional office of the U.S. Department of Health and Human Services' Administration for Children and Families?

- Are you aware that you may arrange for the hearing to be conducted by phone, but you have the right to insist on appearing in person?

- Do you know what kinds of documentation and evidence that you will need to present at the hearing?

- Are you aware that federal hearing regulations afford you an "adequate opportunity" to "review the contents of the case file" and "all documents and records to be used by the agency at the hearing at a reasonable time before the date of the hearing as well as during the hearing. . . ."

- Are you planning on asking medical providers, psychologists, or others to submit written or oral testimony on your behalf?

- Are you aware that if the hearing officer determines that an independent medical assessment is necessary, the cost must be absorbed by the state agency.

- Are you aware that federal hearing regulations give you sufficient time to present your case and to "refute any testimony, including opportunity to confront and cross-examine adverse witnesses."

- Are you aware that the initial hearing and an administrative appeal of a hearing decision within a state agency do not cost any money?

- Are you aware that you may represent yourself or choose to be represented by a lawyer or other person of your choosing?

- Are you aware that federal government will reimburse states that cover transportation and other costs that you incur in connection with the hearing?

- Are you aware that an appeal for a judicial review requires a relatively modest filing fee but that you might want to hire an attorney to file the necessary papers and submit a brief on your behalf?
- Are you aware that if you are denied at the judicial review level, you have the option of contesting the decision in the state appellate court system? Some parents have taken Title IV-E cases all the way to the State Supreme Court.
- Are you aware that you may ask the hearing officer to leave the record open for one or two weeks in order to submit important evidence or documentation that was not presented at the hearing? Such requests are routinely granted.

WHEN THE AGENCY PLAYS DIRTY

There are instances when a county or state agency appears determined to deny your application and takes an aggressive adversarial stance. One common tactic is to reduce the issue of the child's eligibility to one or two issues such as whether a "reasonable, but unsuccessful" attempt was made to place the child with provision for adoption assistance addressed above.

As more adoptive families use the hearing system as a useful tool, hearing officers become more familiar with adoption assistance policy. Right now, however, many hearing officers have limited experience with adoption assistance appeals.

Families should assess the attitude of the agency when preparing for a hearing. If the agency seems determined to deny assistance, the appellants must assume a heavier burden, particularly if the case is likely to be presided over by an inexperienced hearing officer. When parents have a complicated case or are expecting the agency to energetically oppose their claim, it might be a good idea to call the hearing section at the state agency and find out if it has heard many IV-E adoption assistance appeals.

When facing a hostile agency, an inexperienced hearing officer, or a particularly complicated case, families should consult advocacy groups right away. The fact that the appeal may be more difficult doesn't mean that it's not winnable or worth waging only that one must spend more time in preparation.

Remember that federal regulations give you the right to examine the case record and relevant documents, and if the agency refuses, the records can be obtained through subpoena. If you are being denied access to pertinent documents, contact the hearing section at the state agency. They can arrange for subpoenas to be issued if necessary. You can ask for a continuance in a scheduled hearing until you have reasonable time to access records or arrange for witnesses to be present or submit written testimony. As noted earlier, you can also insist on a face to face hearing if you choose.

Parents sometimes discover that the agency has either misrepresented the child's trauma or failed to disclose crucial information about the child's medical or family history. As we will see, misleading or misinforming adoptive parents is not only grounds for revisiting a child's eligibility for adoption assistance, but may be grounds for a lawsuit against the agency.

Chapter 13 reviews legal actions taken against adoption agencies since 1986 for deceiving adoptive families or for withholding information about their child's backgrounds. When parents discover that they have been given false or incomplete information, they would be well advised to consult an attorney with experience in representing plaintiffs' claims of fraud or damages. Appeals for adoption assistance and suits against agencies can be pursued separately and at the same time. In some cases, the threat of legal action provides the family with considerable leverage in dealing with its appeal for adoption assistance. Obtaining adoption assistance does not preclude further legal action.

A complete list of all regional offices of the U.S. Department of Health and Human Services, as well as a list of major adoption advocacy Web sites and organizations, can be found in Part IV of this book.

10

Hearings, Part 2: Applying for Adoption Assistance and Retroactive Payments after a Final Decree of Adoption

Law and order exist for the purpose of establishing justice and . . . when they fail in this purpose they become the dangerously structured dams that block the flow of social progress.
—Martin Luther King, Jr. (1929–1968)

MAKING A GOOD LAW WORK BETTER

Although Title IV-E adoption assistance has provided an essential source of support for children with special needs, time inevitably reveals serious defects in the best of social programs. Throughout the 1980s, the most serious obstacles preventing the program from meeting its intended purpose were federal and state regulations that required agreements for adoption subsidy to be completed prior to the final decree of adoption.

Within a few years after the Adoption Assistance and Child Welfare Act of 1980 went into effect, it became painfully clear that significant numbers of single adults and couples had adopted children without provision for subsidy only to face unexpected, escalating medical and emotional problems that exhausted the family budget and health insurance. When these hard-pressed adoptive parents contacted state agencies for help, they were informed that assistance was not available if the adoption had been finalized.

The long struggle by adoptive families and advocates to remove this regulatory impediment to adoption assistance finally came to fruition when the federal Children's Bureau issued its landmark policy interpretation, PIQ 92-02, on June 25, 1992. While the policy interpretation did not formally change the federal rule requiring adoption assistance to be arranged prior to finalization, it authorized a procedure by which case by case exceptions may be made if the adoptive parents demonstrate that extenuating circumstances prevented them from applying for adoption assistance or completing an adoption assistance agreement prior to finalization.

As might be expected, there is considerable variation among the states in the degree to which they have implemented PIQ 92-02. Ohio moved quickly to amend its state regulations. In September 1992, a rule was enacted that allowed children to become eligible for adoption assistance after finalization. By December 1993, a rule went into effect awarding retroactive payments to most children who became eligible for adoption assistance after finalization. Dozens of children have qualified for adoption assistance and received retroactive payments under this policy.

Minnesota amended its statute to allow adoption assistance to be awarded after finalization but limited retroactive payments to the date of application. Several other states enacted rules to allow families to be considered for adoption assistance after finalization, but made no mention of retroactive payments.

The following list indicates how twenty-nine states have responded to PIQ 92-02:

Provisions for Eligibility and Obtaining Retroactive Payments
Ohio, North Carolina

Provisions for Eligibility; Limits of Retroactive Payments
Oregon, Minnesota, Oklahoma, Maine

Provisions for Eligibility; Retroactive Payments Not Addressed
Colorado, Idaho, New York, Maryland, Arizona, Wisconsin

Provisions for Eligibility More Restrictive Than PIQ 92-02
Virginia, Washington

No Regulations Implementing PIQ 92-02
Alaska, California, Illinois, Massachusetts, Michigan, Montana, Pennsylvania, Kentucky, Indiana, Louisiana, Rhode Island, South Carolina, Texas, Vermont, Wyoming

As the list demonstrates, a number of states have not amended their regulations to respond to PIQ 92-02. The fact that a state has no written procedures does not necessarily mean the agency is resistant to efforts by adoptive parents to obtain adoption assistance after finalization. Vermont, for example, does not have formal regulations addressing PIQ 92-02 but appears to take a family friendly attitude toward requests for postadoptive support. States with no written policies that are less receptive to requests for assistance may still not ignore applications for adoption assistance or deny adoptive parents the right of appeal as prescribed in PIQ 92-02. In 1998, families in Arizona, Idaho, and Montana have not only obtained adoption assistance after finalization but also won retroactive benefits as well. None of the three states had regulations that addressed the issue of retroactive payments, and Montana's regulations did not even mention the question of applying for adoption assistance after a final decree of adoption. States with no written policies may not ignore applications for adoption assistance, may not deny adoptive parents the right of appeal, and may not ignore the rights afforded adoptive parents outlined in PIQ 92-02.

APPEALS THROUGH ADMINISTRATIVE FAIR HEARINGS

PIQ 92-02 requires that applications for adoption assistance after a final decree of adoption be considered through the state's fair hearing system or other administrative appeals process. States also are eligible to receive federal reimbursement at the normal rate for adoption assistance payments if they award retroactive adoption assistance to eligible children and families.

HOW TO OBTAIN A HEARING

Adoptive parents should contact the adoption section in the state human services agency, explain that they adopted a child x years before, and are interested in filing an appeal for Title IV-E adoption assistance. You should inform the state official you are aware that the child's eligibility must be established through an administrative fair hearing. You should then ask how to go about requesting a hearing and ask for any written regulations and procedures on the subject.

If you cannot obtain sufficient information because the state does not yet have clear guidelines on filing an appeal for adoption assistance after finalization, you should not give up. The specific steps for filing an appeal for adoption assistance after a final decree of adoption may vary from state to state, but you should be able to rely on certain basic due process rights.

As noted in the previous section, the right to an administrative fair hearing is triggered by the proposed denial of federal or state assistance. If no other avenue presents itself, you should be able to receive a fair hearing by

- filing an application for Title IV-E adoption assistance with the appropriate state or county agency, as if the child had not yet been adopted. You should retain a copy of the application; or
- writing a letter of petition indicating you are applying for adoption assistance and that you are aware that appeals must be made through the state's administrative fair hearing system as set forth in federal PIQ 92-02. The letter should discuss the extenuating circumstances that you believe are grounds for a reconsideration of your child's eligibility. Finally, you should indicate that you are requesting an administrative fair hearing or information about how to obtain one.

Remember, the application will probably be denied, but federal regulations stipulate that it may not be ignored. If your request for adoption assistance is denied, the denial notice must inform you of your right to appeal the decision and how to schedule an administrative fair hearing.

If there is no response to the application in thirty to forty-five days, or if the response does not contain sufficient information about the appeal process, you should contact the state's office of administrative fair hearings for guidance. Unresponsiveness and an agency's failure to act with "reasonable promptness" to an application are cited as grounds for a fair hearing in federal regulations.

HEARING PROCEDURES AND PRESENTATION OF EXTENUATING CIRCUMSTANCES

Your first responsibility as an adoptive parent is to establish that extenuating circumstances either prevented you from applying for adoption assistance or prevented your child from being determined eligible for adoption assistance. If you succeed in arguing that extenuating circumstances are a factor in your case, then your child's eligibility for adoption assistance should be reconsidered. You may present written documentation, call on witnesses for oral testimony, or present both kinds of evidence to support your argument. PIQ 92-02 lists several types of situations that would constitute extenuating circumstances:

- Relevant facts regarding the child, the biological family or child's background are known and not presented to the adoptive parents prior to the legalization of the adoption
- Denial of assistance was based on a means test of the adoptive family. (According to federal law, the income of the adoptive family has no effect upon the child's eligibility for adoption assistance.)
- Erroneous determination by the state that a child is ineligible for adoption assistance
- Failure by the state agency to advise adoptive parents of the availability of adoption assistance.

Ohio's list of extenuating circumstances also includes situations in which special needs rooted in the child's preadoptive background manifest themselves *after* finalization. This policy is consistent with federal PIQ 88-06, which describes the case of a family that was unable to confirm a diagnosis of junior rheumatoid arthritis affecting their child until after the adoption was completed. The PIQ affirmed that lack of information relevant to the child's eligibility was sufficient grounds for reconsideration after the final decree of adoption.

Suppose, for example, you feel that information about your child's special needs was not available to you at the time of adoption and had you known the extent of the child's problems, you would have applied for or received adoption assistance. At the hearing, you would present statements by medical or mental health professionals that (1) showed the extent of the child's current special needs, and (2) showed that the current special needs either existed or were traceable to conditions that existed at the time of the adoption. Because adoptive parents have worked hard to secure medical or psychological services to address their child's emerging problems, they often have such documentation in abundance. You also might find adoption agency workers to corroborate your testimony.

The point of the presentation is to establish that the child's special needs originated prior to the adoption, but you were either unaware of them or did not recognize their seriousness. The purpose of the adoption assistance program is to help such children. Serious medical or emotional problems may be particularly difficult to recognize in infants or very young children who are simply not old enough to manifest clear symptoms. Adoptive parents and their children should not be punished because of a lack of sufficient information at the time of the adoption.

THE BURDEN OF PROOF FOR ESTABLISHING THE CHILD'S ELIGIBILITY

Assuming you are successful in establishing that extenuating circumstances were a factor in your case, the next issue is whether your child met the eligibility requirements for the Title IV-E adoption assistance program. At first glance, PIQ 92-02 would appear to present a problem for adoptive families, particularly if finalization took place several years before the appeal. When the PIQ is analyzed more carefully, in the broader context of federal adoption assistance law, however, an interpretation more favorable to adoptive families emerges.

In question 7 on page 5 of the PIQ, the author states that federal law does not address the question of the burden of proof in any explicit sense, but notes, "we would expect states to conclude that the adoptive parents have the burden of proving extenuating circumstances and adoption assistance eligibility at a fair hearing." While it appears reasonable enough for adoptive families to assume the burden for establishing the existence of extenuating circumstances, the parents' responsibility with respect to the child's eligibility for adoption assistance requires further analysis and explanation.

Federal law does not explicitly use the term *burden of proof* in discussing questions of eligibility, but the law makes it clear that the state or local agency, not the applicant, is responsible for determining eligibility for federal programs, including IV-E adoption assistance. The applicant has the responsibility of providing information to facilitate the eligibility determination. In most cases involving an appeal for adoption assistance after finalization, the chief contribution of the adoptive family is to provide information about the child's special needs.

Adoptive parents are not expected to assume the primary burden for establishing whether the child meets such requirements as AFDC relatedness or if a judicial determination of best interest has been made when they submit an application for adoption assistance before finalization. Those eligibility requirements pertain to the child's situation at the time he or she was removed from the home of the birth parents, a period before many adoptive families come into the picture and have any relationship with the child. In such cases, the state or local agency assumes responsibility for gathering the facts necessary to determine if the AFDC relatedness and judicial determination of best interest standards are satisfied.

PIQ 92-02, in discussing the burden of proof, fails to distinguish between the state's responsibility for *conducting* eligibility determinations and the adoptive family's responsibility for *responding* to eligibility determinations. If the state contends that the child is not eligible for adoption assistance because he or she did not meet the AFDC relatedness requirement, for example, it should provide documentation for its determinations. At that point, the adoptive family must be able to challenge that claim with evidence of its own.

The following interpretation of PIQ 92-02 should provide some guidance:

1. Extenuating circumstances are most accurately characterized as the *subject* of the hearing, meaning that they are a matter to be determined at the hearing itself, not the *grounds* on which the decision to grant or deny a hearing is made. As an adoptive family, you have a right to an administrative fair hearing if a federal benefit is denied. You should be able to obtain a hearing in virtually every instance in which you petition for adoption assistance after finalization of the adoption.

2. You assume the burden of establishing the existence of extenuating circumstances at the administrative fair hearing.

3. If you succeed in establishing the existence of extenuating circumstances, the next question before the hearing examiner is whether the child met the eligibility requirements for IV-E adoption assistance.

4. The state (agency) is responsible for making eligibility determinations. If the state has determined that the adoptive child does not meet one or more of the eligibility requirements for IV-E adoption assistance, it is responsible for presenting evidence at the hearing to support its determination. If the evidence regarding the child's eligibility is not available at the time of the hearing, the hearing examiner may order the agency to determine eligibility as part of the hearing decision.

5. You share the burden of proof with the agency in that you must *respond* to a determination by the state that the child does not meet one or more of the eligibility requirements for IV-E adoption assistance with evidence of your own. This responsibility, however, *presupposes* that an eligibility determination has been made and communicated to you. If there is no record that an eligibility determination has been made, you must cooperate in presenting information in your possession that may be relevant to the child's eligibility, but you do not assume the entire burden of establishing the child's eligibility.

6. Finally, as part of the hearing rights under federal law, you must be provided "adequate" notice in cases where the state proposes to "discontinue, terminate, suspend or reduce assistance. . . ." [45 CFR Chapter 11, 205.10 (a)(4)] Adequate notice, according to federal regulations means "a written notice that includes a statement of what action the agency intends to take, the reasons for the intended action" and "the specific regulations supporting such action. . . ." The agency's proposed action in such cases is always based on a decision concerning the eligibility of the applicant or recipient. The requirement for adequate notice follows from the agency's responsibility to make eligibility determinations.

One of the key points to remember is that as applicants for adoption assistance after a final decree of adoption, you should be entitled to the same due process rights as adoptive parents who apply for adoption assistance prior to finalization. The agency's response to your application or letter of request for adoption assistance after finalization, in compliance with federal requirements for "adequate notice," should provide some guidance to issues that will arise at the hearing. If the agency, for example, denies your child's eligibility on grounds of failure to meet the AFDC relatedness requirement, you should come to the hearing prepared to respond if you can.

Unfortunately, adoptive families may encounter hearing examiners and agency representatives who have little experience with federal policy interpretations and due process issues pertaining to the adoption assistance program. Applicants should not take it for granted that they will always be fully informed in advance about all the issues that may arise at the hearing. When confronted with eligibility questions for the first time at a hearing, you should point out your right to adequate notice and request that sufficient time be allotted to settle the issue at hand.

Given the inconsistencies that you may encounter, however, it makes good practical sense to learn as much as you can about your child's eligibility prior to the hearing. Agencies are often quite willing to discuss their views as to whether your child meets the requirements for adoption assistance. You should feel free to contact the agency in order to obtain as clear a picture as possible regarding issues that you may need to address.

RETROACTIVE PAYMENTS

According to PIQ 92-02, states may make retroactive payments to adoptive families whose children become eligible for adoption assistance after finalization as the result of a fair hearing decision. States that agree to make retroactive payments may then claim reimbursement for the federal portion of the payment, which is always at least 50 percent and may run as high as 80 percent of the cost.

Basic Argument for Retroactive Payments

The establishment of adoption assistance after finalization is based on the finding that the child would have been determined eligible for adoption assistance except for a lack of information, an error, or an omission. In accordance with PIQ 92-02, establishing the existence of extenuating circumstances authorizes a review of the child's eligibility for adoption assistance. The determination process examines the child's circumstances *prior* to finalization. The issue is not whether the child meets the qualifying standards for IV-E at the time of the hearing, but whether he or she met them during the period preceding the final decree of adoption. To determine that the child qualifies is to affirm he or she *was* eligible for adoption assistance prior to finalization, in some cases as early as the date of the adoptive placement.

Federal hearing regulations at 45 CFR 205.10 (18) stipulate that "When the hearing decision is favorable to the claimant, or when the agency decides in favor of the claimant prior to the hearing, the agency shall promptly make corrective payments retroactively to the date the incorrect action was taken." The "date the incorrect action was taken" is obviously the key phrase for adoptive families. Finding a child eligible for adoption assistance as a result of a postadoptive application and hearing always means that the child met the eligibility requirements *prior* to finalization. Parents should argue that the incorrect action was the failure to find their child eligible for adoption assistance during the period preceding the adoption. Whether the error was one of commission or omission, such as the failure to inform them about subsidy programs, it nonetheless led to an incorrect action. That being the case, retroactive payments should be made promptly back to an appropriate date prior to the final decree of adoption.

Once again, there is no guarantee that this argument will prevail, particularly in light of the fact that PIQ 92-02 states only that federal financial participation is available to states that make retroactive payments. It does not specifically require states to make retroactive payments. States accordingly have taken the position that the decision to pay retroactive benefits is optional.

Nevertheless, it can't hurt to emphasize the point that eligibility for adoption assistance *by definition* means that that the necessary requirements were met prior to finalization. Section 45 CFR 205.10 (18) of the federal hearing regulations dealing with the state's obligation to make "corrective payments" is also worth citing.

Time Frames for Retroactive Payments

Federal law was amended in 1986 to allow adoption assistance payments to begin as early as the date of adoptive placement. Prior to that time, payments could begin no earlier than the date of the interlocutory order or the final decree of adoption.

When the adoptive placement was made on or after October 1, 1986, retroactive payments back to the date of adoptive placement are potentially eligible for federal reimbursement. Retroactive payments are eligible for federal reimbursement back to the interlocutory order or final decree of adoption in cases where the interlocutory or final decree was issued before October 1, 1986.

An Example from Arizona

In December 1998, a tribunal in the Arizona Department of Economic Security handed down an administrative appeal ruling that not only overturned the original hearing decision, but articulated the essential argument for retroactive benefits on behalf of adoptive families. Citing state regulations that required the state to inform adoptive families about adoption subsidy programs, the panel determined that "if the Department had properly followed its responsibilities in November, 1992, this case would not be before the Tribunal six years later."

The appeals tribunal recognized that the family had suffered "significant financial hardship" which adoption assistance payments could have helped to alleviate. Awarding the payments that the family should have been receiving all along could assist the parents in their continuing struggle to meet their adopted children's special needs. "Based on the interpretation policy letters" [PIQ 92-02], the panel awarded retroactive payments back to November 7, 1992, the date the children were placed with the family for adoption. The adoption was finalized in 1993 and, as the preceding section of this chapter notes, after October 1996, retroactive payments back to the date of adoptive placement are eligible for federal reimbursement. In Arizona, the FFP for Title IV-E adoption assistance is 64 percent. A retroactive payment of $40,000 for the family's two children, for example, would be eligible for $25,600 in federal reimbursement.

The appeals panel used Arizona's own adoption assistance payment schedules to calculate the amount of back benefits owed to the family. Arizona has three levels of adoption assistance payments, each "based on the special needs of the child and the intensity of services and care." The tribunal observed that "the children were at the payments Levels 1 and 2 based upon a foster care evaluation done prior to the placement in the adoptive parent's home in November 1992." Since the family did not receive adoption assistance, there was no annual reassessment of the children's special needs and the family's circumstances. In the absence of such periodic reviews, the appeals panel used documentation provided at the hearing to determine the levels of assistance that were appropriate for the children. It found, for example, that one daughter "should have been raised to level 2 as of April 1996 when the multidisciplinary team made their assessment at first grade. After that, she should have been placed at level 3 by June 1997 when she began acting out after her sister was removed." The other child "should have been raised to level 3 in May 1997" when a particularly serious incident occurred at the family's home.

Unfortunately for adoptive families, not all appeals for retroactive payments are affirmed, particularly with such ringing clarity and common sense. Although individual families are winning retroactive adoption assistance benefits in slowly increasing numbers across the country, the decision of the Arizona administrative appeals panel represents more of an ideal than the norm at the present time. As such, it stands as a source of guidance and hope.

For further information about this Arizona case, contact the Arizona Department's Office of Appeals at 207 East McDowell Road, Phoenix, AZ 85004 and ask for a copy of the decision in Arizona Appeal No. 292905 without any identifying information. The family was represented by Jay McCarthy of Hufford, Horstman, McCullough and Mongini, PC, Box B, 323 Leroux St., Flagstaff, AZ. 86002 (520) 774-1453.

Requesting a Hearing to Determine Eligibility and Retroactive Payments at the Same Time

Adoptive parents may pursue eligibility for adoption assistance and retroactive payments as separate appeals. You may also include the issue of retroactive payments in your written request for a hearing to determine your child's eligibility. For instance, you may add a statement such as: "If my child is found eligible for the adoption assistance program, I also request that retroactive adoption assistance payments be awarded from the date of the final decree of adoption (or date of adoptive placement, depending on the date of the adoption)."

A request like that should ensure that you will not have to go through a separate hearing process to consider retroactive payments if the child is found eligible for adoption assistance. If you include retroactive payments as part of the original hearing request, the hearing officer must address the issue of retroactive payments in rendering a decision. Once the initial hearing establishes the child's eligibility, retroactive payments may be awarded without a separate hearing.

THE DECISION TO APPEAL A NEGATIVE HEARING DECISION

PIQ 92-02 authorizes, it does not require, states to make such payments. Most states are reluctant to make retroactive payments on a regular basis. Minnesota limits retroactive payments to a few months by statute. Others have no rules addressing the issue one way or another and simply oppose back payments during the course of the hearing process.

Adoptive families have little to lose by requesting retroactive payments and pursuing their claim through the phases of the hearing process preceding judicial review. Fair hearing and administrative review decisions are usually based on existing state regulations. If there are no state regulations to cover the existing situation, the appeal is usually denied at the initial hearing and administrative review. In practical terms, this means that adoptive families who are challenging a current state policy or raising an issue that is not covered in state regulations may have to file for a judicial review. At that point, they may want to consider hiring an attorney to file the necessary paperwork and to represent them. Before making the decision to secure legal counsel, parents should consult with local and national adoption advocacy groups that might have knowledge or experience with the results of hearings in their state.

The NACAC can provide state profiles as well as the names of individuals who are volunteer advocates. Please consult Information Resources in Part IV for the names of other advocacy organizations.

SUMMARY

If all of this sounds confusing, take heart. The appeals process is not that difficult to negotiate when you proceed one step at a time. Adoption support groups and veteran parents are usually eager to help. Please do not hesitate to call on them when questions arise.

In review, the following recommendations are worth repeating for those of you who have decided to file an appeal for adoption assistance:

1. You must establish that, as a result of extenuating circumstances, your child was denied access to Title IV-E adoption assistance prior to the final decree of adoption. Whatever the extenuating circumstances might have been, presenting documentation that your child's current problems originated prior to finalization will be helpful in verifying that he or she meets the special needs requirement.

2. You should learn as much as you can about IV-E adoption assistance eligibility requirements as they pertain to your child. The state or county agency's response

to your application or letter of petition for adoption assistance may provide some indication of the eligibility issues that are likely to arise at the hearing. Feel free to contact the agency for an explanation of its determination regarding your child's eligibility.

3. If your child needs the assistance, exploring an appeal costs you nothing but time. You are free to change your mind at any stage of the hearing process if you so choose.

In many cases, obtaining retroactive payments will not be easy, but there have been success stories as well as failures. Ohio and North Carolina have policies in place that routinely award retroactive benefits. At this writing, individual families also have been awarded retroactive payments in Arizona, Idaho, Missouri, Montana, and Tennessee.

What If She Won and They Refused

Lakeesha Dawson testified at a fair hearing last year and was immediately hooked on advocacy. In the last few months, she has helped out as a volunteer on three other cases involving thousands of dollars in retroactive adoption assistance for families who were desperate to meet the needs of their disabled children. She is thinking of becoming a lawyer and has been studying law books in her spare time.

Ironically, Lakeesha, herself, is in dire financial straits. Newly divorced, she is broke, in debt, and trying to hang on to the home she shares with her three children who have special needs. One of them, Nathan, does not receive a subsidy and, ironically, his disabilities are the most serious in the household.

Soon after helping the other adoptive families, Lakeesha realized that Nathan could qualify as IV-E eligible and receive retroactive subsidy under PIQ 92-02. She laughed at herself to realize she had helped four other families through this process before she ever realized her own family could benefit from it!

Lakeesha asked for a nonevidentiary hearing, but was denied. The state wanted a fight. Three months after she filed a request for an administrative hearing, the state law changed. Now, it was illegal for the state to pay retroactive IV-E subsidy beyond the "initial date of application." Since Nathan, at age nine years, had missed out on half of his IV-E eligibility, he stood to gain only a few months of retroactive payments under this new law, even if Lakeesha won her hearing.

Outraged, this mother-advocate decided the new law had to be challenged. In order for Nathan to be determined eligible for IV-E as a result of an administrative hearing, the state must find that he met all of the necessary criteria *before* the adoption was final. Had the state acted responsibly at the time, Nathan would have been receiving assistance at least from the date his adoption was finalized. Why should her son be punished for the irresponsible conduct of an adoption agency under the state's jurisdiction?

In her written testimony, Lakeesha asked that if Nathan were found to be IV-E eligible, the state be ordered to pay the full retroactive amount back to the adoption's finalization. She asked the hearing officer to disregard this new state law limiting retroactive, both because it postdated her hearing request date and because it was contrary to simple logic, fairness, and the intent of federal law. If a child met the eligibility requirements prior to the adoption, he would have and should have been receiving assistance since that time.

Lakeesha acknowledged that federal PIQ 92-02 authorized federal financial participation to states that made adoption assistance payments back to the "earliest date of eligibility," but did not explicitly require states to make such payments. On the other hand, she argued that federal hearing regulations as well as logic supported her position. Code of Federal Regulations at 45 CFR 205.10 (18) states "when the hearing decision is favorable to the claimant, or when the agency decides in favor of the claimant prior to the hearing, the agency shall promptly make corrective payments retroactively to the date the incorrect action was taken." In Nathan's case the agency took three incorrect actions. It failed to disclose crucial information about the child's family history. Agency representatives assumed incorrectly that the child was not eligible for adoption assistance. Finally, the agency representative failed to inform the Lakeesha about the potential availability of adoption assistance programs.

She next cited the 1991 U.S. Supreme Court decision in *Sullivan vs. Zebley*, contending that it reinforced the section of the federal hearing regulations and her position. The Zebley decision addressed a group of children who had been turned down for SSI benefits between 1980 and 1991. The court ordered full retroactive payments for all eligible children.

Lakeesha also pointed out that Ohio and North Carolina routinely made retroactive payments back to the original date of eligibility in the case of children who qualified for adoption assistance after finalization. Other states such as Tennessee, Montana, California and Texas had made retroactive payments back to the date of placement or finalization in individual cases. She questioned how a federal entitlement program that was supposed to have uniform eligibility standards could allow an accident of geography to determine access to full retroactive benefits. Benefit levels in federal entitlement programs traditionally differed from state to state, but here was an instance where children in a given state were being categorically denied benefits back to the earliest date of eligibility.

As a final step, Lakeesha consulted with a plaintiff's attorney who felt that she had strong grounds to sue the state for failure to disclose important information about Nathan's family and medical history. She agreed to take the case on a contingency basis and Lakeesha filed suit against the agency shortly after she requested a hearing. The attorney felt that taking legal action at the same time Lakeesha pursued the hearing process might exert pressure on the state to negotiate a settlement that would include retroactive adoption assistance payments.

Lakeesha is hopeful of victory in her administrative hearing. The experiences as advocate and appellant have made her more aware than ever before of what adoptive families confront when they request postadoption support. She recently met with her state representative about drafting legislation to repeal the limit on retroactive payments.

If the hearing goes against Nathan, Lakeesha will consult with her attorney and decide whether to appeal or to concentrate exclusively on her lawsuit. She thinks that she will probably pursue further appeals as far as a judicial review because it is relatively inexpensive and the reasons for her liability action and her argument for retroactive adoption assistance payments have much in common. They both center on the failure of the agency to disclose crucial information about Nathan prior to his adoption.

Lakeesha has discovered an aptitude for the law and advocacy. Win or lose, she hopes to go to law school someday, when she has the time and the money. There are many special needs adoptive families out there who need help just as badly as she does, or more. Lakeesha is confident that she'll have no shortage of clients.

TAKING THE APPEAL ALL THE WAY TO THE STATE SUPREME COURT

In 1998, the state Supreme Courts of Vermont and Nebraska both handed down decisions in cases involving appeals for Title IV-E adoption assistance after the final decree of adoption. The parents won a victory with significant policy implications in the Vermont decision, while the outcome of the Nebraska decision was more of a mixed one for the family.

SSI as the Path to Adoption Assistance in Vermont

In June 1998, the Vermont Supreme Court ruled in favor of an adoptive family in a case involving a postfinalization application for Title IV-E adoption assistance. Because of the issues involved in the case, the decision could have far-reaching implications for adoptive families. The court accepted the parents' argument that their child met the eligibility requirements for federal adoption assistance because he would have qualified for the Supplemental Security Income (SSI) program prior to adoption had an application been submitted. The question of whether a child could claim potential SSI eligibility as means of qualifying for adoption assistance has been a source of considerable controversy in administrative appeals. Because IV-E adoption assistance is a federal entitlement program, the Vermont Supreme Court's decision provides adoptive families in similar situations across the country with a strong argument in their favor. The text of the decision can be found in the Appendix section of this book and in the "Legal Decisions" section of the Adoption Policy Resource Center Web site at www. fpsol.com/adoption/advocates.html.

Policy Issues

In addition to meeting the definition of special needs, children must also satisfy one of two major eligibility requirements for Title IV-E adoption assistance. They must either meet the AFDC relatedness test or the qualifying standards for SSI.

AFDC relatedness is satisfied if a child was actually or potentially eligible for AFDC in the birth family or relative home from which he or she was placed into a foster care or a preadoptive home. It is not necessary for the birth or relative family to have actually been receiving welfare benefits on behalf of the child. The ultimate criterion is that the child would have qualified for welfare benefits had an application been completed.

Federal welfare reform eliminated the AFDC program with passage of the Personal Responsibility and Work Opportunity Reconciliation Act of 1996 (PL 104-193). The AFDC relatedness standard, however, remained in place as an eligibility requirement for IV-E adoption assistance. How can a child meet the AFDC relatedness requirement, when there is no longer an AFDC program? The welfare reform law addresses this apparent conundrum by setting June 1, 1995 as the applicable date for determining AFDC relatedness. The AFDC regulations in effect on that date will be used to calculate eligibility for IV-E adoption assistance and foster care maintenance.

The other path to Title IV-E adoption assistance runs through the children's SSI program. If a child meets all of the requirements for SSI prior to the adoption, then the AFDC connection is not necessary. Furthermore, federal law at 42 U.S. Code Section 673 states that if a child meets the eligibility requirements for SSI and special needs, he or she qualifies for IV-E adoption assistance regardless of whether a state or private agency was involved in the placement. Children placed through independent or inter-country adoptions are potentially eligible.

SSI eligibility consists of an income means test and a disability determination. Prior to finalization of the adoption, the income of the prospective, yet not legal, adoptive parents is not deemed as income to the child for SSI purposes. Only the child's income is counted. Because relatively few children in prefinalized adoptive homes have incomes, the disability determination is the only requirement for obtaining SSI in most cases.

Obstacle: The Income Means Test

Parents applying for Title IV-E adoption assistance after finalization faced several significant obstacles in attempting to use the SSI path. The adoptive parents' income is deemed as income to the child after finalization. In most instances, the family's income is too high for the child to qualify for SSI. The Social Security officials who administer SSI are often unfamiliar with the use of SSI eligibility to qualify for adoption assistance, which has no income means test. Parents whose incomes exceed the means standard for SSI after finalization must establish that prior to the adoption only the child's income was at issue.

Obstacle: The Disability Determination

Social Security officials generally conduct the income means test first. If the family does not qualify, they do not proceed with the disability determination. Because Social Security officials have little or no connection with the adoption assistance program, adoptive parents often have difficulty getting the agency to conduct a disability determination. Advocates recommend that parents refuse to take no for an answer and try to work their way up the bureaucratic chain explaining that they need a disability statement for the IV-E adoption assistance program.

Obstacle: Retroactive Eligibility

A third, and perhaps the most formidable difficulty facing adoptive families involves the claim that the child met the disability requirements for SSI prior to finalization of the adoption. If years have passed since the adoption, families must argue that the child would have qualified had an application been made. In some situations, the child's existing disability is such that he or she would obviously have met the disability standard at an earlier age. The connection is somewhat more tenuous in other cases.

THE SIGNIFICANCE OF THE COURT DECISION

Adoptive families have encountered resistance in their appeals for adoption assistance over the fact that an SSI eligibility determination had not been made prior to finalization of the adoption. The Vermont Supreme Court decision provides adoptive parents with a powerful response to this objection.

The court agreed that, with respect to adoption assistance, the child's eligibility under the statute must be determined on the basis of the child's circumstances prior to the final decree of adoption. The issue question then was how to interpret the eligibility standards when, through no fault of their own, the adoptive parents were deprived of the opportunity to make an application at the proper time.

The court concluded that it was inconsistent to allow parents to apply for adoption assistance after finalization and then categorically deprive them of the means to meet the eligibility requirements. The court reasoned that

if, as the federal Department of Health and Human Services advised SRS (Vermont Department of Social and Rehabilitation Services), the circumstances of this case justify a postadoption application for benefits, then it follows that these circumstances also permit a postadoption application for diagnosis of a condition that meets the SSI disability criteria to substitute for the normal preadoption diagnosis of such a condition. Otherwise, the remedy for the failure to inform the parents of the program would be illusory because the parents could not show what the diagnosis would have been if the child had been examined for this purpose at the time. As a simple matter of logic, mitigating the unfair deprivation of an opportunity to seek benefits is useless unless there is also a mitigation of the similar deprivation of an opportunity to build the requisite medical record.

The Supreme Court decision removes the obstacles that have plagued adoptive families attempting to utilize SSI disability standards as a means of qualifying their child for IV-E adoption assistance after finalization. In particular it affirms three crucial points:

1. The absence of an SSI eligibility determination is not a fatal impediment.
2. The state cannot take the view that since there was no previous SSI eligibility determination, there is no way to address the issue and therefore the child is ineligible. To claim that no decision can be made is to deny parent applicants reasonable access to IV-E adoption assistance as set forth in federal PIQ 92-02.
3. An attempt must be made to reconstruct the child's eligibility for SSI prior to finalization. If the Social Security administration cannot or will not conduct such a reconstruction, the state agency in charge of adoption assistance may do so and indeed must do so.

The full text of the Vermont Supreme Court Decision appears in the Appendix, section 1998, entitled "State Supreme Court Decisions on Title IV-E Adoption Assistance After Finalization."

DELAY WITHOUT ACCOUNTABILITY: *SCHMIDT v. THE NEBRASKA DEPARTMENT OF SOCIAL SERVICES*

The struggle of Jean Schmidt to obtain adoption assistance for her daughter exemplifies two recurring themes in adoption advocacy: (1) Although the Schmidt's victory was inconclusive, parents can use their hearing rights to protect themselves from capricious treatment by the state. (2) Delay is the ally of bureaucratic state children services systems. If justice delayed is justice denied, then states are not sufficiently accountable for errors of omission or commission in handling applications for adoption assistance after finalization.

In November 1998, the Nebraska Supreme Court determined that in denying their application for Title IV-E adoption assistance, the State Department of Social Services failed to comply with federal and state regulations governing an applicant's right to an administrative hearing. Unfortunately, the decision came more than three years after the Schmidts first applied for assistance on the grounds that they finalized the adoption without being told about subsidy programs for special needs children, and discovered, *after* their child was diagnosed with reactive attachment disorder and other problems, that information about their child's family history had not been disclosed prior to the final decree of adoption.

Both situations are cited in federal PIQ 92-02 as "extenuating circumstances" and grounds for examination of a child's eligibility for Title IV-E assistance after an adoption has been finalized. The procedure for determining the existence of extenuating circumstances is the administrative "fair" hearing system. Each state is required to establish administrative hearings as an appeals process for applicants who are denied access to federal and state social programs.

Unfortunately for the Schmidts, their hard won victory was far from complete. The Nebraska Supreme Court addressed only the state agency's failure to follow the regulations governing the family's right of appeal. In declaring the actions taken by the State Department of Social Services to be invalid and in violation of the Schmidts' due process rights, the family was faced with the unenviable prospect of applying for adoption assistance all over again.

The Supreme Court noted that state regulations called for the DSS adoption specialist to review the Schmidts' application for assistance. If the application was denied, then the family had a right to a hearing. Instead of following this procedure, a hearing was held without a formal denial of assistance. After the hearing was held, the director of the DSS determined that the family did not have the right to a review of their child's eligibility for adoption assistance through an administrative hearing after all. The court found, however, that by attempting to deny the Schmidts' right to a hearing on the merits of the IV-E application, the director ended up making both the initial and final determination, which was contrary to state law. Nebraska regulations authorized the DSS Director to review hearing decisions but not to override the hearing process altogether.

The Nebraska DSS compounded procedural blunders with serious policy errors that further confused the issue and prevented its timely resolution. The DSS insisted that the child was not eligible for Title IV-E adoption assistance because she was not a ward of the state at the time of the adoption. The agency cited a 1983 Nebraska statute in support of its position. In staking out its position, the state had apparently missed a series of federal PIQs that confirmed the potential eligibility of children who were placed for adoption by private agencies. The clearest of these interpretations was PIQ 87-5, which addressed the following question:

QUESTION: In some States, statutory requirements for adoption subsidy programs limit eligibility under title IV-E to children when they are committed or relinquished to the State agency. Are these provisions consistent with the requirements of title IV-E, section 473 (a) (2) of the Social Security Act?

INTERPRETATION: No. State statutes which limit access to the Title IV-E Adoption Assistance Program by the addition of eligibility requirements beyond those required under the Federal statute are not in conformance with title IV-E. . . . While it is necessary for a child to be under the responsibility of the State agency in order to be eligible for title IV-E foster care [section 472(a)(2) requirement], there will be

other situations in which children with special needs are in care under the responsibility of private, non-profit agencies without the involvement of the State agency.
When adoption is the goal for such children, and they are determined to be AFDC
or SSI-eligible, the title IV-E agency may not exclude them from consideration or
approval, if they are otherwise found eligible for adoption assistance in accordance
with categories of children who are not in the care of the state agency.

Clearly, the DSS had failed to keep pace with federal policy, which had
from the outset allowed private agency children to participate in the IV-E
adoption assistance program. Ironically, by insisting that children in the
care of private agencies were excluded from the adoption subsidy program,
the state jeopardized its federal funding.

Carol Williams, Associate Commissioner of the U.S. Department of
Health and Human Services and Head of the Children's Bureau, reaffirmed
the children's inclusion of private agency children in responding to a series
of questions submitted by Vermont attorney Gerry Follansbee (Stewart) in
1996. Follansbee asked Ms. Williams, "Is a child with special needs who
is adopted through a private, nonprofit agency eligible for adoption assistance after a final decree of adoption?"

Ms. Williams' answer was unequivocal. "Yes," she wrote, "A child
whose placement and care are the responsibility of a private, nonprofit
agency may be eligible for title IV-E adoption assistance payments after a
final decree of adoption. The child must meet the eligibility requirements
in section 473 (a) (1) of the Social Security Act [section 673 (a) (1) of the
U.S. Code] and be determined by the State to be a child with special needs
in accordance with 473 (c) of the Act [section 673 (c) of the U.S. Code]."
The Schmidts submitted PIQ 87-05 and a copy of Williams' letter as exhibits in support of their appeal.

The Director of the Nebraska DSS also contended that extenuating circumstances did not exist in the Schmidts' case because the family had never
actually applied for adoption assistance. In a stunning display of logic abet-
ted by ignorance of federal policy, the director maintained that PIQs submitted by the Schmidts were not relevant because they only applied to
"reconsiderations" of applications for assistance. Since no decision had ever
been made, there could be no reconsideration. If no extenuating circumstances existed, the Schmidt family was not entitled to a hearing.

As the Nebraska Supreme Court pointed out, all applicants to IV-E adoption assistance are entitled to administrative hearings if they are denied
benefits. In the case of parents applying after finalization, the role of the
hearing is to determine if extenuating circumstances justify a review of the
child's eligibility for adoption assistance. The question of extenuating circumstances has no bearing on a family's right to a hearing.

Federal PIQ 92-02 is the policy document that set forth guidelines
through which parents could apply for adoption assistance after finaliza-

tion. The document lists "failure by the state agency to advise adoptive parents of the availability of adoption assistance" as an extenuating circumstance entitling the family to a review of their child's eligibility. In highlighting this issue, federal officials were attempting to address a long-standing and widely recognized problem. Many families who adopted special needs children had never applied for adoption assistance before finalization because they had insufficient knowledge of subsidy programs. Obviously, such people would not be asking the state to "reconsider" their child's eligibility for adoption assistance but to make a determination that should have been made years before. The idea that parents who had never applied before had no avenue of redress was completely contrary to federal policy. The Schmidts included PIQ 92-02 among their list of supporting documents.

The state's obligation to inform prospective parents extends to private agencies under its jurisdiction. This responsibility was upheld in *Ferdinand v. Department For Children and Their Families*, a May 13, 1991 U.S. District Court decision, as grounds for allowing an adoptive family to apply for and receive adoption assistance after finalization. Like the Schmidts' daughter, the child in the *Ferdinand* case was placed for adoption by a private agency licensed by the state. The federal court justified its position by citing federal adoption assistance regulations at CFR, which stipulate that "the State agency must actively seek ways to promote the adoption assistance program" (See 768 Federal Supplement, 401, District of Rhode Island, 1992 for the *Ferdinand* decision.)

Carol Williams also supported this position in her letter to Attorney Follansbee (Stewart). "The very purpose of the title IV-E adoption assistance program," wrote Williams, "is to encourage the adoption of hard-to-place children. Notification to potential adoptive parents about its availability is an intrinsic part of the program Accordingly, the private nonprofit agency's failure to the parents may be considered an extenuating circumstance. . . ."

To settle any disagreements about the authority of PIQs, Follansbee (Stewart) asked Williams to comment on the "significance of Policy Interpretation Questions issued by the U.S. Department of Health and Human Services" and asked if they were "interpretations of the law." Williams answered that "Policy interpretation questions and other issuances developed by this department are interpretations of statute and are disseminated as a mechanism to further clarify statutes and regulations that are already in place."

As it turned out, the Nebraska DSS not only denied adequate due process to the family, but opposed the application by citing a state law that placed Nebraska's adoption assistance program out of compliance with federal law and subject to fiscal sanctions and thoroughly misinterpreting federal PIQs submitted by the Schmidts.

The family actually cited not one but two extenuating circumstances listed in PIQ 92-02 that justified a review of their daughter's application for adoption assistance. In addition to not being notified about adoption subsidy programs, "relevant facts" regarding the child and her family background were "known and not presented to the adoptive parents prior to legalization of the adoption."

One of the greatest sources of frustrations to adoptive families is that states have a great deal of flexibility to help adoptive children with special needs if they look for reasons to say yes rather than no. The Schmidts' daughter is clearly eligible for adoption assistance and the case could have been resolved years ago in the best interest of the child. Hopefully, a new state administration will be sufficiently chastened by the injustices perpetrated on this family to bring a second appeal to a speedy and successful resolution. The complete text of the Nebraska Supreme Court decision may be found in the Appendix section, entitled State Supreme Court Decisions on Title IV-E Adoption Assistance After Finalization.

ATTORNEYS WITH EXPERIENCE IN ADOPTION ASSISTANCE APPEALS

Attorney: Terry H. Bitting
4444 E. 66th Street, Suite 225
Tulsa, OK 74136
Phone: (918) 494-9989; Fax: (918) 492-7386

Attorney: Sharon Dawn Coppock
2102 Doune Lane
Strawberry Plains, TN 37871-1510
Phone: (423) 933-8173; Fax: (423) 933-3272
E-mail: sdcoppock@aol.com

Attorney: Gary Debele
Walling and Berg
710 4th St., Suite 650
Minneapolis, MN 55415
Phone: (612) 340-1150

Attorney: Jay McCarthy
Hufford, Horstman, McCullough and Mongini, P.C.
Box B, 323 Loroux St.
Flagstaff, AZ 86002
Phone: (520) 774-1453

Attorneys Robert Mello and John Klesh (*See* Previous Section)

Attorney: Sheila Oliver
P.O. Box 8825
Elkins Park, PA 19027-0825
Phone: (215) 635-0604

Attorney: Robert Otte
Morrow, Poppe, Otte, Watermeier and Phillips, P.C.
P.O. Box 83439, Suite 360
201 N. 8th St.
Lincoln, NE 68501-3439
Phone: (402) 474-1731; Fax: (402) 474-5020
E-mail: robot@mid.net

Attorney: Dennis Paul (*See* Previous Section)

Attorney: William Turnipseed
Savell and Williams L.L.P.
245 Peach Tree Center Ave., Suite 2600
Atlanta, GA 30303
Phone: (404) 521-1282; Fax: (404) 584-0026

11

Setbacks and Victories: One Family's Story

No matter how calmly you try to referee, parenting will eventually produce bizarre behavior, and I'm not talking about the children. Their behavior is always normal.

—Bill Cosby (b. 1937)

A NOTE ABOUT THIS CASE

This story is a composite of the true-life experiences of several families. It is representative of what adoptive parents in most states must go through in order to advocate for their children's needs in a retroactive subsidy fair hearing or administrative hearing. It illustrates the long-term nature of advocacy. In this case, the parents renegotiated the contract several times while raising their son.

Some of this composite may seem unrealistic, even outrageous, but every element of it is based on true-life advocacy cases, and typical ones, at that. It is the very unreal nature of the roadblocks adoptive parents face that breaks them down. For example, when told no emphatically by a state worker, the average inexperienced adoptive parent has no reason to believe that the reasoning behind the denial could be faulty. People who have never had reason to mistrust the system are not likely to doubt what they are told. Yet, research tells us that the typical social worker receives inadequate adoption support training, including the proper negotiation of an adoption assistance contract. There's a good chance that no should be yes, or at least, maybe.

The state in this story is referred to as "State X" because of the ever-changing nature of adoption policy and law in the United States. Every parent must realize that many adoption laws are signed by governors every year and that state adoption bureaucrats are constantly reviewing and modifying policy. We are happy to mention states by name in positive examples, but mentioning a state by name in a negative context can be misleading. Not only would it be unfair to the state if it has since changed or improved policies or procedures, it would lead to confusion for parents.

THE ADOPTION

Stan and Judy Hill didn't know if they could have children or not. They hadn't used birth control in quite awhile, and Judy had never been pregnant, but they didn't worry. They wanted children by whatever means God sends them. Pregnancy would be nice, but they had always wanted to adopt, too. Stan's parents are missionaries in China, and he grew up wanting to adopt children with special needs just as his parents had done in their religious travels. Stan, his parents' only biological child, has three sisters who were adopted at various ages from the missions where his folks worked. Judy, an only child, had always wanted to adopt "a child who needs someone."

The Hills filled out an adoption application with Childplace, a local licensed private and nonprofit agency that emphasized special needs placements, on their second wedding anniversary. The agency required a couple to be married at least two years to qualify.

It wasn't expensive. Childplace asked for $600 to do the assessment, or homestudy, but explained that the Hills would be reimbursed that amount by the state after their adoption was finalized in court. This money comes through a federal program many people refer to simply as nonrecurring. In fact, the state would reimburse to the parents up to $2,000 of nonrecurring, or one-time, adoption expenses. The other $1,400 left over from nonrecurring would cover the postplacement supervision by the agency and a few other miscellaneous expenses.

Then the tax credit would take over. Once the legal fees for finalization were paid, that money would come back to them as a tax credit under a new federal law. If they kept their other adoption-related receipts (ones that had not already been reimbursed) to be used in applying for the tax credit, the worker said, this would ultimately be a "free" adoption, as many special needs placements are.

Their worker, Dave, had lots of child-placing experience. He was anxious to help them search, once the homestudy or "family assessment" was completed. Because the Hills were childless, they had no trouble finding a child. Understandably, most social workers like to place waiting children in small families where they will receive lots of attention, and the Hill home fit that bill perfectly.

After just three months of looking at photolistings in books and on-line from all over the country, Stan and Judy were matched to a baby who lived just ten minutes away from them. The little boy was only six weeks old and had been in a foster home waiting to be adopted since birth. Several couples had turned him down because of his risk factors. Judy and Stan said yes even before Dave had a chance to bring them a photograph. The baby had no name. The documents referred to him only as "Baby Boy." Stan told Dave, "We want to name him John, after St. John Bosco, who cared a great deal about children. But we'll call him Johnny."

Childplace gave the Hills as much information as they had, which wasn't much. Johnny's Hispanic birthmother came into the hospital inebriated, gave birth to a beautiful, healthy-looking mixed race (Hispanic/Black) six-pound boy, and then walked out. Ten days later, she signed away her rights in a courtroom and then left town. Nothing was known about the birth father, and the mother could offer no medical history except to say that her father had died from liver disease, and her mother has diabetes. The birth mother admitted that she had not sought prenatal care and that she had drunk beer and wine coolers and smoked tobacco throughout the pregnancy.

The Hills knew that Johnny might develop problems as he grew because of prenatal exposure to alcohol. They had read *The Broken Cord*, by Michael Dorris, a book about the adoption of a child with fetal alcohol syndrome. They loved Johnny at first sight and were thrilled to take him home. They called the handsome child their "baby boy blessing."

THE CONTRACT—NOT

Dave did not offer the Hills an adoption assistance contract for two reasons. One, Johnny appeared to be a healthy baby, even though he had definite risk factors. Two, the state worker he called said that children placed through private agencies in State X can't get adoption subsidies anyway.

Both of these reasons, as the Hills would learn later, should never have prevented Johnny from receiving IV-E eligibility and the family from negotiating a contract, but Stan and Judy didn't know anything about subsidies, so they didn't question the lack of a contract. Medicaid paid the birth mother's medical bill, and after a little initial difficulty with the HMO, the Hills added Johnny to their private health insurance.

Time passed.

JOHNNY'S SPECIAL NEEDS

Johnny grew and gained weight very slowly and cried constantly for the first year. Judy quit her job at the insurance agency because he was too sickly and "high needs" to be left in day care. She and Stan held him night and day and still he cried. All the usual methods parents use to soothe colicky babies, like running a vacuum or driving the baby around the block a few times, simply made Johnny scream louder.

The pediatrician tried many different formulas, but to no avail. One of Stan's sisters, who had recently given birth, supplied breastmilk for several months, which helped dramatically with Johnny's weight gain problem and his chronic constipation. But still Johnny cried and cried. His doctor called it drug withdrawal and "neurological damage" and theorized that Johnny had been exposed in the womb to other drugs in addition to alcohol, possibly cocaine.

In spite of the baby's health problems, the Hills had no regrets about the adoption. They loved their curly-topped brown-eyed son with all their hearts, and they finalized the adoption as soon as the six-month waiting period was up.

When Judy found out she was pregnant right after Johnny's first birthday, they were thrilled that Johnny would have a sibling to play with.

THE FAMILY GROWS

Make that two siblings. Judy gave birth to healthy twin girls. The Hills discussed adopting a brother for Johnny, Nan, and Nina in a few years and settled down to enjoy their three babies.

Because of the twins' above average development patterns, Stan and Judy could clearly see that Johnny's development was delayed. He was a blur of energy and motion, but he walked and talked late according to the child-rearing books. A preschool screening found a mild hearing loss, but it was hoped it would not get worse. Tests showed that Johnny was almost a year behind the average child his age. They called it a developmental delay. Everyone thought he could catch up, but there was no doubt he would need a little extra help. The twins, who by contrast were precocious and advanced for their ages, required less attention from Mom and Dad than their big brother alone did.

Johnny was next diagnosed with an eye-focusing disorder and then with ADHD. He was supposed to wear eyeglasses and do eye exercises, but he broke every pair of glasses he was given within a month and couldn't sit still long enough to do the focusing exercises with his parents.

After several doctors, the Hills found one who had a lot of experience with children like Johnny. Happily, Johnny responded well to a relatively modest dose of the third calming medication they tried. In fact, he was a different child. He was less destructive and impulsive, and he could sit through an entire cartoon for the first time, although not yet through a full half-hour show. He could do his vision exercises now. The Hills were happy. They even talked to Dave about the possibility of adopting one more son so that Johnny could have a brother.

A CONTRACT AT LAST, OR MAYBE NOT

Childplace moved to a bordering state, and Dave started working for DHS as a social worker. The Hills kept in contact with Dave through the special needs adoption support group they had joined shortly before Johnny's adoption finalization. They attended one meeting to hear a parent-advocate talk about an important federal law that was helping adopted children, called Title IV-E, PL 96-272.

At this meeting, Judy was shocked to hear that Johnny probably qualified as a IV-E child, and that they could receive a monthly subsidy to help with his expenses. This was particularly good news because Johnny's needs were such that Judy didn't feel she could go back to work outside the home. Before the adoption, she had made a pretty good living as an insurance adjuster. It was ironic that her twins would have done fine in a quality day care setting, but with Johnny's ADHD and hearing and vision problems, he needed the extra attention he could only get at home. The loss of Judy's salary had long been a cross for the family to bear. Perhaps a subsidy was the answer to their prayers.

Stan called Dave at DHS but received only bad news. Dave said Johnny did not qualify according to what he, Dave, knew about IV-E. He had attended a workshop on this and in Johnny's case, it was too late to apply. Dave said that the application must be made before finalization. Judy was crushed, but Stan called the parent-advocate from the meeting and asked her about Johnny.

The advocate encouraged the Hills to appeal the decision informally to Dave's supervisor because of something called PIQ 92-02. Dave was happy to investigate this Policy Interpretation Question called 92-02. This was a clarification of the IV-E law that said it was okay to go back anytime and apply—if there were extenuating circumstances present. Maybe there was reason to hope, after all.

Extenuating circumstances were defined in 92-02 as circumstances that prevented a family from applying on time for an adoption subsidy. One of the four extenuating circumstances described in PIQ 92-02 was certainly present in Johnny's case: State X and Childplace had never told Stan and Judy that they could apply for a subsidy when they adopted Johnny. Dave himself could attest to that. They had not been informed about the Title IV-E program at all! Armed with this information and Johnny's medical diagnoses, they went to see the State X adoption unit supervisor, a woman Dave had told them would make the final decision. They appealed to this supervisor, Ms. Williams, and asked for an adoption assistance contract and the automatic accompanying Medicad coverage.

Ms. Willliams was sympathetic initially but called back in a few days and firmly denied the application. She agreed that Johnny was a child with special needs, physical, developmental, and educational disabilities, and due to his minority race and to risk factors like prenatal drug exposure, unknown paternity, and lack of prenatal care, he had qualified several times over as a child with special needs from birth. The application was denied because of "federal language" that was lacking in Johnny's paperwork from the court. And, furthermore, she explained, Johnny was adopted from a private adoption agency. In State X, only children coming from DHS foster homes could qualify for subsidies. Judy fought back bitter tears as she listened to Ms. Williams. She felt like she was living an injustice, and she felt powerless to stop it.

Ms. Williams ended their discussion with this statement, "You know, Mrs. Hill, when you adopt a child and finalize the placement, you agree to pay that child's expenses. Johnny really is your responsibility." Judy and Stan had struggled against the idea of accepting money to help them raise their beloved son and had already fought the guilt and the shame they felt over their family's need for help. Judy was further devastated by Ms. Williams' admonitions, so it was difficult to answer her. But she gathered up the rest of her pride. "I assure you," Judy told the administrator, drawing on reserves of courage, "Johnny will never go without anything he needs in our home. We love our son deeply."

The Hills were embarrassed and worried. The denial made no sense to them. It didn't seem possible that a choice of adoption agencies and a few words on a document could prevent a child with special needs from receiving the $400 monthly payment and Medicaid card from the state that he needed so badly.

A few days later, they ran into Dave at the supermarket and told him that they were officially giving up. But they certainly wouldn't be able to afford a second and last adoption. They'd even had to drop their private health insurance. They could barely pay their bills now, including a recent $750 expense for Johnny's first hearing aid. The hearing loss was getting worse instead of better. Their son would simply not have a brother, at least not in the foreseeable future.

Dave encouraged them to try one more time before giving up. "I've heard about this organization called NACAC," he told them. "They have specially trained volunteers called NAATRIN representatives who help parents advocate for subsidies. Maybe you should call the NACAC subsidy Hotline (800–470–6665), before giving up entirely. You have nothing to lose, and I've heard of a recent case where one of Ms. Williams' decisions was overturned in a fair hearing because of the NAATRIN rep."

Could it be that the supervisor was wrong, wondered the Hills. Could people be misinformed two levels up in the bureaucracy? It didn't seem possible. After all, it was and had long been Ms. Williams' job to know the law. They thought about Dave's suggestion and prayed about it. Something told Judy to try one more time and even though he didn't like the stress of fighting on, Stan did not object to a fact-finding mission. Judy called NACAC's toll-free number and was referred to a parent-advocate NAATRIN representative named Melissa who lived just one county away.

Melissa, a single adoptive parent of two grown daughters, had gone through NAATRIN training at NACAC and had already gone to several fair hearings in State X as a NAATRIN volunteer and fair hearing witness. Stan laid out the situation and Melissa listened intently. When she spoke, Stan and Judy could hardly believe their ears.

"Almost 75 percent of the $400 subsidy that State X pays each month to each subsidized family is reimbursed to the state by the federal government. This is called FFP, or Federal Financial Participation, and the specific percentage varies some from state to state, but the bottom line is this: If the states want to receive FFP reimbursement, they must follow the federal IV-E law, even when they don't like it and even when it contradicts state law. If they want to make up their own rules, they can do so under a state subsidy plan, but not under the IV-E subsidy system. There is a PIQ called 87-05, a clarification of IV-E law, that clearly reads if a state wants to access FFP, they have to follow the federal rules. The 'eligibility criteria' in Title IV-E is the 'sole criteria' they may use. No choice!"

Melissa continued, "Other PIQs, like 85-04 and 87-05, say very plainly that you can't discriminate against an otherwise eligible child just because he came through a private adoption agency. States can't get foster care FFP for private agency children, but they can and do obtain adoption assistance FFP for these children." (Note: See Chapters 9 and 10 and the appendices for more information on these issues and for PIQ texts.) "And the federal law is quite clear on the legal language, too, happily. There is a bit of wiggle-room there, provided the intent of the law, the best interests of the child, is clearly respected. For example, the consent can say that 'adoption is in a child's best interests' or that 'continuation in the birth home is contrary to the child's welfare,' or 'words to that effect.' The two phrases are interchangeable according to the PIQs (like 85-07 and 75-21), although some states have tried to insist on exact wording. PL 96-272 demands a balance between making sure that children who can return to their birth homes are given that chance and children who should not be returned to their birth homes are given a chance to be adopted."

Melissa took a breath and went on. "What this law seeks to avoid is 'foster care drift.' Children should not be in familial limbo one moment more than they have to be. And it seeks to remove 'financial disincentives' from the adoption and raising of children with special needs. I'd have to see his documents, especially the Consent, the document that terminated the birth mother's rights, to see if the equivalent language respects the intent of PL 96-272, but I think you have an excellent case and that you should consider requesting an administrative hearing."

This was one more incredible piece of news in a jigsaw of incredible pieces. Stan and Judy embraced, delighted to have hope again. They spoke with Ms. Williams one last time, armed with a new understanding of the law and fresh arguments, but the supervisor did not change her mind. She seemed irritated. This surprised and upset them. Why wouldn't Ms. Williams want the best for Johnny? Shouldn't she be trying to use the law to help Johnny instead of using it to deny him? But Melissa explained that the supervisor's attitude was not based on a personal dislike for the Hill family. Some state administrators have a "gatekeeper mentality" about adoption subsidies instead of a "child's best interest view," guarding money that is mostly federal in origin as if it were their own. In some cases, they simply hate to be proved wrong.

Stan and Judy, now resigned to the inevitable struggle, asked Ms. Williams for the paperwork to begin a fair hearing process. "That is your right, of course," said the supervisor, "but I must tell you, I am almost never overruled."

As Melissa explained, the fair hearing is an informal process. Attorneys can be very helpful, of course, but they are not required. The Hills could not afford an attorney but their income was too high for the free legal aid clinic. So Melissa offered her volunteer services and for the next few weeks, the Hills spoke with her at length until they understood which parts of Title IV-E and which PIQs applied to Johnny's case.

With calculator and PIQ 92-02 in hand, Melissa figured out that the Hills were owed $12,000 for the thirty months of IV-E subsidy Johnny should have received so far. Judy almost fainted. "We could buy Johnny that expensive digital hearing aid he needs and a spare pair of eyeglasses with lightweight plastic lenses and some Tonka trucks that he couldn't destroy within forty-eight hours like he does most toys and a personal computer with speech therapy software for his developmental delays and. . . ."

"Hold on," said Melissa, "don't get your hopes up yet. Fair hearing outcomes are never guaranteed. Anything can happen."

THE FAIR HEARING SUMMARY

The Hills knew they were not required to prepare anything official in writing under State X rules, for the hearing. In another state, they may have been required to submit documents a certain amount of time before the hearing. The Hills could just go in to the hearing and talk. But Melissa strongly recommended that they write down their reasons for believing that their son should receive a IV-E subsidy and back payments to the date of placement in their home. Having something in writing would assure the case was presented in full and give the hearing officer a written reference of their arguments. She called this a "summary."

Stan and Judy visited the Web sites Melissa suggested, downloaded and printed out the relevant PIQs and federal laws, and some state policy, too, although State X stuff was tough to find on the Web. Adoption assistance program details for each state are contained in the state's administrative code, and only a limited number of states have published their administrative codes on the Web so far. They also obtained some essential documents from the National Adoption Information Clearinghouse in Washington, D.C., a federal agency. Stan called NAIC one of the "best uses of tax dollars" he had ever seen in the promotion of the best interests of children.

Judy also called the regional Department of Health and Human Services or DHHS office (see the appendices). She asked for technical assistance and faxed an overview of the case to the federal employees there. They told her that they could provide her with some technical assistance over the phone, but they would not put anything in writing because they had not seen all of the documents in his case. After reviewing the documents from the fax machine, the DHHS people told Judy that Johnny was "probably IV-E eligible." This gave the Hills hope and confidence, but it did little to help the case because DHHS declined their request to write a "letter of support" for the hearing officer.

They typed up their reasons, attached the downloaded documents as exhibits, and gave it all to Melissa to read. "This is good," she said, "but edit it one more time to remove any extraneous paragraphs. Remember, Johnny's best interests and the law is all the hearing officer wants to read about."

Once a final draft was ready, fifty-two pages including exhibits, Stan had four copies made at the quick copy store, one for the hearing officer, one for Ms. Williams, and one for Melissa. They blacked out all identifying information on the fourth copy, to protect their privacy and donated it to the local adoptive parent support group library (in case another family could use the legal research). They kept the original for themselves.

Three days before the hearing, the parents received a copy of Ms. Williams' summary in the mail. It listed all of the same reasons that she had described over the phone when she denied their application. The hearing regulations required Ms. Williams to give them an advance copy of her summary and, in most states, would require the parents to reciprocate, but in State X, the parents were not required to supply an advance copy of their materials.

THE FAIR HEARING

The night before the fair hearing, Stan called Melissa with the news that he and Judy might not be able to make the fair hearing because they were so nervous, they felt ill. Judy had a disabling headache, and Stan was dizzy and nauseous. Melissa had seen various reactions to administrative hearings and she knew just what to say.

"Stan," she began in a calm and sympathetic tone, "Did Ms. Williams

tell you that Johnny is your responsibility or words to that effect, and did
she imply that you had no right to ask for assistance?"

"Yes!" said Stan, "It upset Judy a lot. It made us question this whole
idea. We weren't raised to rely on government handouts. We have been
blessed so far to never need help from the outside."

"Listen to me, Stan. Johnny is not and never has been a healthy, average,
easy-to-place adoptable baby. People were not lined up waiting to adopt
him. Johnny's birth parents abdicated their responsibility to their child.
Because of the birth mother's choices, Johnny has a lot of physical and
educational problems that are in no way your fault. Laws like Title IV-E
recognize that average citizens need help raising an adopted child with
special needs—society's children who are more expensive and difficult to
raise than typical children. Johnny qualifies for these programs and he can
benefit from them. Furthermore, if Judy didn't need to stay home to take
care of Johnny, she could work and you wouldn't have to live on the edge
of financial disaster the way you do. You've made a sacrifice you don't
have to make. What I'm trying to say is this. You mustn't let Ms. Williams'
personal opinion about adoption subsidies change your mind. The federal
government is on your side, so do what you and Judy want to do."

"But, Melissa, how do we know what to fight for and how hard to
fight?" asked Stan.

"Ah, that's the easy part," answered the advocate. "The criterion is el-
egantly simple. You are fighting to meet Johnny's needs, in his best interests. This should be 100 percent about the child and not about anger or
dissatisfaction with Ms. Williams or manipulating the system. Once Johnny
has what he needs and should get legally, you can stop, or, if you think
it's not worth the stress, you can quit now. Not every parent decides to
fight, and I won't respect you any less if you prefer not to go through with
this. No one knows better than I that it is an ordeal."

There was a pause and then Stan said, "We'll be there," with a tone of
quiet determination, "We'll just think of Johnny, and we'll get through it."

A SMALL ROOM WITH A LARGE TABLE

Melissa arrived early at the Department of Human Services and entered
the hearing room with the Hills at her side. The room was filled with a
long wide wooden table surrounded by folding chairs. She greeted Ms.
Williams politely and sat across from her. The administrator did not seem
happy to be facing the state NACAC NAATRIN representative yet again,
but she greeted the Hills with genuine friendliness.

Each side gave a set of documents to the other and a set to the Hearing
Officer, who started a cassette recorder as he began the hearing. His name
was Mr. Garcia, he had a calm and kind demeanor, and he began by
explaining that this was an informal hearing. That's why attorneys were

welcome but not required. Judy noticed a bit nervously that Ms. Williams had brought one of the department's lawyers with her. The Hills were a bit jealous that the state could afford to have legal representation, but they could not.

The department lawyer never spoke but handed brief notes to Ms. Williams that she scrawled throughout the hearing. Ms. Williams went first, describing the department's decision and giving the reasons behind it. The Hills had heard all but the last reason before. The next part, attached as a last minute addendum to the state's case, was new to them. Ms. Williams quoted state subsidy law to explain why she was denying a IV-E subsidy request. Specifically, she read the following lines out loud, emphasizing the second and third words: "Under no circumstances can a state subsidy be granted or an adoption assistance contract be written after the legal finalization of the adoption has taken place. . . ."

The Hills could have raised an objection to the addendum as a violation of the "adequate notice" rule and the "right to inspect" that is specified in the federal hearing regulations, but they did not know the regulations well enough to realize that Ms. Williams was violating them. Melissa noticed the violation, but failed to object because the addendum was about state and not federal subsidy time limits. PIQ 92-02 clearly makes time limits on federal subsidies illegal when extenuating circumstances are present. Melissa was surprised that the department supervisor would bother with a totally irrelevant passage about state subsidies.

Ms. Williams went on to say that federal PIQs are so numerous that they could be used to "prove almost anything" and asked the hearing officer to disregard them as "advisory and not legally binding."

She ended by saying, "I have no reason to believe that this family did not know about adoption subsidies at the time of Johnny's adoption. Subsidy information was not a secret. I'm sorry Johnny has developed disabilities. His adoptive parents were fully informed of the risks and had even read a book about them, according to the postplacement follow-up reports. They finalized the adoption knowing what was ahead of them. The state simply can't afford to do the financial job of the adoptive parents and, in this case, we don't believe there is any reason why we should have to."

Neither Stan nor Judy wanted to do the talking. Stan was afraid he would leave out something important or become angrier than he already was. Judy was afraid she would burst into tears or raise her voice out of frustration. Too much was riding on this, including Johnny's needs and the financial health of their whole family. Melissa agreed to do the talking provided Stan and Judy would interrupt her anytime they wanted to add something.

Melissa read from the summary she had helped the Hills write. She quoted the federal law, the PIQs that applied to the situation, the state law, and even some case law describing similar disputes in other states.

Melissa knew from experience that in State X, IV-E adoption assistance fair hearings were far less common than food stamps and TANF cases. She knew the hearing officer was probably more comfortable hearing a food stamp fraud case than he was a retroactive adoption assistance case, so she started off describing the history and intent and purpose of PL 96-272. Then she addressed the extenuating circumstance that must be proved before there are grounds to ask for retroactive IV-E eligibility and AAP.

"To listen to Ms. Williams," said Melissa to Mr. Garcia, "you might think Stan and Judy Hill are trying to defraud the state of an income-based entitlement that they did not need and should not have. This is not the case, as we shall see. Ms. Williams has provided no evidence that the state made any effort to inform adoptive parents or private licensed agencies about the Title IV-E program even though federal law requires states to inform families. She has provided no evidence that the family knew about this program before Johnny's finalization. And Exhibit 1 is a letter from their social worker, Dave Stein, swearing that he never mentioned the program to them because he did not think Johnny would qualify for it.

"PL 96-272 has nothing to do with relieving Stan and Judy of their parental responsibility," Melissa said firmly. "It is about making special needs adoption affordable for American citizens so that children don't stay in foster care. And the FFP reimburses State X for the majority of IV-E related costs anyway, including retroactive payments. Congress wrote this law in 1980 based on research that clearly showed how state subsidy programs resulted in permanency for children with special needs. Study after study has shown the federal equivalent of subsidies is working. Remove the financial barriers, and good-hearted citizens like Stan and Judy will come forward and take a child or two or three or more out of foster care. Stan and Judy are asking for this help because they need it to meet the needs of a disabled child whom they took into their home."

Melissa sipped her coffee and continued. "Johnny can only qualify for this until he is eighteen years old so his parents are going to advocate for him while it is possible to do so. But after he turns eighteen, you can bet they will still be there for him. As his mom and dad, they will always be there for him. This is a good deal for Johnny and a good deal for society because young adults with families behind them are far more likely to go to college and to become productive tax-payers than are foster children who age out of the system."

Melissa next read from the twenty-five page summary quoting from the federal law, the program regulation, and the PIQs as everyone else followed along in their copy of the summary. She also quoted the intent and purpose of the state subsidy program even though this was a IV-E case, because the intent and purpose of the State X subsidy program mirrored the language of the federal law, almost word for word. Subsidies, whether state or federal, are meant to help foster children find permanency and to make special needs adoption affordable.

The advocate showed that all of the legal language requirements were met in Johnny's paperwork, especially the important "best interests" language. She went through the eligibility paragraphs of PL 96-272 line by line and showed how Johnny had met every single qualification under the federal law. She quoted several different PIQs that proved that Johnny could not be discriminated against simply because he was placed through a private adoption agency and not a state agency, because Childplace, the private agency, met all federal and state requirements as a placing agency.

For almost an hour Melissa read and explained, and Stan and Judy gave testimony. Judy never dared touch the soft drink Stan had set in front of her at the start of the meeting. She was so nervous, she was afraid she would spill it all over herself. Judy had never been a party to a legal proceeding in her life, not even an informal one like this. It was with a huge sigh of relief that she noticed Melissa was finished and the hearing officer was shutting off the tape recorder.

The hearing took about two hours. After leaving the building, the Hills felt as if a great weight had been lifted from their shoulders. They took Melissa to lunch to thank her. Over sandwiches and chocolate cake, Melissa told Stan and Judy to consider the next step in case the decision went against them. "In this state, you get one administrative appeal, and if you lose there, you should hire a lawyer to go further, because the next step is District Court. Hope for the best but make a plan in case it doesn't go well."

THEIR WORST NIGHTMARE

Exactly one month after the hearing, Judy received the decision in the mail. She tore it open as she stood on the front porch next to the mailbox. And then she started to scream, stopping herself only by clamping her free hand on her own mouth. The hope she had clung to was shattered. The last line of the two-page document stood out from the rest of the paragraphs. ". . . in other words, this decision has gone against you."

The good news was that the hearing officer had given them the extenuating circumstance, noting that DHS "had offered no evidence to prove that they had informed the family of their rights under the IV-E program." But Mr. Garcia went on to say that he saw no legal reason why PIQs should be able to supercede a state law that said: "Under no circumstances can a state subsidy be granted or an adoption assistance contract be written after the legal finalization of the adoption has taken place. . . ."

When Stan and Melissa read the decision, there was a minute of shocked silence. Melissa spoke first. "Just about every hearing I am involved in

packs at least one surprise. This one is no exception. I should have addressed this surprise quote from the state law more thoroughly. I just assumed that Mr. Garcia would know that you can't legally apply a state
law about state subsidies to federal subsidies if you intend to access FFP,
as State X does. How could he not understand that there is a big difference
between state subsidies and IV-E subsidies?"

"You did your best, Melissa," said Stan, "and we appreciate it. You have
put a lot of work into this without pay. We have nothing but gratitude for
your help. We'll let you know in a few days if we want to appeal."

"No problem, but remember, you only have thirty days to appeal, no
more than that."

At first, the Hills decided to drop the entire matter. God would see them
through, and maybe in a few years, when Johnny was in school, Judy could
return to the workforce at least part time as an insurance adjuster. They
felt exhausted, drained, betrayed, and cheated. They were angry and sad
and scared all at once. Judy felt like her fourth child had just died because
without a subsidy for Johnny, there was no way they could afford to adopt
and raise another son, even if the new child came with a subsidy. Her grief
was strong.

APPEALING THE HEARING DECISION

A few days later, Johnny accidentally pulled the television set off the
table in the living room and it broke open. The toddler was not hurt, but
this was just one more example of his destructive behavior. His parents
decided that they had to try again, and as Melissa had said, they had
nothing to lose, monetarily, that is.

With Melissa's advice, Judy and Stan wrote an appeal document. It described their reasons for seeking an appeal, the main one being that the
hearing decision was based on a state law that does not and cannot legally
apply to federal IV-E subsidies. Stan also put a stronger emphasis on state
law as it agrees with federal law. They wrote a clear explanation about the
differences between state and federal adoption assistance contracts and why
state law cannot supercede federal law when it comes to federal subsidies.
They also explained in greater detail what PIQs are and what they are
meant to do. Far from being just advisory, PIQs have the force of law and
are meant to be used by state administrators to understand PL 96-272 and
to apply it fairly to all potentially eligible children.

They quoted Carol W. Williams, Associate Commissioner of the U.S.
DHHS, Children's Bureau, (see appendices) on the importance of PIQs:

Q. What is the significance of Policy Information Questions by the U.S. Department
of Health and Human Services and are they interpretations of the law?

A. Policy Information Questions and other issuances developed by this Department are interpretations of statute and are disseminated as a mechanism to further clarify statutes and regulations that are already in place.

Seven weeks after mailing off their appeal summary by certified mail, the decision arrived. The committee that had reviewed Mr. Garcia's decision had decided to uphold his decision. Judy grabbed the mailbox this time and sobbed for five minutes before she could bring herself to read the rest of the document.

Melissa called it "hopeful, overall," but the Hills were completely discouraged. It was a week before they could bear to read it over carefully. The appeals committee had actually overruled Mr. Garcia's application of state subsidy law to a federal subsidy question, calling the action "misplaced." The committee said that the Hills had established Johnny's IV-E eligibility in a legal sense, but they upheld the denial because the Hills had failed to show, as state law requires, how Johnny was "harmed by the substantial violation of his rights." This was the first time Stan, Judy, or Melissa had ever heard that phrase before. There was nothing in PIQ 92-02 or PL 96-272 that required proof of harm. And besides, was harm not implied when a child with special needs is denied money he qualifies for? Once again, they had been stopped by a state law even though only federal law was legally relevant.

AFFORDABLE LEGAL HELP

It was time to hire a lawyer and to appeal to district court, but they had no money for a retainer. In other states they would have been automatically offered discounted legal aid due to the "public assistance" nature of the case, but not in State X.

The lawyers they spoke with asked for retainers of at least $500. They would also need to get a transcript made of the fair hearing from the tape recording. Estimates on the cost of the transcription, reproduction, and postage costs ran as high as $200. Melissa was right that the administrative denial was more good news than bad news, but it seemed that the closer they got to victory, the further away it was. Would the lack of $700 keep them from fighting on?

Judy's uncle was an advocacy attorney, and he suggested that she call her local advocacy, or disability law office, for advice. The advocacy office was staffed by federally paid attorneys who represent parents of disabled children in special education legal disputes with school districts, at no charge to the families. Perhaps they would know of an experienced adoption attorney who would work on a contingency basis, charging them only if they won the case.

Judy called and not only asked for advice on finding a lawyer, she asked the educational advocacy attorneys if they would represent Johnny. At first, they turned Judy down flat because adoption was not part of their mission statement, and they knew nothing about adoption law. But Judy persisted and begged that they reconsider. She took copies of her summary, the appeal summary, and both decisions to the advocacy center. She asked other adoption advocates and adoptive parents to call and ask them to reconsider. A week later, to her great joy, they agreed to write a brief for the court. There would be no charge for their services or for the necessary transcription work. After talking to Judy's friends and reading the materials, it was clear this was a case about the denial of services to a disabled child by a public institution, and such matters were definitely part of their mission statement.

DISTRICT COURT

Stan and Judy did as much of the legal research as they could on the Web, and Ms. Goldberg, the advocacy attorney, approached the awesome task of learning all about PL 96-272 with eagerness. Here was a lawyer with the heart and soul of a child advocate. It was as if Stan and Judy had found someone who "speaks our language." Ms. Goldberg took about two weeks to learn from all of the resources Melissa had suggested and to research case law, and then she wrote a legal brief that the Hills thought was a work of art.

Ms. Goldberg had a way of writing that remained true to the purpose of this legal battle while also communicating how unfair the state had been to Johnny. The brief reflected the pain of Stan and Judy and described their frustration at being unable to access that which the federal law clearly says their son should have. It also addressed the question of whether Johnny was "harmed by the substantial violation of his rights." To prove that this had indeed occurred, Stan and Judy submitted medical evidence of Johnny's special needs and letters from his doctors and teachers describing items and services Johnny could benefit greatly from having, but which the Hills could not afford to provide. Ms. Goldberg also quoted case law and fair hearing regulations on this question and cited the Fourteenth Amendment to the U.S. Constitution:

Amendment XIV—Citizenship rights not to be abridged. Ratified 7/9/1868. Note

1. All persons born or naturalized in the United States, and subject to the jurisdiction thereof, are citizens of the United States and of the State wherein they reside. No State shall make or enforce any law which shall abridge the privileges or immunities of citizens of the United States; nor shall any State deprive any person of life, liberty, or property, without due process of law; nor deny to any person within its jurisdiction the equal protection of the laws.

The Equal Protection Clause of the Fourteenth Amendment to the U.S. Constitution prohibits a state from denying any person within its jurisdiction the equal protection of the laws. In other words, the laws of a state must treat an individual in the same manner as others in similar conditions and circumstances.

Melissa loved the brief, too, and expressed a hope that she could refer other adoptive parents to Ms. Goldberg in the future. As a team, their enthusiasm grew. Stan and Judy spoke at the next adoptive parent support group meeting on the topic "How to Prepare for a Fair Hearing." Judy wasn't even nervous during the speech. Stan and Judy were no longer just support group members. They had unwittingly become parent-advocates. Stan asked to take the NAATRIN training. Melissa now had some more help.

When the team finished the final draft of the brief, Ms. Goldberg submitted it to the court. She received a copy of the state's brief soon after that and sent a copy to the Hills. It was a powerfully written document that painted the adoptive couple as people who went into a risky adoption with their eyes "wide open" and now wanted the court to grant them relief from the financial headaches that they had known were coming. It described Johnny's special needs as "daunting" but "not very much more expensive than the needs of any other child in his age range." This sent Judy reeling with anger. "How dare they make that subjective assessment!" she cried to her husband. "Have they ever lived with Johnny? Have they bought a new TV because their child destroyed the old one? Have they replaced shoes and bedsheets and toys and books and clothing and furniture at three times the average rate with other children? Do they know anything about the cost of eyeglasses or the high cost of new hearing-aid technology?"

The state's brief went on to reiterate much of what Ms. Williams had said and asked that the court not set a precedent by granting the Hills' requests because doing so was not only outside the law, but also the results for the state's adoption assistance budget would be catastrophic.

Ms. Goldberg wrote a counterbrief that also went into the record. It answered the state's points in detail and summed up by explaining that almost three-fourths of the retroactive payment and the future subsidy would be reimbursed to the state anyway, along with 50 percent of the administrative overhead concerning implementation of PL 96-272. "How can the state's budget be so severely strained when the federal government is reimbursing most of the cost to the state?" And she added, "And how can the state ask us to balance the budget on the back of a child with special needs?"

TIME TO WAIT AGAIN

Stan and Judy prayed and tried valiantly not to think about the court action. Weeks passed. Some days passed quickly, but other days found Judy sobbing with worry, and Stan shaking his head over the checkbook. With each passing month, as Johnny grew, his needs became more expensive to meet financially, but the incoming money remained the same.

The Hills tried to concentrate on their options. They had three options if they lost at this level: appeal to the State X Supreme Court; stop appealing, sell their home and the second car, rent a smaller or older house, and try to make do on the savings that would result; or find a job for Judy in the evenings when Stan could stay home with the children.

They hated all of the options, but the third was the worst because it would rob them of precious family time and because it would exhaust them, too. Stan and Judy prayed some more. Time passed slowly.

Weeks became months. The Hills decided to use credit cards to make ends meet but only until the decision came. If it went against them and they could not find the emotional strength to appeal, they would immediately implement the second and third options simultaneously. They kept dread at bay with frequent hugging. Embracing each other became a lifeline. When Judy wanted to cry, Stan hugged. When Stan felt like the stress would break him in two, Judy hugged. And they took delight in Nan, Nina, and Johnny, who never hesitated to hug Mommy or Daddy when the parents stretched out their arms.

THE FIRST DAY OF THE REST OF THEIR LIVES

One day, a Tuesday morning, as Stan lay in bed with the flu and a 102 degree temperature, the phone rang. Judy had been stirring some soup for her husband. Her heart stopped momentarily as it always did when the phone rang during the day. Would it be Ms. Goldberg with bad news? She hugged Johnny for good luck and answered the phone. Ms. Goldberg was indeed on the other end of the line. Her voice was loud and she sounded winded, as if she had been running. There was a lot of noise in the background.

"We won!" she yelled. "I just ran down three flights of stairs to find a free telephone. I'm at the courthouse, the decision has just come down, and we've won. Everything! The court gave Johnny everything we asked for!"

Stan had jumped out of bed when Judy signaled frantically that this was THE PHONE CALL. When Judy started jumping up and down screaming with joy, Stan grabbed the phone and listened while Ms. Goldberg repeated herself. The children began jumping up and down, too, because Mommy and Daddy were jumping. It was great to see Daddy suddenly feeling better. Within moments, everyone was hugging with giant-squeeze bear hugs. Mommy was even hugging the telephone.

The soup scorched the pot.

THE AFTERMATH

A check for the full amount of retroactive subsidy arrived three weeks later. The Hills negotiated a IV-E adoption assistance contract that included the basic rate subsidy, a Level 2 specialized rate because of the ADHD, Medicaid, of course, and reimbursements for extraordinary necessary medical costs not covered by Medicaid, and any health insurance the Hills might have at the time the need arises.

Stan and Judy gave big boxes of chocolates to Melissa and Ms. Goldberg. They took the children to church to thank God, took them out to eat at the family's favorite restaurant, and then wrote out a new budget. They got to keep their house and both old cars, and Judy stopped asking for employment applications.

They used every penny of the retroactive assistance check to meet Johnny's direct and indirect and present and future needs. They bought their son the latest technological marvel in hearing aids. His teachers saw an immediate improvement in his schoolwork as a result of his sharper hearing. They purchased a strong type of athletic eyeglass frames that took Johnny three times as long to break as an ordinary pair of eyeglass frames. They bought him a personal computer with educational software hand-picked by his teachers; super-durable clothing, shoes, and toys; and a bed made of solid hardwood. Johnny had already demolished two other lighter bedframes. They put some of the money into a college IRA for Johnny and used some to buy an almost tip-proof television set.

The win had an extra special long-term effect—it helped other children find permanency. The following year after the court decision, the Hills called Dave. They went on to adopt one more time, but they did not get that brother for Johnny they had planned on. They adopted two brothers for him and for Nan and Nina. The Hills found a sibling group of fraternal twin brothers who were just a little younger than their daughters. One boy had mild asthma and some cerebral palsy, and the other twin had a moderate case of asthma and some skin allergies. They were able to negotiate IV-E adoption assistance contracts on the twins that made the adoption and raising of two more children affordable. By doing most of the labor themselves, Stan and Judy even managed to add another bedroom and bathroom on to their home. Car number two was traded in on a used minivan for the family of seven. They feel that their family is complete.

The budget remains tight, but it is no longer inadequate to meet the needs of the children. Stan and Judy don't have a great deal of spare time to help other families in the support group with contract negotiations and fair hearings, but they offer their aid whenever they can.

Melissa will soon retire as the NACAC NAATRIN representative to go to Russia to teach English. Dave and Ms. Goldberg are encouraging Stan and Judy to take her place as the local NACAC volunteers. They also want them to consider starting a part-time professional advocacy business to serve families at the fair-hearing level and work with attorneys at court level. "If you're good, you'll get plenty of calls from parents and from their lawyers, and if you are getting paid something for your time, you'll be far less likely to burn out on the stress."

The Hills are thinking about it.

12

Parent Groups and Legislators

The good of the people is the greatest law.

—Cicero (106–43 B.C.)

REPRESENTATION

A fair hearing can be an effective short-term solution for an adoption assistance problem, but in the long run, families who adopt must examine
their own state laws and adoption policies to create the most effective and
lasting change. Without child-centered adoption laws, adoptive and foster
families are overly dependent on public agencies in several key respects.
Instead of being actively engaged in formulating policies that affect the lives
of their children in crucial ways, adoptive and foster parents must wait for
policy decisions made by agencies to trickle down. In matters involving
changes to existing laws or regulations, parents are represented by agencies,
even though their interests and those of agencies often diverge. Parents may
testify at public hearings, but the real work of crafting legislation often
goes on at meetings of the various stakeholders held between the hearings.
In spite of the fact that the families are the ones with the most to gain or
lose by the decisions made at such meetings, they are usually absent from
the table.

A few years ago, an adoption triad group was trying to open adoption
records that had been sealed since the 1960s. The group found a sponsor
to draft a bill providing adult adoptees with access to their original birth
certificates. At the public committee hearings that followed the introduction
of the legislation, adoptees presented eloquent testimony about what it was

like to be cut off from their family history. Meanwhile, in between hearings, powerful lobbying groups who were opposed to the bill were meeting with the committee chair and other key committee members. Agency representatives also participated in these discussions. The triad group did not. In the end, the committee yielded to pressure from the opponents and watered down the legislation. The agency, while somewhat neutral on the issue, did not provide strong support to the adoption group.

Given families' difficulties in confronting public agencies that are still opaquely bureaucratic, they need to find an independent voice. One means of establishing a more independent power base is to cultivate a working relationship with key state legislators. In this period where states have assumed responsibility for welfare reform and other social programs, state legislatures have assumed an added significance for adoptive and foster parents. But, if the report cited below is still accurate, child advocates and state legislators often dwell in different, mutually incomprehensible worlds. Adoptive and foster parents must learn some basic realities of the legislative process and culture in order to become effective advocates.

LEGISLATORS AND CHILD ADVOCATES

In 1993, the State Legislative Leader's Foundation began contacting legislators in all fifty states to determine their knowledge of children's issues and attitudes about child advocates. Researchers conducted interviews of eighty-six state senators and ninety-one state representatives. Fifty-four percent of the Speakers of the House and 45 percent of the Senate Presidents participated in the study, along with the chairs of committees dealing with children's issues.

The results of the interviews were published in a 1995 report entitled "Legislative Leaders: Keys to Effective Legislation for Children and Families." The report's preface describes the study as "a portrait of state legislative leaders that describes not only their perceptions and views about children and families and those advocates who speak for them, but also the leaders' innermost convictions and beliefs about the role of state government . . ." The following are excerpts from the Key Findings section of the report.

KEY FINDINGS

The report concludes that state legislators are concerned with children's issues but are not well informed about specific conditions affecting families in their districts. Legislative leaders do not have productive working relationships with child advocacy groups as indicated by the following findings taken directly from the study:

- In the eyes of state legislative leaders, there is no clear discernible legislative agenda for children and families. Instead, there is a plethora of individuals and organizations advocating different agendas for children and families. The leaders get mixed and sometimes contradictory messages.

- To state legislative leaders, groups that advocate for children and families appear to be "liberal" and democratic. Increasingly, the leadership in state legislatures is "moderate" or "conservative" and Republican.

- State legislative leaders are unaware of any cohesive, effective grassroots constituency for children in their states. Generally they do not hear from their constituents on child and family public policy issues.

- Some of the strategies legislative advocates for children and families see as important to their efforts are viewed by legislative leaders as irrelevant or counterproductive (for example, "Children's Day" at the state house, large written reports and legislative "score cards" offered by organizations that are perceived to have little or no political clout).

- State legislative leaders learn anecdotally about issues and not systematically, so their knowledge is often not national or statewide, but limited to what goes on in their districts and what others bring to their attention. Still, our interviews show that most state legislative leaders are not familiar with how children and families are faring in their districts or in their states. They are not informed about the policies and programs that "work" or the evidence of their impact in making a difference in children's lives.

LEGISLATORS' CRITIQUE OF ADVOCATES

The report underscores the extent to which child advocates are not part of the normal legislative process in their respective states. Prominent state legislators viewed advocates as amateurs who were unwilling or unable to develop the practical communication and organizational skills needed to make an impact on policy and budget decisions. In contrast to professional lobbyists, legislators faulted child advocates for

1. the failure to make face-to-face contact and to build long-term relationships with legislators

2. the failure to provide timely accurate information on specific child-related issues

3. the lack of focus on legislative issues

4. the inability to engage in the practical legislative arts of negotiation and compromise

5. the absence of local grassroots organization

SOME PRACTICAL SUGGESTIONS FOR ADOPTIVE AND FOSTER PARENTS

The study indicates that child advocates and legislators dwell in two separate worlds. Where the term advocate is a badge of honor in one realm, to legislators it conjures up images of elitism and moral grandstanding.

On a more positive note, legislators and their staffs are generally more accessible to citizen groups than agency bureaucracies. By learning how legislatures operate, adoptive and foster families can become effective voices on behalf of their children. The following are few suggestions for groups that want to become more active in the legislative process.

Target Key Legislators

The quality of legislative contacts is more important than quantity. Targeting a few key leaders or committee chairs is not only easier from an organizational point of view, it is a key to effectiveness. Talk to established advocacy groups about influential legislators with interest in and jurisdiction over issues impacting adoption. Most state legislatures publish guides listing senators and representatives who are available on request. Information about membership may also be available at state-sponsored sites on the Internet.

Develop Relationships

It is important to establish your credibility and build a relationship of mutual trust with targeted legislators. The legislative process depends on face-to-face contacts. Schedule an initial meeting with the legislator if possible and meet the legislator's aide. Following the initial meeting, you will probably deal primarily with the aide. Once contact is established and the aide knows who you are, continue to meet in person when time permits, but you can also carry on a dialogue by phone, fax, or E-mail.

Provide Clear, Timely, and Accurate Information

As experienced parents, you should already have some credibility. You can enhance your credibility by being able to provide concise accurate information. Try to anticipate questions that an interested, but uninformed person might ask.

Avoid Being Perceived as Too Emotional

The combination of emotional commitment and calm presentation of information is very powerful. It conveys maturity and professionalism.

Be Prepared to Follow Up Again and Again

Legislative aides are accessible, but cannot be expected to have specialized knowledge in many areas. They may be easily distracted by other constituent requests or think the problem is solved after consulting with the state agency. You must be prepared to contact the legislator's office on a regular basis to keep the issue on track. The state agency may provide confusing, incorrect responses to the legislative aide or actually challenge your position. You must be prepared to counter potentially damaging responses that threaten your legislative or policy initiative.

Look for Sources of Technical Assistance

In the beginning, it is helpful for a parent group to obtain advice from persons who understand bureaucratic and legislative cultures and who possess technical knowledge of the policy or legislation in question. This form of consultation helps a fledgling group to develop a context in which to operate and a knowledge of the rules of the game. Individuals with lobbying experience or advocates can often provide this consultative, technical assistance role.

Look for Allies

Your policy or legislative initiative may benefit other groups or organizations. Finding an ally with legislative experience is particularly helpful.

A Grassroots Victory

A small group of concerned advocates gathered in Kate Erickson's living room in April 1997. The state's generous postadoption service subsidy appeared to be in jeopardy. Since its establishment in 1992, postadoption special service subsidy or PASSS program had become the envy of service providers in other states. Like most service subsidy programs, PASSS was used to pay for services that were not covered by private health insurance or Medicaid, but the eligibility standards were minimal. PASSS was designed to respond to existing needs with a minimum of red tape. All adopted children, including those adopted from abroad, are potentially eligible for support. In addition to psychotherapy, residential care, and medical treatment, PASSS funds had been used to fund computer-assisted instruction, pay health insurance premiums, and provide respite care for parents and summer camp experiences for children.

By 1997, annual funding for PASSS had risen from $1.2 to $3.7 million, but county agencies were not making effective use of the subsidy to assist families. Kate contacted the fiscal section of the state's Department of Human Services and received a printout indicating that nearly $1 million in PASSS funds remained unspent in 1996, and spending was again running behind in 1997. As a new budget cycle approached, the advocacy group worried that funding for the program would be cut.

The budget bill passed by the state's House of Representatives on March 22, 1997, did not designate a specific level of funding for the PASSS program for state fiscal years 1998 and 1999. In previous years, a temporary language section of the budget had earmarked a specific amount of a multimillion dollar line item for federal and state adoption subsidies to be specifically set aside for the PASSS program.

Another section of the House-passed bill indicated that individual county agencies could choose to place their PASSS allocation into a general fund and use it for any purpose related to child welfare. Since many counties were not using the state dollars that were earmarked to help adoptive families, Kate and her friends worried what these agencies would do if they had discretion to spend the money any way they chose. The group faced several basic questions:

- Had any funding been appropriated for the PASSS program? If so, how much had been appropriated?

- How could anyone know how much funding had been set aside for PASSS if there were no references to appropriations for the program in the budget bill?

- What assurances did parents have that county agencies would spend any funds on postadoption services?

The advocates realized that they had to act before the Senate voted on the bill. Kate's parent group contacted legislative leaders in both the House and Senate as well as Nancy McKinney, a key staff person in the governor's office who was known to be a strong supporter of adoption. The group expressed its concerns, and Tom Casey, an aide to McKinney and other legislative aides, began making inquiries to the Ohio Department of Human Services for an explanation of the budget bill's effect on the PASSS program.

The parents were impressed by the level of responsiveness they received from the legislative aides and from Casey. With a budget as complex as that of the Department of Human Services, it was not surprising that none of the staffers were aware of any decision to dramatically change the operation of PASSS, and none knew what amount of funding had been appropriated for the program.

The parents and staff aides contacted officials in the Department of Human Services for an explanation of the fate of the PASSS program as rendered in the House budget legislation. Not surprisingly, responses varied to some degree, but more than one department official assured the inquirers that PASSS had been funded at least at the same level of $3.7 million per year as it had received in the previous biennium budget. However, with no specific language earmarking $3.7 million per fiscal year for PASSS, none of the officials initially contacted were able to document their claim. After further perseverance from the parents and the staffers, Kate received a message from the department's fiscal section appearing to confirm that at least $3.7 million had been appropriated for PASSS in state fiscal year 1998 and 1999.

The advocacy group was relieved to learn that funds had been appropriated for PASSS, but the House bill still contained no language that required either the state or county to spend any particular amount of money on postadoption services for children with special needs. As things then stood, the state department had total discretion over the use of PASSS funds, and if county agencies elected to receive their allocation of PASSS funding in the form of a consolidated grant, they could use the money for any purpose that could reasonably be construed as child welfare.

The group set out to restore the earmark for the PASSS program omitted from the House bill. Kate contacted Tom Casey once again and asked Jeanette Wiedemeier Bower of NACAC to send a letter to Ms. McKinney and the director of the Ohio Department of Human Services emphasizing the quality and importance of the program. In an April 29, 1997, response to Wiedemeier Bower, McKinney wrote that although she did not think that the lack of a specific amount set aside for PASSS jeopardized the program, she understood the parents' concerns and stated that the governor "would not oppose an effort on your part to adopt an 'earmark' via an amendment to the state's budget now pending in the Senate."

Casey put the parent group in touch with Brian Burns on the Senate Republican Caucus staff, who brought the matter to the attention of the Chair of the Senate Finance Committee. Kate explained the issue to Burns and once again was pleasantly surprised at how receptive he was. Burns asked her group to send him corrective language and he would present it to the Senator.

Working from a copy of the previous budget bill, the group identified the pertinent funding category or line item and inserted the following language setting aside funds for the PASSS program:

Adoption Assistance—Of the foregoing appropriation item 400–528, not more than $3,700,000 in fiscal year 1998 and not more than $3,700,000 in fiscal year 1999 shall be used in support of postadoption special services subsidy finalization adoption services offered pursuant to section 5153.163 of the Revised Code.

Next, the group moved to the section of the bill that allowed counties to "consolidate state child welfare funds into a consolidated grant." The advocates simply added "With the exception of funds allocated to the postadoption special services subsidy . . ."

After faxing the language to Brian Burns, Kate and the group asked several child welfare groups to contact prominent members of the Senate Finance Committee in support of the proposed changes. Ten days after contacting Burns, she received a fax from him telling her that the senator had agreed to the changes and the amended language would be inserted into the budget bill.

One step remained. The House and Senate versions of the bill had to be reconciled in conference committee. Kate and her group kept in contact with Brian Burns and asked the child welfare groups to contact some key members of the conference committee. On June 30, the last day of the state fiscal year, Kate received word that the final version of the budget legislation contained both of the group's amendments. For each of the next two years, $3.7 million would be set aside for PASSS.

13

Disclosure of Information and the Liability of Adoption Agencies

The law isn't justice. It's a very imperfect mechanism. If you press exactly the right buttons and are also lucky, justice may show up in the answer. A mechanism is all the law was ever intended to be.
—Raymond Chandler (1888–1959)

"WRONGFUL ADOPTION" LAWSUITS

One simple but profound difference between families with biological children and families formed by adoption is that in closed adoptions, adoptive parents are dependent on outside agencies for information about their child's past. Given what we know about the risks associated with severe neglect, sexual abuse, and prenatal drug exposure, it seems astonishing that agencies would fail to disclose crucial information about the children they place for adoption. Nevertheless, withholding unpleasant information has been an all too common practice, although one seemingly motivated more by dangerous good intentions than malice.

In recent decades, an alarming number of families who adopted children without adequate background information found themselves confronting emotional problems and learning disabilities for which they had no explanation. Precious time was wasted and vitally needed services delayed while the parents blamed themselves and searched for answers.

In the 1980s, adoptive parents filed the first in a succession of successful wrongful adoption lawsuits against adoption agencies. The term *wrongful adoption* is actually somewhat misleading because families have taken legal action primarily to recoup the ruinous costs of medical or psychological services, not to dissolve their adoptions. Before the issue of damages could be considered, the court had to address the question of agency's responsibility to inform adoptive parents about their child's family background and medical history.

A number of state appellate and supreme courts have determined that adoption agencies can be held liable for the consequences resulting from presentation of false or misleading information to adoptive parents, and failure to disclose significant facts about the child's background.

The courts have been reluctant to define the extent to which agencies are responsible for collecting and disclosing background information, leaving that decision to state legislatures. Most states have laws and regulations detailing the medical and social information that agencies must provide to prospective parents. Agencies inevitably take steps to provide at least some information about the child's family history. A number of wrongful adoption cases have hinged on the issue of an agency's responsibilities once it has voluntarily disclosed information to the prospective parents. If an agency presents information about the child's family and social history to the adopting parents, does it have an obligation to ensure that the information is reasonably accurate and complete? In a number of state supreme and appellate decisions, the courts have ruled that agencies do have such a responsibility and can be held liable in cases where the information in question was either in the possession of the agency or was reasonably accessible, and the failure to provide accurate and complete information resulted in financial loss.

Falsification of Information: *Burr v. Stark County Board of Commissioners,* 1986 (23 Ohio St. 3d)

In this first major "wrongful adoption" case of the 1980s, the Ohio Supreme Court found that the agency knowingly misrepresented the child's family and medical history, that the parents based their decision to adopt on this false information, and that the agency was therefore liable for the injuries suffered by the family when the child developed serious physical and mental problems. The Supreme Court upheld the trial court's award of $125,000 to the adoptive family. At the time of the decision, medical expenses for Patrick Burr totaled more than $81,000.

Russell and Betty Burr contacted the Stark County Welfare Department in 1964 and expressed their interest in adopting a child. A short time later, the agency informed the Burrs that a seventeen-month-old boy was available for adoption. The agency worker told the Burrs that the boy's mother was an eighteen-year-old unwed mother who was unable to care for the child and work at the same time. She was planning to move to Texas to pursue better employment and surrendered the child to the agency. The infant was described as a "nice big healthy boy" who had been born at the city hospital in Massillon, Ohio.

As time passed, the boy suffered from a range of mental and physical problems. During grade school, he was diagnosed as educable mentally retarded, and by high school began suffering from hallucinations. Eventually, he was diagnosed with Huntington's disease, a genetic condition that attacks the central nervous system.

In order to provide treatment for their son, the Burrs sought and obtained a court order opening records that pertained to the child's family history. It was not until 1982 that the adoptive parents discovered that the agency had deceived them with false information. Their son had been born in a state mental facility where his mother was a patient. She was diagnosed with a "mild mental deficiency, idiopathic with psychotic reactions." The boy's father was unknown but also suspected to be a patient. The story about the birth mother moving to Texas to better her life was completely fabricated. The boy also had been in two foster homes before being placed with the Burrs.

Withholding Information: *M. H. and J. L. H. v. Caritas Family Services,* 1992 (488 N.W. 2d 282)

The Minnesota Supreme Court held that the adoption agency should be accountable for "negligent misrepresentation" of a child's medical and genetic history. The court found that the agency, having volunteered facts about the child's background to the adoptive parents, could be held accountable for misleading the parents by withholding information. In this particular case, the agency told the adoptive parents that there was incest in the child's family history, but did not reveal that the child's birth parents were brother and sister. The child subsequently exhibited severe behavioral and emotional problems.

The trial court found the agency guilty of negligent misrepresentation. However, the award to the family was limited because the court ruled that the agency was not liable for emotional damages suffered by the adoptive parents.

Intentional and Negligent Misrepresentation: *Gibbs v. Ernst,* 1994 (647 A.2d 882 Pa.)

The Pennsylvania Supreme Court held that "the traditional common law causes of action grounded in fraud and negligence do apply to the adoption setting." Agencies can be held liable for damages resulting from deliberate presentation of false or misleading information (intentional misrepresentation) as well as for negligent misrepresentation. In the court's opinion, an agency assumes a duty to the adoptive parents when it provides them with information about the child's background. Negligent misrepresentation occurs when an agency does not make a reasonable effort to determine if the information is accurate and the adoptive family suffers injury as a result of the agency's carelessness. The Supreme Court's decision paved the way for the case to be remanded to a lower court for trial, based on the merits of the parents' charges.

In 1983, foster parents Jayne and Frank Gibbs approached Concern Professional Services for Children and Youth about the possibility of adopting a healthy white infant. The agency informed the Gibbs that there was a two-year waiting period and encouraged them to explore the adoption of an older child. The family broadened their search and applied to adopt either a healthy infant or a child who was "hard to place" because of age. The couple made it clear that they did not want to adopt a child with mental or emotional problems or one with a history of physical or sexual abuse.

The agency placed five-year-old Michael with the Gibbs family in November 1984. Michael was repeating kindergarten at the time, and in addition to being behind at school, he was described by the agency as hyperactive. The agency assured the couple that Michael had been in foster care for only two years with the same family prior to his placement for adoption. They were also told that Michael's birth mother had neglected him and subjected him to verbal abuse.

The Gibbs family requested additional information about Michael's psychological and emotional history, and at a meeting prior to finalization, asked representatives of Concern if there was anything in the file that had not been disclosed to them. The representatives claimed that Concern had provided them with everything they had been given by the Northhampton Department of Children and Youth up to that date and that Northhampton had promised additional information. The couple was assured that Concern would check all of the child's records and make sure that all available information was provided to them prior to the final decree of adoption.

Michael began exhibiting severe behavioral problems almost immediately after the final decree of adoption in October 1985. He tried to suffocate his cousin, attempted to amputate the arm of another child, hit another cousin over the head with a lead pipe, started a fire, and caused Mrs. Gibbs to burn her hands by putting Chlorox bleach in a cleaning solution. Michael was eventually admitted to residential care and placed in the custody of the Department of Human Services in Philadelphia.

In 1989, a Department of Human Services caseworker informed the couple that Michael had been in ten different foster homes and had been severely abused both sexually and physically. Michael's biological parents had both abused him, and his birth mother had once attempted to cut off his penis. The boy's violence toward other children was clearly apparent during his placements in foster care. As a result of this information, the Gibbs family filed suit against Concern and the Northhampton Department of Children and Youth in April 1990.

The Statute of Limitations: *Quentin Meracle and Nancy Meracle, Plaintiffs-Appellants, v. Children's Service Society of Wisconsin,* 1989 (138, 437 N.W.2d 532, 149 Wis. 2d 19)

In several wrongful adoption cases, the agency moved to have the family's complaint dismissed on grounds that the state's statute of limitation for filing damage claims had expired. At issue was the event that started the legal clock ticking on the statute of limitations. Was it the point at which an agency provided false or misleading information or failed to disclose pertinent facts? Was it when the parents discovered the agency's negligence? Did the parents have to confront or actually experience some form of damages as a result of the agency's actions or omissions?

State appellate courts have generally determined that the agency's action or negligence alone does not start the clock on the statute of limitations. The adoptive parents must discover that they had been misled and face damages as a consequence.

On October 10, 1979, Quenton and Nancy Meracle met with a social worker from the Children's Service Society of Wisconsin (CSS) to consider the placement of Erin, a twenty-three-month-old girl. In their initial inquiries, the Meracles indicated that they wanted to adopt a child of at least average intelligence who had no disabling condition. The agency representative told them that Erin's paternal grandmother had died of Huntington's disease. According to the parents' testimony, the social worker went on to tell them that the degenerative brain disease was genetically transmitted from one generation to another. If Erin's father did not have Huntington's, the chance that Erin would contract the disease was no greater than that of the average child. The Meracles were told that Erin's father had tested negative for Huntington's and, therefore, the child was at very low risk to get it. The agency placed Erin with the Meracles on October 18, 1979, and the adoption was finalized on November 12, 1980.

On February 8, 1981, Nancy Meracle watched a segment of the television program *60 Minutes,* which dealt with Huntington's disease. The show indicated that there was no reliable test for Huntington's, thereby throwing the agency worker's claim into doubt. A pamphlet acquired from the library further confirmed the fact that there was no test for the disease.

More than three and one-half years passed, and then, on September 27, 1984, a neurologist diagnosed Erin as having Huntington's disease. The Meracles consulted an attorney and filed a suit against the CSS agency on September 25, 1985. The complaint was later amended to include two insurance companies.

The defendants moved to have the case dismissed on the grounds that the Meracles had first learned that there was no test for Huntington's disease in 1981, and the three-year statute of limitations for filing such complaints had expired. On September 8, 1986, CSS and American Home

Insurance moved for summary judgment contending that the complaints was barred both by public policy and by the three-year statute of limitations. The Milwaukee County circuit court agreed that the statute of limitations had expired and granted the dependents motion for summary judgment on February 10, 1987.

The Meracles appealed and the court of appeals divided the family's complaint into two separate claims. The appellate court upheld the decision that the statute of limitations had run out on any claim for emotional distress arising from the fear that Erin would contract Huntington's disease. However, the court found that the statute of limitations had not expired on the claim for future medical expenses and emotional distress arising from Erin's actual contraction of the disease. The clock did not start ticking on that three-year time limit for filing a compliant until September 1984.

The Wisconsin Supreme Court agreed with the appellate decision. Under Wisconsin law, it concluded that "a cause of action will not accrue until the plaintiff discovers, or in the exercise of reasonable diligence should have discovered, not only the fact of injury but also that the injury was probably caused by the defendant's conduct or product." The high court recognized that the Meracles learned of the agency's negligence in 1981 when they found out that there was no reliable test for Huntington's disease. At that time, however, they had suffered "no injury" in the court's words, which would "support a cause of action."

The court rejected the agency's argument that the Meracles could have taken legal action to recoup the $1,000 adoption fee and the subsequent cost of caring for Erin from the time the child was adopted until she contracted the disease in 1984. Those expenses, noted the court, "are costs which would have been incurred in any case during the adoption of a child. These were ordinary expenses pursuant to that end. It is only the extraordinary expenses, the unexpected expenses resulting from Erin's special needs, which are actionable."

In 1981, the Meracles knew only that Erin's grandmother had Huntington's disease. Based on the information provide by their agency, they did not did not have any particular reason to anticipate extraordinary medical expenses. On the other hand, noted the court, "the Meracles did suffer an injury which could form the basis for a cause of action in 1984 when they learned that Erin had developed Huntington's disease." At that point, the parents could show "with reasonable medical certainty" that extensive medical care would be required for their child. "They were now certain to incur future expenses because of the adoption which they allege was induced by the affirmative misrepresentation that Erin's father had tested negative for the disease and therefore that Erin would not contract it. In 1984, the Meracles had 'a claim capable of present enforcement.' " The Wisconsin Supreme Court rejected the Meracles' claim of emotional distress both before and after 1984 but agreed that CSS was guilty of negligent misrepresentation.

Mohr v. Massachusetts, 1991 (Bristol County Superior Court, Case No. 87–0152)

A Massachusetts jury awarded the Mohrs $3.8 million in compensation for medical and living expenses for their adopted daughter Elizabeth. The judgment was later reduced to $200,000 in compliance with limitations imposed by the Massachusetts Tort Claims Act. The family did not discover that the child's mother had been institutionalized for schizophrenia, or that Elizabeth had been diagnosed as mentally retarded with cerebral atrophy when she was an infant, until ten years after they adopted her.

The agency told the Mohrs that Elizabeth had been abused while in foster care but was otherwise a healthy child. Elizabeth was eventually diagnosed with schizophrenia and spent much of her childhood in institutions. By the time the case went to trial, Elizabeth was an adult and was able to live at home. Although the state appealed the decision, on August 14, 1995, the Massachusetts Supreme Court upheld the award.

Juman v. Louise Wise Services, 1994 (608 N.Y.S. 2d 612 Sup.), 1994 and 1995 (620 N.Y.S. 2d 371 A.D. 1 Dept.)

In *Juman v. Louise Wise Services,* New York state courts upheld the family's right to file suit against the adoption agency even though the adopted child had reached adulthood. On February 9, 1994, The Supreme Court of New York County recognized wrongful adoption as an extension of the law pertaining to fraud and held that in order to determine if fraud had occurred, the agency was required to provide pertinent information and records sought by the adoptive family. The New York State Supreme Court, Appellate Division, upheld the lower court's decision on January 10, 1995, even though the adoptee had died during the course of the litigation.

Louise Wise Services, a private nonprofit agency, placed an infant for adoption with the Juman family. The adoption was finalized on May 13, 1966, when the child was approximately sixteen-months old. By 1994, the adoptee, then a man of twenty-eight, had suffered a history of psychological problems requiring periodic hospitalization. At the time the family filed suit against the agency, he was being treated for schizophrenia.

The legal action by the adoptive family was apparently initiated as a result of information discovered by the adoptee when, as an adult, he sought information about his birth family. With the assistance of an adoption search group, the adoptee located a maternal uncle who informed him that his birth mother had a long history of mental illness and had undergone a frontal lobotomy prior to his birth. Louise Wise Services had not disclosed this information to the Juman family at the time of the adoptive placement. According to agency records presented to the court, the family was told only that the birth mother sought professional help for "emotional difficulty" following the untimely death of a close boyfriend and subsequent pregnancy.

The adoptive parents sought to recover the sizable cost of their son's psychological treatment and filed a motion asking the court to compel the agency to comply fully with their request for information pertaining to his birth family and subsequent mental illness. The court affirmed that principles of fraud under common law were applicable to adoption and that the adoptive family could bring suit against the agency for wrongful adoption. In recognizing the tort of wrongful adoption as a legitimate cause for legal action, the court cited previous wrongful adoption cases such as *Burr v Board of County Commissioners of Stark County* (Ohio, 1986); *Meracle v Children's Service Society of Wisconsin* (1989); and *Roe v Catholic Charities of the Diocese of Springfield Illinois* (1992).

The court determined that in order to determine if fraud had occurred, the agency was required to provide the following information and records sought by the adoptive family.

1. Information on the child's medical history and that of the child's birth parents, "including any psychological information . . . which might be a factor influencing the child's future health in compliance with existing Services Law 373-a." The court noted that the agency was required to comply with the current law on disclosure of medical histories even though the law was enacted in 1983, many years after the child's 1966 adoption.

2. Information about the child's family history, including the mental health history of the child's birth mother, in compliance with the state's existing domestic relations law requiring extensive disclosure of the child's medical history and family background, even though the law was not enacted until 1989, more than twenty years after the child's adoption.

3. Information about agency procedures, including the names and addresses of agency employees and former employees who might be called as witnesses.

4. Additional information about the birth family to be disclosed to the adoptive parents as a result of their having demonstrated "good cause." Good cause, noted the court, "may be established by psychological trauma or medical need . . . , or even by concern for the possibility that a genetic or hereditary factor might be passed on to the adoptee's issue." In this particular case, the adoptee's history of mental illness, including schizophrenia, was deemed good cause.

As a means of safeguarding the identity of the birth family, the court ordered the agency to submit complete answers to the adoptive family's questions along with the pertinent records to the court for an in camera inspection before any information was released to the family.

In compelling the adoption agency to provide the information requested by the adoptive parents, the judge noted that

> the state's interest is even more pronounced when dealing with a child with special needs. If a child awaiting adoption has special physical or psychological needs, the state has an interest in ensuring that the placement will be such that the child's needs will be fully met. In furtherance of this goal, federal and state programs providing subsidies to adoptive parents have been established (see, e.g., Adoption Assistance Act, 42 USC 673). To qualify for these subsidies most programs require the prospective parents to apply before the adoption is finalized. When the agency withholds information that the child has special needs, generally to increase his chances of adoption, special protection will be lost to the child and public policy vitiated.

Mallette v. Children's Friend and Service (661 A.2d 67 Rhode Island)

The Mallettes did not initiate a suit against the agency until years after the adoption of their son. The Rhode Island Supreme Court determined that in spite of the fact that the state had no law requiring adoption agencies to disclose pertinent information to prospective adoptive parents, an agency can be held liable for negligent representation once it voluntarily undertakes to make information available. When the agency, Children's Friend and Service (CFS), "began allegedly volunteering information concerning Christopher's and his biological mother's medical and genetic background," stated the court, "the agency assumed a duty to refrain from making negligent misrepresentations."

The Mallettes' complaint alleged that the agency informed them that the birth mother had learning disabilities as the result of a childhood head trauma, but failed to disclose the more alarming information in its possession. Eight years after the final decree of adoption, the family discovered that Christopher's birth mother had been diagnosed with "macrocephaly, pseudoepicanthal folds, a high arched palate, tachycardia, small clinodactyl of the fifth fingers, trembling of the hands, and poor coordination." Medical history documents described the biological mother as "mildly to moderately retarded" with only a possibility that the condition was due to head trauma and noted that the child's maternal grandmother was considered "intellectually limited."

At the time of the court case, Christopher Mallette was thirteen-years-old and afflicted with mental retardation and severe emotional problems. The Supreme Court, noting that the Mallettes, like other adoptive parents,

"remain at the mercy of adoption agencies for information," remanded the
case back to the Superior Court for trial.

The Influence of Information on the Parents' Decision to Adopt: *Cesnik v. Edgewood Baptist Church,* 1996 (United States Court of Appeals, Eleventh Circuit, No. 95-8151)

The dependence of adoptive parents on the agency for information about
the child and his or her birth family is a common factor in a number of
wrongful adoption cases. Testimony by the parents that they would not
have proceeded with the adoption had they complete information about
the child undoubtedly strengthens the claims for damages against an adoption agency. However, is such a claim essential? After a child is placed for
adoption, a bond forms between parent and child. As we noted earlier,
parents file "wrongful adoption" suits primarily to help care for their child,
not to end the adoption. Whatever their qualms might have been at one
time had they been better informed, their commitment to the child during
the course of legal proceedings remains unshakable.

In most instances, the parents did not encounter serious medical or psychological problems and did not discover that they had been misled about
their child's background until after the adoption was finalized. But, what
if the parents discover that the agency has withheld or falsified information
before finalization? Do the parents have any grounds to file claims against
an agency if they go through with the adoption because of their growing
attachment to the child? A 1996 decision by the United States Court of
Appeals for the Eleventh Circuit in *Cesnik v. Edgewood Baptist Church*
suggests that parents may have grounds for a suit if they discover that the
adoption agency has falsified or withheld information before the adoption
has been finalized.

In *Cesnik*, the U.S. Court of Appeals for the Eleventh Circuit reversed
the decision of the U.S. District Court for the Middle District of Georgia
to dismiss a Minnesota couple's entire suit against a church-based adoption
agency in Georgia for deliberately misrepresenting the health status of two
children placed with them for adoption. The federal appeals court ruled
that the trial judge erred in dismissing two claims brought by the adoptive
family. The court found that there were sufficient grounds to allow the
family's suit to go forward in two areas: (1) The allegation that the Edgewood Baptist Church through its adoption agency breached its contract
with the family when it misrepresented the state of their children's health,
and (2) The allegation that the church through its adoption agency used
the mails and wires (phones) to defraud the family in violation of the Rack-
eteer Influenced and Corrupt Organizations (RICO) Act.

The court of appeals remanded the case back to the U. S. District Court for retrial with the stipulation that the appellants reorganize and clarify their claims against the church and its agents.

Blane and Kristi Cesnik of St. Cloud, Minnesota, were the adoptive parents of four children with severe mental and physical problems at the time of the court of appeals decision. The two youngest children were adopted through New Beginnings Adoption and Counseling Agency, operated by Edgewood Baptist Church in Georgia. In November 1989, the Cesniks spoke with Ms. D., director of New Beginnings and expressed an interest in adopting a healthy infant. Ms. D. contacted the Cesniks shortly thereafter to tell them about a baby boy born on November 20, 1989.

Ms. D. told the family that she had reviewed the medical records and results of the tests that the Cesniks asked to be performed and everything indicated that the infant was in perfect health. She informed the family that the child's birth mother had received prenatal care since her sixth week of pregnancy and that there were no indications of substance abuse.

Ms. D. delivered the child to the Cesniks on December 10, 1989. The family named him Caleb. The child soon developed health problems. When the medical records arrived some months after Caleb's placement, they showed that he was born prematurely, that his birth mother had received no prenatal care and had tested positive for opiates and barbiturates at the time of her delivery. Caleb was soon diagnosed with cerebral palsy, asthma, developmental disorders and, as time passed, with behavior problems. Doctors attributed the child's problems to drug and alcohol exposure and his birth mother's lack of prenatal care.

When confronted with the discrepancy between her statements and the child's medical records, Ms. D. told the Cesniks that the birth mother's records had been mixed up with those of another woman with the same name and that the birth mother had lied about her drug abuse. The Cesniks went through with the adoption, which was finalized on July 10, 1990.

The family again contacted New Beginnings about adopting a healthy infant in December 1990. Incredibly, the same pattern of events was repeated. Ms. D. testified that the child was healthy, that the birth mother did not use drugs, and had received adequate prenatal care. After she delivered the child, Eli, to the Cesniks, he developed multiple problems including cerebral palsy, pseudobulbar palsy, asthma, and fetal alcohol syndrome. Once more, the medical records completely contradicted her assurances. Ms. D. even offered the same explanation about the switching of records and the duplicity of the birth mother as she had in the initial adoption.

The Cesniks made inquiries regarding adoption subsidies for the two boys from the state of Georgia. Shortly thereafter, on July 21, 1991, Ms. D. visited the family in their Minnesota home and indicated that if the Cesniks did not keep quiet about what had transpired and cease their discussion of the boys' medical and psychological condition, she could withdraw her approval of Eli's adoption. The Cesniks finalized the adoption on September 21, 1991.

The family filed a formal complaint against New Beginnings with the Georgia Department of Human Resources in August 1992. The state found irregularities and ordered the agency to take corrective action. On December 9, 1993, the Cesniks filed suit in the United States District Court for the Middle District of Georgia against the Edgewood Baptist Church, the pastor, Ms. D., and the social worker hired to work with Eli and Caleb's birth mothers.

The court of appeals characterized the family's suit as a "shotgun complaint, which is so muddled that its is difficult to discern what the appellants are alleging beyond the mere names of certain causes of action." In rendering its verdict, the court divided the Cesniks' claims into three counts.

Count 1 encompassed the claim of "Wrongful Placement and Adoption," which included the common law torts of "negligent breach of duty; negligent hiring, training, supervision, discipline and retention of personnel, negligence per se; breach of fiduciary relationship; misrepresentation; fraud in the inducement of the act; undue influence; duress; and intention infliction of emotional distress." The appeals court agreed with the trial judge that the two-year statute of limitations for such claims had expired. The key date, according to the court, was August 8, 1991, the date that New Beginnings gave consent to Eli's adoption. Up to that time, the Cesniks, in the court's opinion, had reason to fear reprisals on the part of the adoption agency if they initiated legal action. After that date the family was free to act.

Count 2 involved "Breach of Contract." The trial court had rejected the Cesniks' claim, reasoning that the parents could have prevented the problems they suffered by simply returning the children to the agency. The appeals court acknowledged that the family could have returned the children but asked whether "they were required to do so or suffer the consequences?" The court's answer was no. It found the Cesniks' situation as "analogous to a seller misrepresenting the quality of goods being sold to a buyer." In such cases, the buyer has two options. "He can rescind the transaction by returning the goods to the seller and demanding a return on the purchase price, or he can stand on the transaction and sue for damages—measured by the difference in value between the goods as represented and the goods as received. Here, the Cesniks kept the children and seek to recover the expenses they will incur in excess of those that would have incurred had the children not been disabled." The court of appeals agreed with the district court's dismissal of the family's complaint against the individual parties, but upheld the family's complaint against the church, allowing it to go forward.

Count 3 involved claims of federal and state conspiracy under the RICO Act. The court of appeals acknowledged that the family's claims under the RICO statute were "woefully deficient," but that the trial court did not dismiss the Cesniks' arguments because they "inadequately pled." Rather, the trial judge rejected the claim on the grounds that the family had presented no evidence in support of either "a conspiracy" or "predicate acts of mail or wire fraud."

The appeals court disagreed, holding that "a reasonable jury could find from the evidence in the record that defendant Ms. D. misrepresented the boys' health for the purpose of inducing the Cesniks to accept them for adoption, that the appellee (the pastor) participated in or was aware of the scheme, and that their contact implicated the church." Regarding the second point, the appeals court found that the facts supported the existence of a "scheme to defraud and several uses of the mails and wires in furtherance of that scheme." The court of appeals allowed the complaints against Ms. D. and the pastor to go forward, while agreeing with the district court that the complaint against the agency social worker should be dismissed.

The *Cesnik* decision is consistent with the emotional dynamics of adoption in that it recognizes the significance of the period between the child's placement in an adoptive home and the final decree of adoption. The Cesniks had become attached to the children and proceeded with the adoptions even after learning that they had been misinformed about the birth mothers. Although we are not attorneys, the federal appeals ruling appears to argue that proceeding with the adoption after discovering that the child may be at risk for emotional or medical problems does not necessarily preclude the parents from filing a suit against the agency at a later time if serious problems materialize. A family's chances of prevailing obviously depend on the circumstances of the case and the laws of the state of jurisdiction. Adoptive parents who find themselves in a situation comparable to that of the Cesniks are well advised to consult an experienced plaintiffs attorney. A list of attorneys with experience in initiating wrongful adoption suits appears at the end of the chapter.

A RECENT CASE

On March 10, 1998, the Supreme Court of Montana reversed a lower court decision and in doing so recognized negligent misrepresentation as a cause of action by adoptive parents. The decision in *Jackson v. State of Montana*, which is reproduced in full below, relied on previous appellate decisions such as *Mohr v. Massachusetts* and *Gibbs v. Ernst*.

Meracle v. Children's Service Society of Wisconsin, Mallette v. Children's Friend and Service, and M. H. and J. L. H. v. Caritas Family Services

EUGENE E. JACKSON AND PEGGY J. JACKSON, INDIVIDUALLY AND AS PARENTS AND NEXT FRIENDS OF AARON JON JACKSON, PLAINTIFFS AND APPELLANTS, v. STATE OF MONTANA, A GOVERNMENTAL ENTITY, THE DEPARTMENT OF FAMILY SERVICES, A STATE AGENCY, AND JOHN AND JANE DOES I-IV, DEFENDANTS AND RESPONDENTS.

1998 MT 46, No. 96-688, March 10, 1998

APPEAL FROM: District Court of the Thirteenth Judicial District, In and for the County of Yellowstone, The Honorable Robert W. Holmstrom, Judge presiding.

In April 1994, adoptive parents Eugene and Peggy Jackson filed an action based in negligence with the District Court for the Thirteenth Judicial District in Yellowstone County against the State of Montana, the Department of Family Services, and John and Jane Does I-IV (the State). The Jacksons primarily alleged the State negligently misrepresented, and failed to disclose to them, certain material facts regarding the psychological and medical background of their adoptive son's birth mother and putative father.

On August 7, 1995, the State filed an initial motion for summary judgment with respect to all counts contained in the Jacksons' complaint. The Jacksons amended their complaint in November 1995, and the State filed a supplemental motion for summary judgment in April 1996. On November 6, 1996, the District Court issued an order granting the State's original and supplemental motions for summary judgment. It is from this order that the Jacksons presently appeal. For the reasons discussed below, we reverse.

We find the following issues dispositive on appeal:

Did the District Court err in concluding the State had neither a common law nor a statutory duty to fully and accurately disclose to the Jacksons information in its possession regarding the psychological and medical background of their adoptive son's birth mother and putative father?

Did the District Court err in implicitly concluding the State sufficiently established the absence of any genuine issue of material fact regarding a causal connection between the State's allegedly negligent conduct and the Jacksons' injuries?

Factual and Procedural Background

Lawrence John Allen Russell (later renamed Aaron Jon Jackson by his adoptive parents and hereinafter referred to as Aaron) was born on November 8, 1983, to Deborah Annette Russell, his biological mother. Aaron's two putative fathers are Brian Scott and Robert T. Stevens. Russell spent much of her pregnancy incarcerated at the Women's Correctional Center at Warm Springs, Montana, during which period she underwent a psychological evaluation by clinical psychologist, Dr. B. A. Peters. Dr. Peters concluded that Russell had a Full Scale I.Q. of 73, and wrote that certain test scores "strongly suggest" the presence of an "organic or psychiatric impairment." Dr. Peters additionally described Russell's thinking as "disorganized, unconventional, diffused, possibly at times delusional" and characterized her as an "emotionally immature and inappropriate" young woman who "is making a marginal psychological adjustment." Ultimately, Dr. Peters diagnosed Russell with borderline intellectual functioning and inadequate personality.

In January 1984, Russell fed her infant son soda pop, meat, and vegetables, which caused him to aspirate and led to his hospitalization. As a result of this incident, the State began providing child protective services to Russell and Aaron. In February 1984, social worker Marylis Filipovich prepared a social study in which she noted Russell's "IQ is approximately 70, and functions as though she is retarded." In conclusion, Filipovich remarked that "besides [Russell's] low functioning, she seems to be quite disturbed and will need professional counseling."

In the following months, the State continued to provide child protective services to Aaron, Russell, and Aaron's two putative fathers, Brian Scott and Robert Stevens. The State, in fact, entered into a service treatment agreement with Russell and Scott, and into a second such agreement with Russell and Stevens. Moreover, the State arranged for Russell to undergo a psychological evaluation by clinical psychologist Kenneth Collier, on June 7, 1984. In his report, Dr. Collier noted that "people who produce similar clinical profiles are seen as having a long-standing and chronic emotional disturbance, most likely a personality disorder, though a paranoid disorder should be considered." Dr. Collier described Russell as "clinically intellectually dull" and his ultimate diagnosis was one of "Paranoid Personality Disorder with mild mental retardation."

In December 1983, Aaron's putative father, Stevens, was treated on an inpatient basis by Dr. R. V. Edwards of the Veterans Administration Medical Center in Sheridan, Wyoming. In his written report, Dr. Edwards noted that Stevens complained of "feelings of unreality as though things were floating" and diagnosed him with a "schizophrenic disorder, paranoid type." The State acquired a copy of Dr. Edwards' evaluation prior to Aaron's adoption in 1986.

On August 1, 1984, social worker Dave Wallace submitted a report to the court on behalf of the State which chronicled Russell's difficulties and recommended that the State receive permanent custody of Aaron and that he be made available for adoption. Among the items referenced in the report were Dr. Peters' and Dr. Collier's psychological evaluations, as well as Filipovich's social study. In addition, copies of Dr. Peters' and Dr. Collier's reports were attached to the report.

On December 31, 1984, the District Court issued an order terminating the parental rights of Russell, Scott, and Stevens, and awarded permanent legal custody of Aaron to the State with the right to consent to his adoption. Roughly one month later, resource worker Betty Petek contacted the Jacksons and informed them that Aaron was available for adoption.

The Jacksons had applied with the State to become adoptive parents just one week after Aaron's birth, in November 1983. To become adoptive parents, the Jacksons completed a written application and participated in personal interviews with Petek. During the course of this application process, the Jacksons advised Petek that they could not provide care for a child that had, or might be at risk for developing, a mental disorder. On March 10, 1984, Petek completed the Jacksons' adoptive home study and recommended that they "be approved for the adoption of one Caucasian child, either sex, infancy through two years of age," noting that they would consider adopting a child with "a minor correctable handicap." In accordance with Petek's recommendation, the Jacksons were approved as adoptive parents on May 1, 1984.

Thus, in January 1985, shortly after Aaron became available for adoption, Petek contacted the Jacksons and informed them of Aaron's availability. That evening, the Jacksons discussed the possibility of adopting fifteen-month-old Aaron and agreed between the two of them that "if the family history was acceptable . . . and if the child appeared normal looking physically, that would probably take him." On January 28, 1985, the Jacksons met with Petek and Wallace to discuss Aaron's family background, and the possibility of initiating visits with Aaron.

During this visit, the Jacksons specifically asked Wallace and Petek whether there was any history of mental illness in Aaron's family. Although they were each aware of the reports completed by Dr. Peters, Dr. Collier, and Dr. Edwards, as well as Filipovich's social study, neither Wallace nor Petek disclosed the content of these evaluations to the Jacksons in response to their inquiry. In Wallace's actual possession at the time of this meeting were Filipovich's social study, a January 9, 1985, social history update, and his August 1, 1984, report to the court to which copies of Dr. Peters' and Dr. Collier's evaluations had been attached. Wallace generally referred to the documents in his possession to answer the Jacksons' questions during the visit, but did not provide them with copies and did not disclose the various psychological evaluations.

Instead, Peggy Jackson's deposition testimony indicates that Wallace and Petek provided the Jacksons with the following background information during this January 28, 1985, meeting:

"They told us that Aaron was removed from his parents, that they determined the mother not capable of caring for him, that when he was very little, that she had attempted to feed him some sort of solid food and pop and he aspirated and was hospitalized. . . .

"We talked about family. They mentioned that she came from a family, how they termed it was, several generation welfare family, it was low economic status. They felt the family was socially inept. They mentioned, well, when we asked what the mother was like, they told us that physically she was healthy.

"There may have been a possibility of some drug usage, but they felt that was minimal, because they told us she had been incarcerated for most of her pregnancy on a criminal charge.

"We asked why she was unable to take care of Aaron, and we were told that she moved around a lot and that she didn't meet his needs for feeding him or caring for him physically and that she didn't appear to even have the interest to stick it out and stay with him and learn those skills."

In the weeks following their meeting with Wallace and Petek, the Jacksons visited with Aaron on a number of occasions, and entered into an adoptive placement agreement with the State on March 5, 1985. On January 2, 1986, the District Court issued an order finalizing Aaron's adoption.

Although the State's records included Dr. Peters' and Dr. Collier's psychological evaluations of Russell, Filipovich's social study, and Dr. Edwards' report concerning Aaron's putative father, Stevens, the State never disclosed the content of these evaluations to the Jacksons prior to the finalization of Aaron's adoption in January 1986.

Aaron began to exhibit behavioral problems, and on December 16, 1987, the Jacksons took Aaron to the Child Study Center at the Children's Clinic in Billings, Montana, where Dr. Paul R. Crellin performed a pediatric and pediatric neurological evaluation. Aaron's behavior had become such that he "could not seem to keep attention, was disruptive, frustrated, was always going fast and 'furious,' and this was becoming more and more of a problem" for those around him. Dr. Crellin concluded that "Aaron had significant attention deficit disorder with hyperactivity" and noted that it was "impossible to tell whether or not this is a genetic trait that he inherited from his mother or father, or whether it has to do with the chemical or substance abuse that the mother had during her pregnancy."

The record in this case documents Aaron's continuing history of psychological and emotional problems. On February 7, 1989, for example, clinical psychologist Dr. Ned N. Tranel evaluated Aaron and concluded that he "displays a host of features of attention deficit disorder with and without hyperactivity." Clinical psychologist Dr. William Dee Woolston first saw Aaron in October 1991, and continues to treat him. In a December 1994 report, Dr. Woolston explained that he had diagnosed Aaron with pervasive developmental disorder, learning disorder, and attention deficit hyperactivity disorder. In November 1991, Aaron was hospitalized at the

Deaconess Psychiatric Center Youth Treatment Unit where he began a course of psychopharmaceutical treatment. On the date of Aaron's discharge, Dr. J. Earle diagnosed Aaron with psychotic disorder, history of attention deficit hyperactivity disorder, and pervasive developmental disorder.

Aaron was readmitted into the Deaconess Medical Center on two separate occasions in December 1992, and has since seen Dr. Woolston for ongoing psychotherapy. Aaron has additionally been under the continuous care of Dr. John Talbot Blodgett, a child and adolescent psychiatrist.

On April 6, 1994, the Jacksons filed a negligence action in District Court against the named defendants in this case. In their original complaint, the Jacksons asserted claims against the State for breach of contract, negligent misrepresentation, negligent disclosure, and negligent supervision. On August 7, 1995, the State filed a motion for summary judgment with respect to each count leveled against it in the Jacksons' complaint. The Jacksons subsequently abandoned their claim for breach of contract, and on September 22, 1995, the parties attended a final pretrial conference. As a result of the pretrial conference, the District Court vacated the trial date and issued a new scheduling order.

The Jacksons obtained permission from the District Court to amend their complaint, and on November 6, 1995, filed an amended complaint, which omitted their original breach of contract claim and added an additional cause of action for negligence based upon the doctrine of informed consent. The amended complaint additionally contained a revised caption pursuant to which the Jacksons sought to bring suit, not only in their individual capacities, but also "as parents and next friends of Aaron Jon Jackson."

In response to the amended complaint, the State renewed its original motion for summary judgment and filed a supplemental motion for summary judgment on April 19, 1996. On November 6, 1996, the District Court issued an order granting the State's original and supplemental motions for summary judgment. It is from this order that the Jacksons presently appeal. For the reasons stated below, we reverse the order of the District Court.

Standard of Review

This Court's standard of review in appeals from summary judgment rulings is de novo. *Treichel v. State Farm Mut. Auto. Ins. Co.* (1997), 280 Mont. 443, 446, 930 P.2d 661, 663 (citing *Motarie v. Northern Montana Joint Refuse Disposal Dist.* [1995], 274 Mont. 239, 242, 907 P.2d 154, 156; *Mead v. M.S.B., Inc.* [1994], 264 Mont. 465, 470, 872 P.2d 782, 785). This Court reviews a summary judgment order entered pursuant to Rule 56, M.R. Civ. P., based on the same criteria applied by the district court. *Treichel*, 280 Mont. at 446, 930 P.2d at 663 (citing *Bruner v. Yellowstone County* [1995], 272 Mont. 261, 264, 900 P.2d 901, 903).

In proving that summary judgment is appropriate:

The movant must demonstrate that no genuine issues of material fact exist. Once this has been accomplished, the burden then shifts to the non-moving party to prove by more than mere denial and speculation that a genuine issue does exist. Having determined that genuine issue of material fact do not exist, the court must then determine whether the moving party is entitled to judgment as a matter of law. [This Court] reviews the legal determinations made by the District Court as to whether the court erred. *Bruner*, 272 Mont. at 264-65, 900 P.2d at 903.

Moreover, the "moving party has the burden of showing a complete absence of any genuine issue as to all facts considered material in light of the substantive principles that entitle the moving party to judgment as a matter of law and all reasonable inferences are to be drawn in favor of the party opposing summary judgment." *Kolar v. Bergo* (1996), 280 Mont. 262, 266, 929 P.2d 867, 869.

Discussion

The crux of the Jacksons' "wrongful adoption" suit is their allegation that the State negligently misrepresented, and failed to disclose to them, certain material facts regarding the psychological background of their adoptive son's birth mother and putative father. To determine whether Montana law recognizes a cause of action for "wrongful adoption," such as the one initiated in the present case, we must simply determine "whether longstanding common law causes of action should be applied to the adoption context." *Gibbs v. Ernst* (1994), 647 Pa. A.2d 882, 886. Indeed, a number of courts have recognized "that the question of whether to recognize causes of action for 'wrongful adoption' simply requires the straightforward application and extension of well-recognized common law actions, such as negligence and fraud, to the adoption context and not the creation of new torts." *Mallette v. Children's Friend and Service* (1995), 661 R.I. A.2d 67, 69 (citing *Roe v. Catholic Charities of the Diocese of Springfield* [1992], 588 (Ill) N.E. 2d. 354, 357, appeal denied, 602 N.E. 2d 475 [1992]); see also *Gibbs*, 647 A.2d at 886.

Here, the Jacksons have brought a negligence-based action against the State, specifically alleging claims for negligent misrepresentation, negligent nondisclosure, negligence based on a lack of informed consent, and negligent supervision. The present appeal thus requires us to determine whether these "long-standing common law causes of action should be applied to the adoption context" and whether they constitute viable claims in the present case. *Gibbs*, 647 A.2d at 886.

Issue 1

Did the District Court err in concluding the State had neither a common law nor a statutory duty to fully and accurately disclose to the Jacksons information in its possession regarding the psychological and medical background of their adoptive son's birth mother and putative father?

As noted, the Jacksons have asserted four negligence-based claims against the State, including claims for negligent misrepresentation, negligent non-disclosure, negligence based on lack of informed consent, and negligent supervision. It is well established that a plaintiff in a negligence action must prove the existence of a duty, breach of duty, causation, and damages. See e.g., *Kitchen Krafters v. Eastside Bank of Montana* (1990), 242 Mont. 155, 161, 789 P.2d 567, 571, overruled in part on other grounds by *Busta v. Columbus Hosp. Corp.* (1996), 276 Mont. 342, 370, 916 P.2d 122, 139. Thus, the presence of a legal duty is an essential element of each of the Jacksons' negligence-based claims at issue on appeal.

We have recognized that "the existence of a legal duty is a question of law to be determined by the district court." *Yager v. Deane* (1993), 258 Mont. 453, 456, 853 P.2d 1214, 1216. We review such a conclusion of law by the district court to determine whether the court's interpretation of the law is correct. *Carbon County v. Union Reserve Coal Co.* (1995), 271 Mont. 459, 469, 898 P.2d 680, 687.

On appeal, the Jacksons urge the District Court erred in concluding the State owed them no duty of care upon which they may now premise their claims for negligence and negligent misrepresentation. The Jacksons first argue the court erred in concluding the State had no common law duty to fully and accurately disclose certain background information regarding the psychological health of Aaron's birth parents. The Jacksons next contend the court similarly erred in concluding the State had no statutory duty to disclose the background information which the Jacksons allege was withheld in this case.

In contrast, the State argues it had neither a common law nor a statutory duty to disclose in the present case. More specifically, the State argues it had no common law duty because it made no misleading statements to the Jacksons regarding Aaron's familial background. The State next contends the imposition of either a common law or statutory duty to disclose the background information allegedly withheld in the present case would conflict with the State's statutory duty to maintain confidentiality of the birth parents' medical records.

Thus, with respect to our discussion in the present case, we must first determine whether the lower court erred in concluding the State owed no common law or statutory duty to the Jacksons to either disclose or avoid negligently misrepresenting certain information in its possession regarding the psychological background of their adoptive son's birth mother and putative father.

A. Common Law Duty: Negligent Misrepresentation

We turn initially to the question of whether the State had a common law duty sufficient to support the Jacksons' negligence-based claims in the present case. Of central importance to the Jacksons' suit is their claim for negligent misrepresentation, in which they allege the State misrepresented certain material facts regarding Aaron's family background. This Court has long recognized the common law tort of negligent misrepresentation. See, e.g., *Kitchen Krafters*, 242 Mont. at 65, 789 P.2d at 573. In *Kitchen Krafters*, we set out the following elements of a claim for negligent misrepresentation:

(a) the defendant made a representation as to a past or existing material fact;

(b) the representation must have been untrue;

(c) regardless of its actual belief, the defendant must have made the representation without any reasonable ground for believing it to be true;

(d) the representation must have been made with the intent to induce the plaintiff to rely on it;

(e) the plaintiff must have been unaware of the falsity of the representation; it must have acted in reliance upon the truth of the representation and it must have been justified in relying upon the representation;

(f) the plaintiff, as a result of its reliance, must sustain damage. *Kitchen Krafters*, 242 Mont. at 165, 789 P.2d at 573.

To succeed with a claim for negligent misrepresentation, a party need not demonstrate an intent on the part of a defendant to misrepresent, but must merely show "a failure to use reasonable care or competence in obtaining or communicating . . . information." *Barrett v. Holland & Hart* (1992), 256 Mont. 101, 107, 845 P.2d 714, 717. See also *Batten v. Watts Cycle and Marine, Inc.* (1989), 240 Mont. 113, 117, 783 P.2d 378, 381, cert. denied, 494 U.S. 1087 (1990). For liability to arise, "it not necessary that the negligent misrepresentation constitute constructive fraud, nor actual fraud." *Bottrell v. American Bank* (1989), 237 Mont. 1, 21, 773 P.2d 694, 706. Rather, a "want of ordinary care" on the part of a defendant may, under certain circumstances, give rise to liability for negligent misrepresentation. *Bottrell*, 237 Mont. at 21, 773 P.2d at 706. The presence of a duty to exercise due care is thus a requisite element of any claim for negligent misrepresentation. We have previously held that "the existence of a duty of care [in a negligence-based action] depends upon the foreseeability of the risk and upon a weighing of policy considerations for and against the imposition of liability." *Singleton v. L. P. Anderson Supply Co., Inc.* (1997), 943 Mont. P.2d 968, 971, 54 St. Rep. 738, 739 (quoting *Maguire v. Department of Institutions* [1992], 254 Mont. 178, 189, 835 P.2d 755, 762).

Public Policy

Among those policy considerations this Court will weigh in determining whether to impose a duty are (1) the moral blame attached to a defendant's conduct; (2) the prevention of future harm; (3) the extent of the burden placed on the defendant; (4) the consequences to the public of imposing such a duty; and (5) the availability and cost of insurance for the risk involved. [68] *Singleton*, 943 P.2d at 971, 54 St. Rep. at 739 (citing *Phillips v. City of Billings* [1988], 233 Mont. 249, 253, 758 P.2d 772, 775). See also, *Estate of Strever v. Cline* (1996), 278 Mont. 165, 172, 924 P.2d 666, 670.

As the question of whether public policy weighs in favor of the imposition of a duty upon the State to use due care in disclosing information regarding an adoptive child's birth parents is one of first impression in Montana, we turn for initial guidance to case law from other jurisdictions. Courts in a number of other states have, under certain circumstances, recognized a cause of action for negligent misrepresentation in the adoption context and the concomitant presence of a duty on the part of an adoption agency to use due care in disseminating medical background information to potential adoptive parents. See, e.g., *Mohr v. Commonwealth* (1995), 653 Mass. N.E. 2d 1104; *M.H. and J. L. H. v. Caritas Family Services* (1992), 488 Minn. N.W.2d 282, 288, *Gibbs v. Ernst* (1994), 647 Pa. A.2d 882, 891-92; *Mallette v. Children's Friend and Service* (1995), 661 R.I. A.2d 67, 71; *Meracle v. Children's Service Society of Wisconsin* (1989), 437 Wisc. N.W.2d 532, 537. But see *Michael J. v. Los Angeles County, Department of Adoptions* (1988), 201 Cal. App. 3d 859, 874-75; *Richard v. Vista Del Mar Child Care Service* (1980), 106 Cal. App. 3d 860, 866-68.

In recognizing that an adoption agency may owe such a duty to use reasonable care, these courts have invariably premised that duty "on the adoption agencies' voluntary dissemination of health information concerning the child to potential adopting parents." *Mallette*, 661 A.2d at 70. Courts have commonly recognized that a duty on the part of the adoption agency to use due care may arise only when the agency "begins volunteering information to potential adopting parents." *Mallette*, 661 A.2d at 70. See also *Caritas*, 488 N.W. 2d at 288 (concluding that adoption agencies must "use due care to ensure that when they undertake to disclose information about a child's genetic parents and medical history, they disclose that information fully and adequately . . ."); *Meracle*, 437 N.W 2d at 537 (where an adoption agency makes affirmative misrepresentations about a child's health and background, it has assumed a duty); *Gibbs*, 647 A.2d at 890 (recognizing that "an adoption agency has assumed the duty to tell the truth when it volunteers information to prospective parents"). Thus, courts will, under certain circumstances, impose upon adoption agencies a duty to use due care and to refrain from making negligent adoptive parents.

SUMMARY

Withholding or falsifying information is a common basis for pursuing adoption assistance after finalization, as well as for wrongful adoption lawsuits. Filing an appeal for adoption assistance does not preclude legal action to recover damages. On the contrary, the two actions may be taken simultaneously if the adoptive family so chooses.

As we observed in Chapter 9, filing a liability claim or the threat of such a claim can sometimes induce the state to pay more serious attention to an adoptive family's appeal for postadoption assistance. In a 1998 case, the state of Idaho settled with an adoptive family for $100,000 after the parents pressed a claim for wrongful adoption at the same time they pursued retroactive payments through the administrative hearing process.

Parents should obviously consult competent legal counsel before suing an agency for wrongful adoption. The purpose of this chapter is to make families and advocates aware that exploring legal action might be a viable alternative when:

- you are faced with burdensome costs in caring for a child with special needs
- you have reason to believe that the agency either presented you with false or misleading information about your child's background or failed to disclose crucial information
- you agreed to an adoptive placement before you discovered the truth about your child's background
- the missing facts about your child's background are directly related to the child's special needs and the costs that you have incurred or will incur as a result of the cost of care and services

Most of the lawsuits discussed in this chapter involved adoptions that took place fifteen or twenty years ago. Increasing awareness of the dire consequences of inadequate disclosure has led to improvement in state laws and agency practices. The cases serve to remind us that providing complete information about a child's background is an essential step in preparing adults for adoptive parenthood, and families who are suffering crushing financial burdens related to inadequate disclosure of information may have an avenue of redress.

ATTORNEYS WITH EXPERIENCE IN WRONG
ADOPTION CASES

For the complete text of many of the cases listed below, see the Adoption Policy Resource Center Web site at http://www.fpsol.com/adoption/advocates.html

Attorney: Kenneth J. Cardinal
Firm: Solo Practicioner
758 N. Fifteenth St.
Sebring, OH 44672–1316
Phone: (330) 938–2161
Fax: (330) 938–1556
Case: *Burr v. Stark County Board of Commissioners*, 1986 (23 Ohio St. 3d 69)

Attorney: Sheldon S. Rosenfeld
441 Villa Blanca
Encita, CA 92024–6772
Case: *Michael J. v. Los Angeles County Department of Adoptions* (201 1988. CA 496, 247 Cal. Rptr. 504, 201 Cal. App. 3d 859)

Attorneys: Kay Nord Hunt and Stacy DeKalb
Firm: Lommem, Nelson, Cole and Stageberg
1800 IDS Center, 80 South 8th St.
Minneapolis, MN 55402
Phone: (612) 339–8131
Case: *M. H. and J. L. H. v. Caritas Family Services*, 1992 (448 N.W. 2d 282, Minn.)

Attorney: Samuell A. Morimino
Firm: Wiseman, Shaikewiez, McGivern, Wahl, Flavin and Hesi, and Morimino, P. C.
3517 College Avenue
Alton, IL 62002
Phone: (618) 465–2541
Case: *Roe v. Catholic Charities*, 1992 (588 N.E. 2d 354, Ill. App. 5 Dist.)

Attorney: Samuel C. Totaro, Jr.
Firm: Kellis, Totaro and Soffer
Suite 100, 3325 Street Rd.
Bensalem, PA 19020–2025
Phone: (215) 244–1045
Fax: (215) 244–0641
Case: *Gibbs v. Ernst*, 1994 (647A.2d 882 Pa)

Attorney: Stephan P. Sheehan
Firm: Wistow and Barylick
61 Weybosset St.
Providence, RI 02903–2824
Phone: (401) 831–2700

Case: *Mohr v. Massachusetts*, (Bristol County Superior Court, Case 87–0152, 1991). The Supreme Judicial Court granted an application for direct appellate review (SJC-06600, 1995).
Case: *Mallett v. Children's Friend and Service*, 661 A. 2d 67 (R.I. 1995)

Attorney: Leonard R. Sperber
94 Willis Avenue
Minneola, NY 11501–2611
Phone: (516) 739–3979
Case: *Juman v. Louise Wise Services*, 1994 (608 N.Y.S. 2d 612, Sup.); (608 N.Y.S.2d 612 Sup. 1994); *Juman v. Louise Wise Services*, 1995 (620 N.Y.S. 2d 371 A.D. 1 Dept.)

Attorney: Timothy C. Ferris
Firm: Brett and Daugert
300 North Commercial, Box 5008
Bellingham, WA 98227–5008
Phone: (360) 733–0212
Fax: (360) 647–1902
E-mail: brettlaw@brettlaw.com

Attorney: Robert Mello and John Klesh
1795 Williston Rd.
South Burlington VT 05403
Phone: (802) 862–3200
Case: *Hogan v. The Elizabeth Lund Home, Inc,*. 1997 (Chittenden Superior Court, Chittendon County, VT)

Attorney: Richard Alexander
Firm: The Alexander Law Firm
152 N. Third St. #600
San Jose, CA 95112
Phone: (408) 289–1776
Fax: (408) 287–1776
E-mail: access@alexanderlaw.com
Web site: http://consumer/awpaye.com/article/adopt.shtml.
Also: 1300 Mercantile Library Building
414 Walnut Street
Cincinnati, OH 45202
Phone: (513) 723–1776
Fax: (513) 421–1776

Attorney: Dennis Paul
Firm: Placek, McIlvaine, Paul and Hoffman
200 Smokerise Dr.
Wadsworth, OH 44281–9460
Phone: (330) 334–1536

Attorney: Roger W. Frickle
Firm: Edwards Law Firm, Ltd.

P.O. Box 20039
Billings, Montana 59104
Phone: (406) 256–8155 and 1-(800) 566–8155
Fax: (406) 256–8159
Case: *Jackson v. State of Montana*, 1998 (No. 96–688, MT. 46)

AFTERWORD: A FAILED ATTEMPT AND LESSONS LEARNED

In 1981, while teaching fifth grade in a public school, one of the authors of this book, Rita Laws, tried to adopt one of her students, a mentally retarded foster child named Tommy. Tommy was fourteen, tall and handsome with long, straight brown hair and, in spite of years of abuse and neglect in his birth home, had a kind heart and a sweet disposition. He was every teacher's favorite pupil, the kind of person who brought sunshine into the room with him. He loved animals and was gifted with an ability to care for them intuitively.

Tommy lived with an experienced career foster mother who was parenting four other foster children in her home. She fully supported the idea of Tommy becoming Rita's son. A homestudy was completed and, for several months, Tommy spent weekends at Rita's house learning about and caring for every small animal that happened onto the acreage.

Not knowing anything about adoption or state bureaucracies outside of education, Rita expected to be treated like a consumer, to be afforded the services she needed to complete the adoption, and have them in a timely manner. From the start, she and Tommy's social worker seemed to be at odds about what was best for Tommy, but they quarreled most often about how long the adoptive placement was taking. One day, a frustrated and bewildered Rita raised her voice at the social worker who immediately responded by saying she was "unfit" to be an adoptive parent. After that, Tommy was no longer allowed to see his teacher outside of school.

Rita refused to give up and spoke with several supervisors in the adoption unit who first said she could not adopt Tommy because he was a Native American. So Rita produced proof of her Native American ancestry and tribal membership. Next, they said Tommy had to be placed with his biological sister who lived in another county. Rita agreed to adopt the entire sibling group. But nothing worked. Tommy would shortly be moved to the other side of the state to an adoptive home with his sister, and the social worker refused to give Rita a forwarding address.

On the day Tommy was to leave, his foster mother took him by his teacher's house at his request to say good-bye. Rita tried not to cry because she didn't want to dampen Tommy's happiness over being reunited with his sister. But when Tommy put his arms around her and started sobbing, she did too. For a long time they held on to one another, and then Tommy, who had an IQ of 62, spoke with his usual profound insight.

"I know you did everything you could to adopt me, Rita. Don't worry, my sister will take good care of me. And someday, we'll all be in heaven and you can be my mom then." Rita never saw or heard from Tommy again.

PAINFUL LESSONS WITH A SILVER LINING

Sadly, first-time adoption disaster stories are not rare. However, if the adoptive parent decides to try again, the process can be and often is mastered. A wiser Rita adopted successfully eight times after Tommy left over the next two decades, seven sons and one daughter, because the lesson she learned with her initial adoption experience remained with her: Don't raise your voice to the person who has the power. Put another way: Work within the system to help a child, but if you must challenge the system, do so effectively.

Prospective adoptive parents often expect to be treated like the tax-paying citizen consumers that they are, but this expectation can get them into trouble. For example, many desperate prospective parents will turn to their senators or representatives to break the bureaucratic log jam. While this is an effective strategy for many other problems, and has been known to occasionally result in an adoption, it is actually one of the least effective tools in adoption advocacy. The state adoption bureaucracy has been around a long time, will outlast any politician, and operates under its own rules and traditions, not under any consumer code.

However, depressing as this reality can be, there is another lesson to be learned that is hopeful: Bureaucracies do not hold ultimate power. That rests with the courts and the law, and the law says above all else that the *best interests* of the child are paramount. Period. Where senators and representatives are most effective is in partnership with parents and advocates to pass child-centered state and federal adoption legislation.

Adoptive parents serve children and their families best when they try first to work within the system, calmly and patiently, working up the chain of command, and attempting to understand why the bureaucracy operates the way it does. If that fails, they should turn to the law for help, using the administrative hearing process, appeals, and courts if necessary. They should also form support groups and work with legislators to enact or change laws so that children with special needs and their families are better served. No one should have to lose a child in order to learn how to work within a bureaucracy. No one should have to suffer financial devastation to give a child with special needs permanency.

ASFA AND THE FUTURE

The Adoption and Safe Families Act of 1997 has shortened the amount of time foster children will wait to enter permanency planning. This will continue to result in a rapid increase in the number of foster children who need adoptive homes right now. This is the time to recruit, encourage, and keep special needs adoptive families.

Special needs adoption is a challenging and uniquely joyous way to grow a family. It should be a simple thing to match waiting children to well-prepared families. However, until the system is more child-centered and all state administrators are working to encourage adoption and protect children with special needs, books like this one will be necessary.

The good news is that the outlook is not bleak. Both authors have worked with state administrators who are compassionate and caring, as well as knowledgeable of the intent and scope of the federal adoption assistance laws. There is reason to hope such people will grow in number as the federal law continues to "age" and accomplish the goals it was intended to produce.

For every bureaucrat who sees the federal law as a tool for getting children into permanency, and for every parent who becomes educated about the rights of their adopted children with special needs, the adoption assistance program grows a little stronger. The stronger it becomes, the more effective it is at removing the financial barriers that keep children in foster care. And with each child who leaves the insecurity of foster care for the stability and permanence of adoption, our society is better off and our nation's future, brighter.

PART III

DOCUMENT APPENDICES

WORD INDEX TO POLICY INTERPRETATION
QUESTIONS OR PIQs

The following unique and highly useful tool was developed by Dr. L. Anne Babb of The Family Tree for the Web site, Homes For Kids (www. homes4kids.org). It is included here with her permission.

Federal PIQs are important documents that clarify aspects of the federal adoption assistance law. If you are interested in a particular issue relating to federal foster care or adoption assistance, look below by alphabet letter section to search for your area of concern and the corresponding PIQs.

Since new PIQs are issued every month or so, this list should not be considered complete. If you don't find what you need here, talk to a child advocate, support group leader, or adoption attorney, and see the Web sites section for links to pages where the full text of PIQs can be downloaded.

A

AAP: Adoption Assistance Payments
    PIQ 86-01 and federal income tax; addendum to PIQ 85-06
Adoption agency, definition
    PIQ 85-02, definitions and intent of law
    PIQ 85-04, adoption assistance eligibility and private nonprofit agencies
    PIQ 87-05, Title IV-E AAP and agency responsibility
Adoption Assistance Payments
    See AAP

C

Case review, foster care
  PIQ 81-01
Certification of relative foster homes
  PIQ 85-11
Changes in statute, regulation, or policy
  PIQ 92-02, do not constitute grounds for fair hearing appeal of AAP denials
Child born to prison inmate or patient in hospital
  PIQ 86-03, eligible for IV-E, if other conditions are met
Child support
  PIQ 85-12, State may require adoptive parents to pay, if child in residential
    treatment or other out-of-home facility while child is in State custody
Concurrence of adoptive parents needed in negotiating amount of AAP
  PIQ 81-02
Court involvement necessary in relinquishment
  PIQ 85-03, children voluntarily relinquished
  PIQ 86-02, nature of court involvement and court orders
Custody
  PIQ 83-06, of State not required for IV-E eligibility
  PIQ 85-02, of agencies other than State agency acceptable
  PIQ 85-04, of children by private nonprofit agencies acceptable
  PIQ 85-12, if child in state custody but adoptive parents still retain parental rights
    and responsibility, child still eligible for IV-E AAP even if living away from
    the home of adoptive parents
  PIQ 87-05, of public, private, or no agency, depending on situation of child
  PIQ 89-02, of child, and placement responsibility, and bearing on IV-E ongoing
    AAP or nonrecurring expense reimbursement (private and public agency chil-
    dren, and children adopted independently, can qualify)
  PIQ 91-01, Indian tribal custody issues

D

Date of placement
  PIQ 83-06, definition of
  PIQ 91-01, date of placement definitions for IV-E FC and AAP
  PIQ 92-02, for purposes of receiving AAP, is the date on which the child enters
    the adoptive family home and begins to live with the adoptive parents, or the
    date on which the AAP contract is signed; AAP contracts should reflect the
    date on which the child was physically placed
Deaths of adoptive parents, and continuation of IV-E AAP to guardian
  PIQ 84-04, continuation of AAP after deaths of adoptive parents
Delinquent and status offenders
  PIQ 82-10
  PIQ 88-03, Title IV-E and adjudicated delinquents
  PIQ 91-03, judicial determinations and "contrary to the welfare" language in
    Section 472(a)(1)
Denial of AAP
  See Fair hearings

V

Varying rates for IV-E foster care
  PIQ 86-04, Title IV-E and varying foster care rates; should also apply to FFP for
    DOC/LOC AAP payments
Voluntary placements of children in foster care or adoption
  PIQ 82-06, covering early AAP agreements (pre-1980)
  PIQ 83-06, timelines the same for voluntaries and involuntaries
  PIQ 85-03, definitions identifying voluntaries and involuntaries
  PIQ 89-01, IV-E and children voluntarily relinquished
  PIQ 89-03, Title IV-E foster care FFP for voluntary placements

W

Waivers under Section 1115(a) of the Social Security Act
  PIQ 96-02, Section 1115(a) waivers and Title IV-E eligibility, as affected by the
    Personal Responsibility and Work Opportunity Reconciliation Act (PRWORA)
    of 1996 (Public Law 104-193)

ADOPTION AND SAFE FAMILIES ACT (ASFA) OF 1997, P.L. 105-89: SUMMARY

(REVISED AS OF 11/13/97—House agreed to Senate amendment with amendment)
TABLE OF CONTENTS:

·Title I: Reasonable Efforts and Safety Requirements for Foster Care and Adoption Placements ·Title II: Incentives for Providing Permanent Families for Children ·Title III: Additional Improvements and Reforms ·Title IV: Miscellaneous ·Title V: Effective Date

Title I: Reasonable Efforts and Safety Requirements for Foster Care and Adoption Placements—Amends title IV part E (Foster Care and Adoption Assistance) of the Social Security Act (SSA) to emphasize that, in meeting the "reasonable efforts" requirement of family preservation and reunification, the paramount concern of a State plan for foster care and adoption assistance shall be the health and safety of the child. States that reasonable efforts to preserve and reunify the family shall not be required on behalf of certain parents, including those who have murdered or committed felony assault against another child, or who would otherwise pose a serious risk to a child's health or safety. Declares that nothing in such Act shall be construed as precluding State courts from exercising their discretion to protect the health and safety of children in individual cases, including cases other than those described in the Act.

(Sec. 102) Includes the safety of the child in State case planning and review system requirements.

(Sec. 103) Delineates circumstances compelling a State to file a parental rights termination petition and concurrently initiate selection of a qualified adoptive family for certain children in foster care or under State responsibility.

(Sec. 105) Makes the Federal Parent Locator Service available to child welfare services for enforcement of child custody or visitation orders.

(Sec. 106) Requires State plans for foster care and adoption assistance to provide procedures for criminal records checks for prospective foster and adoptive parents.

(Sec. 107) Requires a case plan for a child for whom the State's goal is adoption or placement in another permanent home to document State agency efforts to accomplish that goal.

Title II: Incentives for Providing Permanent Families for Children—Authorizes the Secretary of Health and Human Services to award an adoption incentive grant to an incentive-eligible State meeting specified criteria whose number of foster child or special needs adoptions for a fiscal year exceeds a base number calculated according to a specified formula. Includes among such criteria the provision of State health insurance coverage for children with special needs for whom an adoption assistance agreement is in effect between the State and the adoptive parents.

(Sec. 201) Authorizes the Secretary to provide technical assistance to States, local communities, and the courts to reach their targets for increased numbers of adoptions and alternative permanent placements for children in foster care. Authorizes appropriations for FY 1998 through 2000.

(Sec. 202) Requires a State plan for child welfare services to contain assurances for State plan development using cross-jurisdictional resources to effect timely adoptive or permanent placements for waiting children. Denies Federal assistance eligibility where a State has impeded the placement of a child for adoption outside of the jurisdiction with responsibility for handling the case.

Instructs the Comptroller General to study and report to the Congress on improved procedures to facilitate the interjurisdictional adoption and permanent placement of children.

(Sec. 203) Directs the Secretary to: (1) develop a set of outcome measures for rating State placements for adoption and foster care, and to report annually thereon to the Congress; and (2) develop a performance-based incentive payment system.

Title III: Additional Improvements and Reforms—Authorizes the Secretary to authorize up to ten State child welfare demonstration projects in each of FY 1998 through 2002. Requires the Secretary to consider demonstration project proposals designed to address: (1) barriers that result in delays to adoptive placements for children in foster care; (2) the impact of parental substance abuse problems upon the placement of children; and (3) kinship care.

Prohibits the Secretary from authorizing a State demonstration project if it fails to provide health insurance coverage for certain children with special needs. Requires the Secretary to consider the effect of a State demonstration project upon specified court orders concerning the State's non-compliance with certain Federal requirements for child welfare services and foster care and adoption assistance.

(Sec. 302) Changes the mandatory annual dispositional hearing for a child in foster care to an annual permanency planning hearing.

(Sec. 303) Requires the Secretary to report to a child welfare advisory panel on the extent to which children in foster care are placed in kinship care, and subsequently to certain congressional committees, following such panel's review and comment on the report.

(Sec. 304) Mandates that independent living programs be designed, among others, for children with respect to whom foster care maintenance payments are no longer being made because the child has accumulated assets of up to $5,000 which are otherwise regarded as resources in determining eligibility for Federal foster care benefits.

(Sec. 305) Authorizes appropriations for family preservation and support services for FY 1999 through 2001, including family reunification, adoption promotion and support services.

(Sec. 306) Mandates that State plans for foster care and adoption assistance provide health insurance coverage for children with special needs.

(Sec. 307) Provides for the continuation of eligibility for adoption assistance payments on behalf of children with special needs whose initial adoption has been dissolved.

(Sec. 308) Requires State plans for foster care and adoption assistance to incorporate standards to ensure quality services for children in foster care.

Title IV: Miscellaneous—Expresses the sense of the Congress that the States should have procedures in effect for a chronically ill or near-death parent, without surrendering parental rights, to designate a standby guardian for the minor children, to take effect on the parent's death, mental incapacity, or physical debilitation (with consent).

(Sec. 404) Revises requirements governing the Contingency Fund for State Welfare Programs. Specifies a reduction in appropriations to offset certain increases in State remittances. Instructs the Secretary to submit recommendations to the Congress for improving the Fund's operation.

(Sec. 405) Instructs the Secretary to report to certain congressional committees regarding the scope of substance abuse in the child welfare population, and the outcomes resulting from the services provided to such population.

(Sec. 406) Expresses the sense of the Congress that, to the greatest extent practicable, all equipment and products purchased with funds made available under this Act should be American-made.

Title V: Effective Date—Sets forth the effective date of this Act.

P.L. 96-272 TITLE IV-E, 1980

UNITED STATES CODE
TITLE 42—The Public Health and Welfare
CHAPTER 7—Social Security
SUBCHAPTER IV—Grants to States for Aid and Services to Needy Families With Children and For Child Welfare Services
PART E—Federal Payments for Foster Care and Adoption Assistance

§673. Adoption assistance program
(a) Agreements with adoptive parents of children with special needs; State payments; qualifying children; amount of payments; changes in circumstances; placement period prior to adoption; nonrecurring adoption expenses
(1)
(A) Each State having a plan approved under this part shall enter into adoption assistance agreements (as defined in section 675(3) of this title) with the adoptive parents of children with special needs.
(B) Under any adoption assistance agreement entered into by a State with parents who adopt a child with special needs, the State—
(i) shall make payments of nonrecurring adoption expenses incurred by or on behalf of such parents in connection with the adoption of such child, directly through the State agency or through another public or nonprofit private agency, in amounts determined under paragraph (3), and
(ii) in any case where the child meets the requirements of paragraph (2), may make adoption assistance payments to such parents, directly through the State agency or through another public or nonprofit private agency, in amounts so determined.

(2) For purposes of paragraph (1)(B)(ii), a child meets the requirements of this paragraph if such child—

(A)

(i) at the time adoption proceedings were initiated, met the requirements of section 606(a) of this title or section 607 of this title or would have met such requirements except for his removal from the home of a relative (specified in section 606(a) of this title), either pursuant to a voluntary placement agreement with respect to which Federal payments are provided under section 674 (or 603) of this title or as a result of a judicial determination to the effect that continuation therein would be contrary to the welfare of such child.

(ii) meets all of the requirements of subchapter XVI of this chapter with respect to eligibility for supplemental security income benefits, or

(iii) is a child whose costs in a foster family home or child-care institution are covered by the foster care maintenance payments being made with respect to his or her minor parent as provided in section 675(4)(B) of this title.

(B)

(i) received aid under the State plan approved under section 602 of this title in or for the month in which such agreement was entered into or court proceedings leading to the removal of such child from the home were initiated, or

(ii)

(I) would have received such aid in or for such month if application had been made therefor, or

(II) had been living with a relative specified in section 606(a) of this title within six months prior to the month in which such agreement was entered into or such proceedings were initiated, and would have received such aid in or for such month if in such month he had been living with such a relative and application therefor had been made, or

(iii) is a child described in subparagraph (A)(ii) or (A)(iii), and

(C) has been determined by the State, pursuant to subsection (c) of this section, to be a child with special needs. The last sentence of section 672(a) of this title shall apply, for purposes of subparagraph (B), in any case where the child is an alien described in that sentence.

(3) The amount of the payments to be made in any case under clauses (i) and (ii) of paragraph (1)(B) shall be determined through agreement between the adoptive parents and the State or local agency administering the program under this section, which shall take into consideration the circumstances of the adopting parents and the needs of the child being adopted, and may be readjusted periodically, with the concurrence of the adopting parents (which may be specified in the adoption assistance agreement), depending upon changes in such circumstances. However, in no case may the amount of the adoption assistance payment made under clause (ii) of par-

agraph (1)(B) exceed the foster care maintenance payment which would have been paid during the period if the child with respect to whom the adoption assistance payment is made had been in a foster family home.

(4) Notwithstanding the preceding paragraph,

(A) no payment may be made to parents with respect to any child who has attained the age of eighteen (or, where the State determines that the child has a mental or physical handicap which warrants the continuation of assistance, the age of twenty-one), and

(B) no payment may be made to parents with respect to any child if the State determines that the parents are no longer legally responsible for the support of the child or if the State determines that the child is no longer receiving any support from such parents. Parents who have been receiving adoption assistance payments under this section shall keep the State or local agency administering the program under this section informed of circumstances which would, pursuant to this subsection, make them ineligible for such assistance payments, or eligible for assistance payments in a different amount.

(5) For purposes of this part, individuals with whom a child (who has been determined by the State, pursuant to subsection (c) of this section, to be a child with special needs) is placed for adoption in accordance with applicable State and local law shall be eligible for such payments, during the period of the placement, on the same terms and subject to the same conditions as if such individuals had adopted such child.

(6)

(A) For purposes of paragraph (1)(B)(i), the term "nonrecurring adoption expenses" means reasonable and necessary adoption fees, court costs, attorney fees, and other expenses which are directly related to the legal adoption of a child with special needs and which are not incurred in violation of State or Federal law.

(B) A State's payment of nonrecurring adoption expenses under an adoption assistance agreement shall be treated as an expenditure made for the proper and efficient administration of the State plan for purposes of section 674(a)(3)(B) (FOOTNOTE 1) of this title.

(b) Aid to families with dependent children

For purposes of subchapters XIX and XX of this chapter, any child—

(1)

(A) who is a child described in subsection (a)(2) of this section, and

(B) with respect to whom an adoption assistance agreement is in effect under this section (whether or not adoption assistance payments are provided under the agreement or are being made under this section), including any such child who has been placed for adoption in accordance with applicable State and local law (whether or not an interlocutory or other judicial decree of adoption has been issued), or

(2) with respect to whom foster care maintenance payments are being made

under section 672 of this title, shall be deemed to be a dependent child as defined in section 606 of this title and shall be deemed to be a recipient of aid to families with dependent children under part A of this subchapter in the State where such child resides. For purposes of the preceding sentence, a child whose costs in a foster family home or child-care institution are covered by the foster care maintenance payments being made with respect to his or her minor parent, as provided in section 675(4)(B) of this title, shall be considered a child with respect to whom foster care maintenance payments are being made under section 672 of this title.

(c) Children with special needs

For purposes of this section, a child shall not be considered a child with special needs unless—

(1) the State has determined that the child cannot or should not be returned to the home of his parents; and

(2) the State had first determined

(A) that there exists with respect to the child a specific factor or condition (such as his ethnic background, age, or membership in a minority or sibling group, or the presence of factors such as medical conditions or physical, mental, or emotional handicaps) because of which it is reasonable to conclude that such child cannot be placed with adoptive parents without providing adoption assistance under this section or medical assistance under subchapter XIX of this chapter, and

(B) that, except where it would be against the best interests of the child because of such factors as the existence of significant emotional ties with prospective adoptive parents while in the care of such parents as a foster child, a reasonable, but unsuccessful, effort has been made to place the child with appropriate adoptive parents without providing adoption assistance under this section or medical assistance under subchapter XIX of this chapter.

FEDERAL PIQS AND OTHER ISSUANCES

Instead of issuing a large number of regulations, the U.S. Department of Health and Human Services, through its Children's Bureau, has published periodic policy interpretations including Information Memoranda (IM), Policy Announcements (PA), Policy Interpretations (PI) and Policy Information Questions (PIQs). PIQs are responses to questions submitted to the Children's Bureau by individual states about the Title IV-E adoption assistance and foster maintenance programs. A number of the PIQs provide useful information to adoptive parents who are applying for adoption assistance.

As Carol Williams, Associate Commissioner and head of the Children's Bureau, has noted, "Policy Information Questions and other issuances by this Department are interpretations of statute and are disseminated as a mechanism to further clarify statutes and regulations that are already in place." Ms. Williams makes an important point for adoptive families. PIQs apply to the date the law went into effect, not to the date that the policy announcement is made. For example, PIQ 87-05 affirms that certain children who are not in the care of the state, including those placed by private agencies, are candidates for adoption assistance. Even though the policy interpretation was not issued until 1987, it establishes that private agency children have always been potentially eligible for adoption assistance because the relevant section of federal law has not changed since its enactment in 1980. The letter containing Ms. Williams' statements is reprinted below.

The following section presents a sample of PIQs that address questions of significance for adoptive families. A complete listing of federal policy issuances may be found at the U.S. Department of Health and Human Services Web site at http://www.acf.dhhs.gov/programs/cb/policy. The Adoption Policy Resource Center at www.fpsol.com/adoption/advocates.html also features a number of PIQs.

Response by Carol W. Williams, Associate Commissioner of the U.S. Department of Health and Human Services, Children's Bureau to Questions Submitted by Attorney Geraldine Follansbee (Stewart): April 5, 1996

Carol Williams is head of the Children's Bureau, the division of the U.S. Department of Health and Human Services that is responsible for publishing federal interpretation pertaining to the Title IV-E adoption assistance program. Her responses to Ms. Follansbee's (now Ms. Stewart) questions affirm that children adopted through private agencies have the same access to adoption assistance as children placed through public agencies. Ms. Williams also makes the very significant point that PIQs and other policy statements issued by the Children's Bureau are interpretations and clarifications of existing law, not changes or amendments.

Would grounds for a fair hearing exist if a private, nonprofit agency fails to notify or advise adoptive parents of the availability of adoption assistance for a child who was in the care and under the responsibility of the private, nonprofit agency?

Yes. Grounds for a fair hearing exist when a private, nonprofit agency fails to notify adoptive parents of the availability of adoption assistance for a child in its care. The very purpose of the Title IV-E adoption assistance program is to encourage the adoption of hard-to-place children. Notification to potential adoptive parents about its availability is an intrinsic part of the program. Accordingly, the private, nonprofit agency's failure to the parents may be considered an "extenuating circumstance," which justifies a fair hearing.

Is a child with special needs who is adopted through a private, nonprofit agency eligible for adoption assistance after a final decree of adoption? If yes, what is the procedure that must be followed to obtain adoption assistance?

Yes. A child whose placement and care are the responsibility of a private, nonprofit agency may be eligible for Title IV-E adoption assistance payments after a final decree of adoption. The child must meet the eligibility requirements in section 473 (a) (1) of the Social Security Act [section 673 (a) (1) of the U.S. Code] and be determined by the State to be a child with special needs in accordance with 473 (c) of the Act [section 673 (c) of the U.S. Code].

In order to obtain adoption assistance after finalization, the adoptive parents' request for subsidy must either be denied or the agency must fail to notify the adoptive parents regarding the availability of subsidy. The parents may then request a fair hearing under section 471 (a) (12) of the Act. The fair hearing process requires that participants be advised of their right to a hearing, that they may be represented by an authorized representative, and that there be a timely notice of the date and place of the hearing.

Each state Title IV-B/IV-E agency is required to have a fair hearing process in place that addresses the procedure that the adoptive parents must follow. It should be noted that it is acceptable for states to have written guidance regarding the types of situations that would constitute the grounds for a fair hearing, in order to assist fair hearing officers. State policies, however, may not define the grounds for a fair hearing more narrowly than does federal policy. (See ACYF-PIQ-83-4, dated October 26, 1983, and ACYF-PIQ-88-06, dated December 2, 1988, for further guidance.)

What is the significance of Policy Information Questions issued by the U.S. Department of Health and Human Services and are they interpretations of the law?

Policy Information Questions and other issuances developed by this department are interpretations of statute and are disseminated as a mechanism to further clarify statutes and regulations that are already in place.

INTRODUCTION TO PIQ 92–02

PIQ 92–02: Applying for Adoption Assistance after Finalization

May an adoptive family apply for and obtain adoption assistance for a child after the final decree of adoption?

Yes. PIQ 92-02 is the landmark policy interpretation that set forth procedures through which families can apply for and obtain adoption assistance after finalization. The policy issuance and its implications are discussed extensively in Chapter 10.

Administration for Children and Families
U.S. DEPARTMENT OF HEALTH AND HUMAN SERVICES
Administration on Children, Youth and Families

1. Log No. ACF-PIQ-92-02
2. Issuance Date: June 25, 1992
3. Originating Office: Children's Bureau
4. Key Word: Fair Hearing and Extenuating Circumstances

POLICY INTERPRETATION QUESTION

TO: State Agencies Administering or Supervising . . . Title IV-E of the Social Security Act, Indian Tribes and Indian Tribal Organizations
SUBJECT: Clarification Regarding ACYF-PIQ-88-06, Dated December 2, 1988, and Situations Which Would Constitute "Extenuating Circumstances" for the Purpose of a Fair Hearing for Denial of Title IV-E Adoption Assistance

LEGAL AND RELATED REFERENCES: Sections 473(a) and (c), 471(a)(12) and 1132(a) of the Social Security Act, 45 CFR 1356.40(b)(1), 45 CFR 95.7, ACYF-PIQ-83-4, Dated October 26, 1983 and ACYF-PIQ-88-06, Dated December 2, 1988

BACKGROUND: Policy Interpretation Question, ACYF-PIQ-88-06, dated December 2, 1988, set forth conditions, after the finalization of an adoption, under which a State may reverse an earlier decision to deny title IV-E adoption assistance benefits. It stated that Federal regulations at 45 CFR 1356.40(b)(1) require that the adoption assistance agreement be signed and in effect at the time of or prior to the final decree of adoption. However, if the adoptive parents were denied benefits and there are extenuating circumstances, the adoptive parents may request a fair hearing. The policy issuance goes on to state that, if the hearing determines that all of the facts relevant to the child's eligibility were not presented at the time of the request for assistance, the State may reverse the earlier decision to deny benefits under title IV-E.

INTERPRETATION TO: Questions raised with regard to what constitutes "extenuating circumstances" for the purpose of a fair hearing under the title IV-E adoption assistance program.

QUESTION 1: The case situation described in ACYF-PIQ-88-06 spoke to a child's medical condition which was not properly diagnosed prior to adoption as being grounds for a fair hearing. Would a change in Federal statute, regulation or policy constitute grounds for a fair hearing as well?

RESPONSE: No. Changes in Federal statute, regulation or policy normally are effective only prospectively. Since the previous statute, regulation or policy is in effect until such a change is made, a change would not constitute grounds for a fair hearing.

QUESTION 2: With respect to the State agency's responsibilities in the administration of the program, some concern has been expressed over the seeming paradox between notifying and advising prospective adoptive parents of the adoption assistance program and making a reasonable, but unsuccessful, effort to place a child without adoption assistance as required by section 473 (c)(2)(B) of the Social Security Act. Please clarify this issue.

RESPONSE: In an effort to find an adoptive home for a child, the agency should first look at a number of families in order to locate the most suitable family for the child. Once the agency has determined that placement with a certain family would be the most suitable for the child, then full disclosure should be made of the child's background, as well as known and potential problems. If the child meets the State's definition of special needs with regard to specific factors or conditions, then the agency can pose the question of whether the prospective adoptive parents are willing to adopt without a subsidy. If they say that they cannot adopt the child without a subsidy, the agency would meet the requirement in 473(c)(2)(B) that there be a reasonable, but unsuccessful, effort to place the child without providing adoption assistance.

It was the intent of Congress, with the establishment of the adoption assistance program, to increase significantly the number of children placed in permanent homes. Thus, it is reasonable to conclude that it was not the intent of Congress that a child remain unnecessarily in foster care while the agency "shops" for a family which might be less suitable but is willing to adopt the child without a subsidy, if it has already found a suitable placement for the child.

QUESTION 3: Would grounds for a fair hearing exist if the State agency fails to notify or advise adoptive parents of the availability of adoption assistance for a child with special needs?

RESPONSE: Yes. The very purpose of the title IV-E adoption assistance program is to encourage the adoption of hard-to-place children. State notification to potential adoptive parents about its existence is an intrinsic part of the program and the incentive for adoption that was intended by Congress. Thus, notifying potential adoptive parents is the State agency's responsibility in its administration of the title IV-E adoption assistance program. Accordingly, the State agency's failure to notify the parents may be considered an "extenuating circumstance" which justifies a fair hearing.

QUESTION 4: Would grounds for a fair hearing exist if the State agency erroneously determines that a child is ineligible for adoption assistance?

RESPONSE: Yes. If the basis for denial of adoption assistance is the erroneous determination by the State that the child does not meet the eligibility criteria set forth in section 473 of the Act, the adoptive parents may request a fair hearing under section 471(a)(12) of the Act. If the hearing determines that the State erred in its assessment of the child's eligibility for adoption assistance, the State may reverse the earlier decision to deny benefits under title IV-E. (See 45 CFR 205.10, ACYF-PIQ-83-4, dated October 26, 1983, and ACYF-PIQ-88-06, dated December 2, 1988, for guidance.) The types of situations which would constitute grounds for a fair hearing include: (1) relevant facts regarding the child, the biological family or child's background are known and not presented to the adoptive parents prior to the legalization of the adoption; (2) denial of assistance based upon a means test of the adoptive family; (3) erroneous determination by the State that a child is ineligible for adoption assistance; and (4) failure by the State agency to advise adoptive parents of the availability of adoption assistance.

If applicants or recipients of financial benefits or service programs under titles IV-B or IV-E believe that they have been wrongly denied financial assistance or excluded from a service program, they have a right to a hearing. It is the responsibility of the fair hearing officer to determine whether extenuating circumstances exist and whether the applicant or recipient was wrongly denied eligibility.

QUESTION 5: May a State establish policies defining the factual circumstances which constitute an extenuating circumstance for the purpose of a fair hearing?

RESPONSE: It is permissible for States to have written guidance regarding the types of situations which would constitute the grounds for a fair hearing in order to assist fair hearing officers. However, State policies may not define the grounds for a fair hearing more narrowly than Federal policy.

QUESTION 6: May a State agency change its eligibility determination and provide adoption assistance based upon extenuating circumstances without requiring the applicant to obtain a favorable ruling in a fair hearing?

RESPONSE: No. However, if the State and the parents are in agreement, a trial-type evidentiary hearing would not be necessary. The undisputed documentary evidence could be presented to the fair hearing officer for his or her review and determination on the written record.

QUESTION 7: Who has the burden of proving extenuating circumstances and adoption assistance eligibility at a fair hearing?

RESPONSE: The Federal statute does not address the point explicitly. We would expect States to conclude that the adoptive parents have the burden of proving extenuating circumstances and adoption assistance eligibility at a fair hearing. However, as stated in the previous response, if the State agency is in agreement that a family had erroneously been denied benefits, it would be permissible for the State to provide such facts to the family or present corroborating facts on behalf of the family to the fair hearing present corroborating facts on behalf of the family to the fair hearing officer.

QUESTION 8: After the legalization of an adoption, if a fair hearing determines that a child has been wrongly denied benefits under the title IV-E adoption assistance program, what is the earliest date from which the assistance may be provided?

RESPONSE: Prior to the passage of the Tax Reform Act of 1986, the statute required that there be an interlocutory or final decree of adoption prior to receipt of adoption assistance. Therefore, after the effective date of a State's title IV-E State plan, the earliest date from which adoption assistance may be provided is from the time of the interlocutory or final decree of adoption for those children adopted on or before October 1, 1986. As of October 1, 1986, with the passage of the Tax Reform Act of 1986, the requirement that there be an interlocutory decree prior to providing adoption assistance was rescinded and adoption assistance payments may begin when the adoption assistance agreement is signed and the child is placed in the adoptive home.

If a State chooses to pay adoption assistance retroactively from the earliest date of the child's eligibility in accordance with Federal and State statutes, regulations and policies, the State may claim Federal financial participation for this expenditure. For cases in which there was no signed adoption assistance agreement, the earliest date of eligibility would be that of the interlocutory or final decree for assistance provided before October 1, 1986, or placement in an adoptive home for assistance provided after October 1, 1986. States should sign a new agreement backdated to the earliest date of eligibility for the child. The two-year restriction in section 1132(a) of the Social Security Act applies to the date of claim for actual expenditures, and, thus, would not apply in this situation.

Wade F. Horn, Ph.D.   Commissioner

INTRODUCTION TO PIQ 90-02

PIQ 90-02: The Use of Income Means Tests

May a state agency use an income means test to determine the amount of adoption assistance?

No. A state may not use an income means test as the sole basis for determining the amount of adoption assistance. Federal policy interpretations such as PIQ 90-02 and PIQ 92-02 clearly anticipate a negotiation process in which the child's background, anticipated needs and the family's overall situation are the subject of a constructive dialogue.

Unfortunately, there are few guidelines for customizing adoption assistance agreements as individually negotiated family support plans and states generally fall back on payment categories based on such factors as the child's needs and the severity of the child's medical, emotional or development problems. Many states have a "standard" payment category with age gradations and one or two "special" payment categories for children with more serious problems.

The payment schedules usually form the context of negotiations between the parents and the agency. The parents, for example, might contend that their child falls into a particular "specialized care category," because the child has a reactive attachment disorder, autism or severe mental retardation, but the potential amount of assistance is not open-ended. The rate schedules for "specialized care" establish the outer limits of support that the state will offer.

Let us suppose, for instance, that the state has two payment schedules, one for a "typical" child with special needs and one for a child with "severe" special needs. A family is planning to adopt a six-year-old child. The regular adoption assistance payment rate for a six-year-old child with special needs is a maximum of $385 per month. The parents present evidence that their child has been diagnosed with a reactive attachment disorder and contend that the regular rate is inadequate to meet the child's anticipated care needs. The agency agrees that the child fits into a severe special needs category and offers the adoptive family $600 per month, which is the maximum payment on the rate schedule for a child of six.

Federal funding regulations further limit the ability of parents to negotiate a completely customized plan of support. Title IV-E adoption assistance is funded by federal dollars, but requires a nonfederal match. The rate of federal financial participation (FFP) in a state's IV-E program is the same as the FFP in the state's Medicaid program. The federal share ranges from lows of 50 percent to highs of 80 percent. In many states, the federal share is around 60 percent of the cost of adoption assistance payments.

Federal law specifies that FFP is available for adoption assistance payments up to the rate a child would receive were he or she in a family foster home rather than an adoptive placement. For example, suppose a child with severe emotional problems were placed in a special foster home where the care givers were paid $1,500 per month for his care. If the child is placed in an adoptive home and qualifies for Title IV-E adoption assistance, FFP would be available for a monthly adoption assistance payment of up to $1,500. In Ohio, the FFP for a $1,500 adoption assistance payment would be approximately $900.

Federal funding limits and the absence of clear guidelines for assessing the "needs of the child and the circumstances of the family" result in states' reliance on payment schedules. Foster care rates usually function as de facto ceilings on adoption assistance payments. The maximum figure in the rate schedule is the normal payment.

Suppose that the regular adoption assistance schedule in State A is as follows: $345—ages 0 through 5; $370—ages 6 through 12 and $460—ages 13 through 18. A family adopting a three-year-old child might expect the agency to offer an adoption assistance payment of $345 per month, unless evidence is presented that the child meets the state's severe special needs category. The agency could offer less, but once again in the absence of clear guidelines about how to assess a child's needs or a family's circumstances, it is somewhat difficult to argue that the Smith family should be treated any differently from the Jones family.

Adoptive parents may explore service subsidies in addition to adoption assistance payments as part of an overall plan of support. Most states have some form of program that pays for services that are not covered by health insurance or Medicaid. Parents also may appeal agency decisions regarding program eligibility or the amount of adoption assistance. By becoming well-informed, families have the opportunity to help design a somewhat individualized postadoptive support plans for their child. Federal funding patterns and the difficulty of translating general terms such as family circumstances into levels of support makes it difficult for families to negotiate payments above specified rate schedules.

Foster care rates function as payment ceilings for adoption subsidy programs in most states. The NACAC survey found that rate schedules for adoption assistance were matched with regular foster care rates in twenty-one states. Foster care rates exceed adoption assistance payment schedules in seventeen states and the District of Columbia. Surprisingly, adoption assistance rate schedules appear to be higher than regular foster care rates in seven states. These rates represent maximum payments for "regular" child with special needs in particular age categories. It is nor clear whether in these relatively few cases, states were willing to absorb the cost of payments over the foster care rate or if they routinely offer adoption assistance at the foster care rate and only agree to the maximum payment on rare occasions.

ACYF-PIQ 90-02: Title IV-E, Adoption Assistance, Means Test

1. Log No. ACYF-PIQ 90-02

2. Issuance Date 10–02–90

3. Originating Office: Children's Bureau

4. Key Word: Title 10-E

5. Adoption Assistance

6. Means Test

POLICY INTERPRETATION QUESTION:

TO: State Agencies Administering or Supervising Administration of Title IVE of the Social Security Act, Indian Tribes and Indian Tribal Organizations (ITOs)

SUBJECT: Title IVE Adoptive Assistance Agreements and the Use of a Means Test

STATEMENT OF PROBLEM

Public Law (P.L.) 96-272, the Adoption Assistance and Child Welfare Act of 1980, established a program of adoption assistance for "children with special needs." This landmark legislation was intended to provide, for the first time, Federal financial participation with States in a program of incentives and supports to families adopting certain children who, because of a variety of specific conditions, could not be adopted without assistance.

The legislative history of P.L. 96-272 indicates that Congress at first considered the inclusion of a "means test" as a requirement under the Title IV-E adoption assistance program. At one point in Committee discussion, a family would not have been eligible to receive adoption assistance if its income exceeded 150 percent of the State median income for a family of four. However, this restriction was later dropped after the Committee noted that "we should not design a program to foster adoptions only in those families with the least financial capacity to care for these children with special needs." (See Congressional Record Senate §11704, August 3, 1979.)

In the years since the enactment of P.L. 96-272, States have developed their Title IV-E adoption assistance programs to comply with the State Plan requirements in section 471 and the program in section 473 of the Social Security Act (the Act). Recently, however, questions have been raised by a number of States, through the Regional Offices of the Office of Human Development Services, indicating that there is still uncertainty about the use of a means test and the appropriate method for negotiating an adoption assistance agreement with potential adoptive parents in relation to a children who is eligible for assistance under Title IV-E.

BACKGROUND: In order to be eligible for ongoing adoption assistance payments under Title IV-E, a child must be eligible for Aid to Families With Dependent Children, Title IV-E Foster Care, or Supplemental Security Income for the Blind and Disabled and meet the definition of a child with special needs according to section 473 (c) of the Act. Under that section, the State Title IV-E agency makes a determination as to whether a child is a child with special needs, according to the following factors:

The child cannot or should not be returned to the home of the parents;

there exists a specific factor or condition (such as the child's age, ethnic background, emotional, physical or mental handicap, or membership in a minority or sibling group) because of which it is reasonable to conclude that the child cannot be placed for adoption without providing adoption assistance; and, except where it would be against the best interests of the child, a reasonable, but unsuccessful, effort has been made to place the child without adoption assistance.

The Title IV-E regulations at 45 CFR 1356.40 (c) prohibit the use of a means test in the process of selecting suitable adoptive parents for a child with special needs and in negotiating an adoption assistance agreement (including the amount of the adoption assistance payment). This means that, once a child is found eligible under section 473 (c) of the Act, the child's adoptive parents may not be rejected for adoption assistance or have payments reduced without their agreement because of the level of their income or other resources. The purpose of the adoption assistance program is to provide incentives for families of any economic stratum and to remove barriers to the adoption of child with special needs.

Section 473(a)(3) of the Act states that the amount of the adoption assistance payment shall be determined through an agreement between the adoptive parents and the State or local agency and that the agreement "shall take into consideration the circumstances of the adopting parents and the needs of the child. . . ." The language is interpreted to pertain to the parents' ability to incorporate the child into their household in relation to their lifestyle, standard of living, and future plans and to their overall capacity to meet the immediate and future needs (including educational needs) of the child.

In some States, however, the language has been used to justify extensive investigation of the financial circumstances of the potential adoptive parents at the time of adoption and at yearly recertification periods subsequent to the adoption. There is no statutory requirement for such investigations; thus, Federal reimbursement is not available for costs associated with them.

Section 473(a)(4)(B) of the Act indicates that there are only two reasons (other than the child's age) why parents become ineligible for payments after the child is adopted: (1) the State determines that the parents are no longer legally responsible for the support of the child and (2) the State determines that the child is no longer receiving any support from the parents. The parents may also request termination of payments and services. Events not related to these conditions that occur subsequent to the adoption have no applicability to Title IV-E eligibility.

LEGAL AND RELATED REFERENCES: Section 473 of the Social Security Act; 45 CFR 1356.40 (c); and ACYF-PIQ 82-02, dated January 19. 1982

INTERPRETATION TO: Questions raised by Regional Offices regarding the development of an adoption assistance agreement and the use of a means test.

QUESTION 1: Can a State use criteria, such as State median income adjusted for family size or a sliding income scale, in determining the potential adoptive family's eligibility for adoption assistance?

RESPONSE: No. The regulations at 45 CFR 1356.40 (c) prohibit the use of a means test in determining eligibility for adoption assistance payments. Therefore, States are prohibited from using criteria such as State median income or sliding income scales to determine the eligibility of adoptive parents to receive adoption assistance payments on behalf of a child with special needs.

QUESTION 2: Should State policy describe the procedure used by the State to determine eligibility for and the amount of adoption assistance?

RESPONSE: Yes. The Title IV-E State Plan requires inclusion of State statutory, regulatory, and policy references for each Federal statutory and regulatory requirement under Title IV-E. As a result, States must address the procedures in place which meet the requirements regarding eligibility for and amount of adoption assistance as set forth in section 473 of the Act and 45 CFR 1356.40 (c).

QUESTION 3: Can the State median income adjusted to family size be used as a guide to establish consistency in determining amounts of payment?

RESPONSE: No. The use of such guidelines is not appropriate to the process. During the negotiation of an adoption assistance agreement, it is important to keep in mind that the circumstances of the adopting parents and the needs of the child must be considered together. As stated in the Background section, this means the overall ability of a singular family to incorporate an individual child into the household. Families with the same incomes or in similar circumstances will not necessarily agree on identical types or amounts of assistance. The uniqueness of each child/family situation may result in different amounts of payment. Consistency is not the goal.

QUESTION 4: Some States use the family's income as one of the factors considered in determining the amount of the adoption assistance payment, since Policy Interpretation Question ACYF-PIQ 82-02, dated January 19, 1982, states: "If Mississippi uses the means test, in conjunction with the needs of the child, to determine the amount of assistance, it is a permissible tool." When determining the amount of the monthly payment, are all factors of consideration given equal weight? When setting the amount of the monthly payment, can the family's income be the major factor in determining the amount of monthly payment?

RESPONSE: Policy Interpretation Question ACYF-PIQ 82-02 predated the Final Rule, dated May 23, 1983, which takes precedence over previously written policy issuances. The regulations at 45 CFR 1356.40 (c) specifically prohibit the use of a means test for prospective adoptive parents in determining their eligibility for payments. Sections 473(a)(1), (2) and (3) of the Act clearly indicate that eligibility for adoption assistance is related to the child and not the parent; therefore, the negotiation should focus on the needs of the child. As stated in the Background section, section 473(a)(3) allows for the circumstances of the adopting parents to be taken into consideration, in conjunction with the needs of the child, in determining the amount of adoption assistance. In doing so, the State should consider what it would take to incorporate a specific child, with his or her specific needs, into a particular household.

QUESTION 5: Can the State deny an adoption assistance payment to potential adoptive parents who have chosen to defer their maximum income potential while pursuing a higher education? For instance, an infant is considered to be a child with special needs because of a combination of medical problems and minority status. A family is interested in adopting but will need help with the medical expenses, as the child will need corrective surgery plus ongoing medical care. The prospective adoptive parents are both medical students and have two years to complete their internships. They request monthly adoption assistance payments for two years and ongoing medical assistance after that time. Can the State deny cash payments or limit assistance to medical care?

RESPONSE: No. The State cannot deny adoption assistance payments because the adoptive parents have chosen to defer their maximum income potential while pursuing a higher education. The adoptive parents' income is not relevant to the child's eligibility for adoption assistance payments. As stated in an earlier response, the eligibility for adoption assistance is related to the child and not the parent.

The example can be used, however, to demonstrate the process described in response to previous questions; that is, that adoption assistance agreements are developed for individual situations. In this case, the discussion of payment would take into consideration the parents' plans and their request for assistance to meet the needs of the child during a specific period. This, too, could be adjusted at some time in the future. If agreement cannot be reached between the agency and the adoptive parents, they have the right to request a fair hearing.

QUESTION 6: In a similar situation, parents already receiving assistance payments return to school for a one year training program and request an increase in the amount of payment for that period of time to meet the needs of the child. Can the agency deny this request based on the voluntary nature of the change in income level or the fact that the modification in income may not relate to the original need or circumstances at the time of the initial agreement?

RESPONSE: The State cannot arbitrarily reject such requests. Section 473(a)(3) requires the State to consider the circumstances of the adopting parents when determining the amount of payment and allows for periodic readjustment depending upon changes in such circumstances. The statute does not limit the changes in circumstances to those which are beyond the parents' control. As in the response to question 5 above, the agency should consider such requests in a renegotiation of the adoption assistance agreement with regard for the parents' plans for meeting the needs of the child during a specific time period. If the agency refuses to consider a renegotiation of the adoption assistance agreement, the adoptive parents have the right to request a fair hearing.

DISCUSSION: The Title IV-E Adoption Assistance Program has a broad purpose and, unlike other public assistance programs in the Social Security Act, it is intended to encourage an action which will be of lifelong social benefit to a certain category of children and not generally to meet short-term monetary needs during a temporary period of economic crisis.

Under Title IV-E, the term "adoption assistance" means, literally, to assist the adoption of children with special needs. Experience in public child welfare agencies has shown that, in the past, many children with special problems and disabilities have grown up in foster homes or institutions, without the security of belonging to a family of their own. Assisting in the adoption of such children is not only beneficial for the children and enriching for families, but is also cost-beneficial to State agencies in that administrative costs in the adoption assistance program can be far less than in the foster care program.

Means testing concepts such as those illustrated in the examples cited in this policy issuance are not appropriate in the Title IV-E adoption assistance program and should not be acted upon in the negotiation of an agreement with prospective adoptive parents. Adoptive parents are selected for their ability to provide permanent and stable homes for child with special needs and are not expected to change their long-term plans because of the adoption of such children. Under the title IV-E program, even though adoption assistance payments are made, the agency does not control or participate in family choices regarding lifestyle or career plans.

Wade F. Horn Ph.D.   Commissioner

INTRODUCTION TO PIQ 87-05

PIQ 87-05: The Eligibility of Children for Adoption Assistance Who Are Not in the Care of the State

May a state categorically deny access to adoption assistance in the case of children who are not in care or custody of the state?

No. Children with special needs who meet the eligibility standards for SSI, children placed by private agencies and children adopted by relatives may all qualify for adoption assistance if they meet the eligibility requirements. A state may not enact laws, regulations or policies that are more restriction than what is allowed under federal law.

1. Log No. ACYF-PIQ-87-05 12/17/87
2. Originating Office: **Children's Bureau**
3. Key Word: State Adoption Subsidy Requirements—Title IV-E

POLICY INTERPRETATION QUESTION

TO: State Agencies Administering or Supervising the Administration of Title IV-E of the Social Security Act and Indian Tribes and Indian Tribal Organizations
SUBJECT: Request for Clarification of State Adoption Subsidy Requirements in relation to Section 473(a)(2) of the Social Security Act (the Act)

SUMMARY OF REPLY: Title IV-E does not require that States, in all cases, have a responsibility for placement and care (or custody) of a child as a prerequisite to adoption assistance under the Federal program. Further, there are no Title IV-E provisions which would allow States to attach eligibility requirements for adoption assistance under that title in addition to those cited in the Federal statute.

LEGAL AND RELATED REFERENCES: Section 473 of the Social Security Act; ACYF-PIQ-85-3, Issued March 19, 1985; ACYF-PIQ-85-4, Issued April 16, 1985

QUESTION: In some States, statutory requirements for adoption subsidy programs limit eligibility under Title IV-E to children who are committed or relinquished to the State Agency. Are these provisions consistent with the requirements of Title IV-E, section 473(a)(2), of the Social Security Act?

INTERPRETATION: No. State statutes which limit access to the Title IV-E Adoption Assistance Program by the addition of eligibility requirements beyond those required under the Federal statute are not in conformance with Title IV-E. The Act establishes the eligibility criteria in section 473(a)(2) as the sole criteria. It does not set forth the listed criteria as minimums or as examples of eligibility criteria.

The eligibility requirements for the Adoption Assistance Program are found in section 473(a)(2) of the Act. While this section references the requirements of the Title IV-A AFDC program, the Title IV-E foster care program, and the Title XVI SSI program, it does not specify, in addition, that a child must be under the legal custody or responsibility of the Title IV-E administering agency, through commitment or relinquishment, to be eligible for Title IV-E adoption assistance. While it is necessary for a child to be under the responsibility of the State agency in order to be eligible for Title IV-E foster care (section 472(a)(2) requirement), there will be other situations in which children with special needs are in care under the responsibility of private, nonprofit agencies without the involvement of the State agency. When adoption is the goal for such children, and they are determined to be AFDC or SSI-eligible, the Title IV-E agency may not exclude them from consideration or approval, if they are otherwise found eligible for adoption assistance in accordance with section 473.

If a State does not have responsibility for placement and care of the otherwise eligible child, the child may be eligible for Title IV-E adoption assistance under any of the following circumstances:

1. At the time the adoption petition is filed, the child is eligible for AFDC while living with a specified relative (section 473(a)(2)(A)(i));
2. The child meets the eligibility requirements for the SSI program prior to the finalization of the adoption (section 473(a)(2)(A)(ii): or adoption (section 473(a)(2)(A)(ii); or
3. The AFDC-eligible child is placed in foster care through a voluntary placement agreement (or relinquishment) with a private, nonprofit agency (no Title IV-E payment is made) and a judicial determination is subsequently made (following an initiation of court proceedings within six months of removal of the child from the home of a relative) to the effect that continuation in the home would be contrary to the welfare of the child. This action would satisfy the requirements in sections 473(a)(2)(A)(i) and 473(a)(2)(B)(ii)(II) and the child would be considered judicially removed.

In any of the above circumstances, the adoption assistance agreement must be negotiated between the prospective adoptive parents and the State title IV-E agency, with the involvement of other relevant agencies, as appropriate (section 5(3)).

Dodie Livingston   Commissioner

INTRODUCTION TO PIQ 81-02

PIQ 81-02: Age Limits on Adoption Assistance Payments

May a state arbitrarily cut off adoption assistance payments for all children when they reach the age of 18?

No. PIQ 81-02 specifies that states may not categorically limit adoption assistance payments to child with special needs under the age of eighteen. Section 473(a)(3)(A) of the 1980 Federal Adoption Assistance and Child Welfare Act (USC 673(a)(3)(A) states that "no payment may be made to parents with respect to any child who has attained the age of eighteen (or, where the State determines that the child has a mental or physical handicap which warrants the continuation of assistance, the age of twenty-one)." The state must set reasonable criteria for determining if a child has a "mental or physical handicap" and any child who meets those criteria is eligible for adoption assistance payments to the age of twenty-one.

A state, in short, may determine that an individual child does have a mental or physical handicap, but it may not arbitrarily determine that no children will receive adoption assistance payments to the age of twenty-one. Nor may it set criteria that are so stringent that few if any children would qualify. PIQ 81-12 is reprinted below.

1. Log No.: ACYF-PIQ-81-2

2. Issuance Date: December 8, 1981

3. Originating Office: Children's Bureau

4. Key Word: Duration of Adoption Assistance Payments

P.L. 96-272
POLICY INTERPRETATION QUESTION

TO: Mr. Roy Fleischer
Regional Program Director
Region IX–ACYF

SUBJECT: Duration of adoption assistance payments under the Adoption Assistance Program, section 473 of the Social Security Act

STATEMENT OF REPLY: States may limit the duration of payments under an adoption assistance agreement for individual eligible children to a period which may end prior to the child's eighteenth birthday, if the decision is made on a case-by-case basis, taking into consideration the provisions of section 473(a)(2) of the Act. States may not have a blanket policy which limits the duration of all adoption assistance payments to a date earlier than the eighteenth birthday of eligible children, although a time limit may be set in individual cases, depending on the needs of the child and circumstances of the parents.

LEGAL REFERENCES: Social Security Act, section 473.

INTERPRETATION TO: A letter from the Department of Social Services of the California Health and Welfare Agency

QUESTION: California currently has an existing program, "Aid for the Adoption of Children, which permits subsidy payments up to the age of majority, but limits the payments period for five years unless the need for financial assistance was related to a chronic health condition . . . [Will] . . . the California program, with the five-year limitation . . . qualify as an approved plan under proposed Federal regulations implementing section 473 [?]"

ANSWER: No. The existing California adoption subsidy program would not qualify as an approvable plan under section 473 of the Act. Section

473(a)(2) states: "The amount of the adoption assistance payments shall be determined through agreement between the adoptive parents and the State or local agency administering the program . . . which shall take into consideration the circumstances of the adopting parents and the needs of the child, and may be readjusted periodically, with the concurrence of the adopting parents." The only mandatory limits on duration of payment in the law are found in section 473(a)(3) where it is stated at (A): "no payment may be made to parents with respect to any child who has attained the age of eighteen (or, where the State determines that the child has a mental or physical handicap which warrants the continuation of assistance, the age of twenty-one)" and at (B), that no payments may be made if the parents "are no longer legally responsible for the support of the child" or ". . . the child is no longer receiving any support from the parents." [Author's **Note:** See PIQ 85-12 for an interpretation of the criteria for continuing eligibility for adoption assistance, including situations when the child is placed outside the home.]

Thus, age of the child, legal responsibility for the support of the child, and actual receipt of support are the three conditions upon which a State may base limit or duration of payment for all eligible children on in an approved Title IV-E Adoption Assistance Program.

Therefore, to qualify as an approved Title IV-E plan, a State's plan may not have a blanket policy which would in all cases limit the duration of adoption assistance payments to a date earlier than the eighteenth birthday of eligible children.

In addition, based on section 16120 of the California Welfare and Institutions Code, which was attached to California's request for interpretation of the Act, it would appear that the California program does not meet the statutory requirements for adoption assistance payments to be made pursuant to an adoption assistance agreement in amounts determined through agreement between the adoptive parents and the State, taking into consideration the circumstances of the adoptive parents and the needs of the child being adopted. Neither does the program appear to prohibit payment under the circumstances listed in section 473(a)(3) above.

The intent of the statute is to provide continuing support to eligible "special needs" children and to encourage and expand the possibility of permanent homes for these children. Therefore, we believe that it was not congressional intent to give States the option to limit the duration of all adoption assistance payments arbitrarily to a period which may end prior to the child's eighteenth birthday.

However, since Congress did not require States to make payments in all cases until the child is eighteen, States may limit the duration of payments for individual children to a period which may end prior to the child's eighteenth birthday, if the decision is made on a case-by-case basis, taking into consideration the provisions of 473(a)(2) of the Act.

Since the adoption assistance agreement is the basis upon which adoption assistance payments are made, the terms of this agreement determine both the amount and duration of payment, considering the unique needs of the individual child, and the circumstances of the adopting parents. Section 473(a)(2) allows for readjustment of the adoption assistance "with the concurrence of the adopting parents . . . depending upon changes in such circumstances." Therefore, the State may place a limit on duration of payment in the initial adoption assistance agreement or at any subsequent time with the concurrence of adopting parents, based on the circumstances of the parents and according to the needs of the specific child.

Warren Master, Acting Commissioner, Administration for Children, Youth and Families

FEDERAL REGULATIONS ON ADMINISTRATIVE FAIR HEARINGS

[Code of Federal Regulations]
[Title 45. Volume 2, Parts 200 to 499]
[Revised as of October 1, 1997]
From the U.S. Government Printing Office via GPO Access
[CITE: 45CFR205.10, Pages 20–24]
TITLE 45—PUBLIC WELFARE

CHAPTER II—OFFICE OF FAMILY ASSISTANCE (ASSISTANCE PROGRAMS), ADMINISTRATION FOR CHILDREN AND FAMILIES, DEPARTMENT OF HEALTH AND HUMAN SERVICES
PART 205—GENERAL ADMINISTRATION—PUBLIC ASSISTANCE PROGRAMS—Table of Contents

Sec. 205.10 Hearings

(a) State plan requirements. A State plan under title I, IV-A, X, XIV, or XVI(AABD) of the Social Security Act shall provide for a system of hearings under which:

(1) The single State agency responsible for the program shall be responsible for fulfillment of hearing provisions which shall provide for:

(i) A hearing before the State agency, or

(ii) An evidentiary hearing at the local level with a right of appeal to a State agency hearing. Where a State agency adopts a system of evidentiary hearings with an appeal to a State agency hearing, it may, in some political subdivisions, permit local evidentiary hearings, and in others, provide for a single hearing before the State agency. Under this requirement hearings shall meet the due process standards set forth in the U.S. Supreme Court decision in Goldberg v. Kelly, 397 U.S. 254 (1970) and the standards set forth in this section.

(2) Hearing procedures shall be issued and publicized by the State agency. Such procedures shall provide for a face-to-face hearing or, at State option, a hearing by telephone when the applicant or recipient also agrees. Under this provision, the State shall assure that the applicant or recipient is afforded all rights as specified in this section, whether the hearing is face-to-face or by telephone;

(3) Every applicant or recipient shall be informed in writing at the time of application and at the time of any action affecting his claim:

(i) Of his right to a hearing, as provided in paragraph (a)(5) of this section;

(ii) of the method by which he may obtain a hearing;

(iii) That he may be represented by an authorized representative, such as legal counsel, relative, friend, or other spokesman, or he may represent himself.

(4) In cases of intended action to discontinue, terminate, suspend or reduce assistance or to change the manner or form of payment to a protective, vendor, or two-party payment under

Sec. 234.60

(i) The State or local agency shall give timely and adequate notice, except as provided for in paragraphs (a)(4) (ii), (iii), or (iv) of this section. Under this requirement:

(A) Timely means that the notice is mailed at least 10 days before the date of action, that is, the date upon which the action would become effective;

(B) Adequate means a written notice that includes a statement of what action the agency intends to take, the reasons for the intended agency action, the specific regulations supporting such action, explanation of the individual's right to request an evidentiary hearing (if provided) and a State agency hearing, the circumstances under which assistance is continued if a hearing is requested, and if the agency action is upheld, that such assistance must be repaid under title IV-A, and must also be repaid under titles I, X, XIV or XVI (AABD) if the State plan provides for recovery of such payments.

(ii) The agency may dispense with timely notice but shall send adequate notice not later than the date of action when:

(A) The agency has factual information confirming the death of a recipient or of the AFDC payee when there is no relative available to serve as new payee;

(B) The agency receives a clear written statement signed by a recipient that he no longer wishes assistance, or that gives information which requires termination or reduction of assistance, and the recipient has indicated, in writing, that he understands that this must be the consequence of supplying such information;

(C) The recipient has been admitted or committed to an institution, and further payments to that individual do not qualify for Federal financial participation under the State plan;

(D) The recipient has been placed in skilled nursing care, intermediate care or long-term hospitalization;

(E) The claimant's whereabouts are unknown and agency mail directed to him has been returned by the post office indicating no known forwarding address. The claimant's check must, however, be made available to him if his whereabouts become known during the payment period covered by a returned check;

(F) A recipient has been accepted for assistance in a new jurisdiction and that fact has been established by the jurisdiction previously providing assistance;

(G) An AFDC child is removed from the home as a result of a judicial determination, or voluntarily placed in foster care by his legal guardian;

(H) For AFDC, the agency takes action because of information the recipient furnished in a monthly report or because the recipient has failed to submit a complete or a timely monthly report without good cause. (See Sec. 233.37);

(I) A special allowance granted for a specific period is terminated and the recipient has been informed in writing at the time of initiation that the allowance shall automatically terminate at the end of the specified period;

(J) The agency has made a presumption of mismanagement as a result of a recipient's nonpayment of rent and provides for post hearings in such circumstances;

(K) An individual's payment is suspended or reduced for failure to meet a payment after performance obligation as set forth at Sec. 233.101(b)(2)(iv) (B) or (C) of this chapter. In addition to the contents set forth in paragraph (a)(4)(i)(B) of this section, the adequate notice must advise the individual of the right to have assistance immediately reinstated retroactive to the date of action at the previous month's level pending the hearing decision if he or she makes a request for a hearing and reinstatement within 10 days after the date of the notice.

(iii) When changes in either State or Federal law require automatic grant adjustments for classes of recipients, timely notice of such grant adjustments shall be given which shall be "adequate" if it includes a statement of the intended action, the reasons for such intended action, a statement of the specific change in law requiring such action and a statement of the circumstances under which a hearing may be obtained and assistance continued.

(iv) When the agency obtains facts indicating that assistance should be discontinued, suspended, terminated, or reduced because of the probable fraud of the recipient, and, where possible, such facts have been verified through collateral sources, notice of such grant adjustment shall be timely if mailed at least five (5) days before action would become effective.

(5) An opportunity for a hearing shall be granted to any applicant who requests a hearing because his or her claim for financial assistance (including a request for supplemental payments under Secs. 233.23 and 233.27) is denied, or is not acted upon with reasonable promptness, and to any recipient who is aggrieved by any agency action resulting in suspension, reduction, discontinuance, or termination of assistance, or determination that a protective, vendor, or two-party payment should be made or continued. A hearing need not be granted when either State or Federal law requires automatic grant adjustments for classes of recipients unless the reason for an individual appeal is incorrect grant computation.

(i) A request for a hearing is defined as a clear expression by the claimant (or his authorized representative acting for him), to the effect that he wants the opportunity to present his case to higher authority. The State may require that such request be in written form in order to be effective;

(ii) The freedom to make such a request shall not be limited or interfered with in any way. The agency may assist the claimant to submit and process his request;

(iii) The claimant shall be provided reasonable time, not to exceed 90 days, in which to appeal an agency action;

(iv) Agencies may respond to a series of individual requests for hearing by conducting a single group hearing. Agencies may consolidate only cases in which the sole issue involved is one of State or Federal law or policy or changes in State or Federal law. In all group hearings, the policies governing hearings must be followed. Thus, each individual claimant shall be permitted to present his own case or be represented by his authorized representative;

(v) The agency may deny or dismiss a request for a hearing where it has been withdrawn by the claimant in writing, where the sole issue is one of State or Federal law requiring automatic grant adjustments for classes of recipients, where a decision has been rendered after a WIN hearing before the manpower agency that a participant has, without good cause, refused to accept employment or participate in the WIN program, or has failed to request such a hearing after notice of intended action for such refusal, or where it is abandoned. Abandonment may be deemed to have occurred if the claimant, without good cause therefor, fails to appear by himself or by authorized representative at the hearing scheduled for such claimant.

(6) If the recipient requests a hearing within the timely notice period:

(i) Assistance shall not be suspended, reduced, discontinued or terminated (but is subject to recovery by the agency if its action is sustained), until a decision is rendered after a hearing, unless:

(A) A determination is made at the hearing that the sole issue is one of State or Federal law or policy, or change in State or Federal law and not one of incorrect grant computation;

(B) A change affecting the recipient's grant occurs while the hearing decision is pending and the recipient fails to request a hearing after notice of the change;

(C) The recipient specifically requests that he or she not receive continued assistance pending a hearing decision; or

(D) The agency has made a presumption of mismanagement as a result of a recipient's nonpayment of rent and provides for the opportunity for a hearing after the manner or form of payment has been changed for such cases in accordance with Sec. 234.60 (a)(2) and (a)(11).

(ii) The agency shall promptly inform the claimant in writing if assistance is to be discontinued pending the hearing decision; and

(iii) In any case where the decision of an evidentiary hearing is adverse to the claimant, he shall be informed of and afforded the right to make a written request, within 15 days of the mailing of the notification of such adverse decision, for a State agency hearing and of his right to request a de novo hearing. Unless a de novo hearing is specifically requested by the appellant, the State agency hearing may consist of a review by the State agency hearing officer of the record of the evidentiary hearing to determine whether the decision of the evidentiary hearing officer was supported by substantial evidence in the record. Assistance shall not be continued after an adverse decision to the claimant at the evidentiary hearing.

(7) A State may provide that a hearing request made after the date of action (but during a period not in excess of 10 days following such date) shall result in reinstatement of assistance to be continued until the hearing decision, unless (i) the recipient specifically requests that continued assistance not be paid pending the hearing decision; or (ii) at the hearing it is determined that the sole issue is one of State or Federal law or policy. In any case where action was taken without timely notice, if the recipient requests a hearing within 10 days of the mailing of the notice of the action, and the agency determines that the action resulted from other than the application of State or Federal law or policy or a change in State or Federal law, assistance shall be reinstated and continued until a decision is rendered after the hearing, unless the recipient specifically requests that continued assistance not be paid pending the hearing decision.

(8) The hearing shall be conducted at a reasonable time, date, and place, and adequate preliminary written notice shall be given.

(9) Hearings shall be conducted by an impartial official (officials) or des-

ignee of the agency. Under this requirement, the hearing official (officials) or designee shall not have been directly involved in the initial determination of the action in question.

(10) When the hearing involves medical issues such as those concerning a diagnosis, an examining physician's report, or a medical review team's decision, a medical assessment other than that of the person or persons involved in making the original decision shall be obtained at agency expense and made part of the record if the hearing officer considers it necessary.

(11) In respect to title IV-C, when the appeal has been taken on the basis of a disputed WIN registration requirement, exemption determination or finding of failure to appear for an appraisal interview, a representative of the local WIN manpower agency shall, where appropriate, participate in the conduct of the hearing.

(12) The hearing shall include consideration of:

(i) An agency action, or failure to act with reasonable promptness, on a claim for financial assistance, which includes undue delay in reaching a decision on eligibility or in making a payment, refusal to consider a request for or undue delay in making an adjustment in payment, and discontinuance, termination or reduction of such assistance;

(ii) Agency decision regarding:

(A) Eligibility for financial assistance in both initial and subsequent determinations,

(B) Amount of financial assistance or change in payments,

(C) The manner or form of payment, including restricted or protective payments, even though no Federal financial participation is claimed.

(13) The claimant, or his representative, shall have adequate opportunity:

(i) To examine the contents of his case file and all documents and records to be used by the agency at the hearing at a reasonable time before the date of the hearing as well as during the hearing;

(ii) At his option, to present his case himself or with the aid of an authorized representative;

(iii) To bring witnesses;

(iv) To establish all pertinent facts and circumstances;

(v) To advance any arguments without undue interference;

(vi) To question or refute any testimony or evidence, including opportunity to confront and cross-examine adverse witnesses.

(14) Recommendations or decisions of the hearing officer or panel shall be based exclusively on evidence and other material introduced at the hearing. The transcript or recording of testimony and exhibits, or an official report containing the substance of what transpired at the hearing, together with all papers and requests filed in the proceeding, and the recommendation or decision of the hearing officer or panel shall constitute the exclu-

sive record and shall be available to the claimant at a place accessible to him or his representative at a reasonable time.

(15) Decisions by the hearing authority shall:

(i) In the event of an evidentiary hearing, consist of a memorandum decision summarizing the facts and identifying the regulations supporting the decision;

(ii) In the event of a State agency de novo hearing, specify the reasons for the decision and identify the supporting evidence and regulations. Under this requirement no persons who participated in the local decision being appealed shall participate in a final administrative decision on such a case.

(16) Prompt, definitive, and final administrative action shall be taken within 90 days from the date of the request for a hearing.

(17) The claimant shall be notified of the decision in writing and, to the extent it is available to him, of his right to appeal to State agency hearing or judicial review.

(18) When the hearing decision is favorable to the claimant, or when the agency decides in favor of the claimant prior to the hearing, the agency shall promptly make corrective payments retroactively to the date the incorrect action was taken.

(19) All State agency hearing decisions shall be accessible to the public (subject to provisions of safeguarding public assistance information).

(b) Federal financial participation. Federal financial participation is available for the following items:

(1) Payments of assistance continued pending a hearing decision.

(2) Payments of assistance made to carry out hearing decisions, or to take corrective action after an appeal but prior to hearing, or to extend the benefit of a hearing decision or court order to others in the same situation as those directly affected by the decision or order. Such payments may be retroactive in accordance with applicable Federal policies on corrective payments.

(3) Payments of assistance within the scope of Federally aided public assistance programs made in accordance with a court order.

(4) Administrative costs incurred by the agency for:

(i) Providing transportation for the claimant, his representative and witnesses to and from the place of the hearing;

(ii) Meeting other expenditures incurred by the claimant in connection with the hearing;

(iii) Carrying out the hearing procedures, including expenses of obtaining an additional medical assessment.

[38 FR 22007, Aug. 15, 1973, as amended at 44 FR 17941, Mar. 23, 1979; 45 FR 20480, Mar. 28, 1980; 47 FR 5673, Feb. 5, 1982; 47 FR 47827, Oct. 28, 1982; 51 FR 9202, Mar. 18, 1986; 53 FR 36579, Sept. 21, 1988; 57 FR 30425, July 9, 1992]

FEDERAL ADOPTION ASSISTANCE REGULATIONS

There are few federal agency regulations that pertain to the adoption assistance program. The existing rules are reproduced below. Paragraph (f) specifying that "The State agency must actively seek ways to promote the adoption assistance program" was cited in *Ferdinand v. Department for Children and Their Families*, a May 13, 1991 U.S. District Court decision, as grounds for allowing an adoptive family to apply for and receive adoption assistance after finalization. See 768 Federal Supplement, 401, District of Rhode Island, 1992 for the *Ferdinand* decision. The rules also explicitly forbid an income means test to be used in determining eligibility for Title IV-E adoption assistance.

[Code of Federal Regulations]
[Title 45, Volume 4, Parts 1200 to end]
[Revised as of October 1, 1997]
From the U.S. Government Printing Office via GPO Access
[CITE: 45CFR1356.40]

TITLE 45—PUBLIC WELFARE
  CHAPTER XIII—OFFICE OF HUMAN DEVELOPMENT
SERVICES, DEPARTMENT OF HEALTH AND HUMAN
SERVICES
  PART 1356—REQUIREMENTS APPLICABLE TO
TITLE IV-E
  TABLE OF CONTENTS

Sec. 1356.40

Adoption assistance program: Administrative requirements to implement section 473 of the Act.

(a) To implement the adoption assistance program provisions of the title IV-E State plan and to be eligible for Federal financial participation in adoption assistance payments under this part, the State must meet the requirements of this section and sections 471 (a), 473 and 475(3) of the Act.

(b) The adoption assistance agreement for payments pursuant to section 473(a)(2) must meet the requirements of section 475(3) of the Act and must:

(1) Be signed and in effect at the time of or prior to the final decree of adoption. A copy of the signed agreement must be given to each party; and

(2) Specify its duration; and

(3) Specify the nature and amount of any payment, services and assistance to be provided under such agreement and, for purposes of eligibility under title XIX of the Act, specify that the child is eligible for Medicaid services; and

(4) Specify, with respect to agreements entered into on or after October 1, 1983, that the agreement shall remain in effect regardless of the State of which the adoptive parents are residents at any given time.

(c) There must be no income eligibility requirement (means test) for the prospective adoptive parent(s) in determining eligibility for adoption assistance payments.

(d) In the event an adoptive family moves from one State to another State, the family may apply for social services on behalf of the adoptive child in the new State of residence. However, for agreements entered into on or after October 1, 1983, if a needed service(s) specified in the adoption assistance agreement is not available in the new State of residence, the State making the original adoption assistance payment remains financially responsible for providing the specified service(s).

(e) A State may make an adoption assistance agreement with adopting parent(s) who reside in another State. If so, all provisions of this section apply.

(f) The State agency must actively seek ways to promote the adoption assistance program.

[48 FR 23116, May 23, 1983, as amended at 53 FR 50220, Dec. 14, 1988]

1998 STATE SUPREME COURT DECISIONS ON TITLE IV-E ADOPTION ASSISTANCE AFTER FINALIZATION

ENTRY ORDER
SUPREME COURT DOCKET NO. 97-441
JUNE TERM, 1998

Kevin and Diane Hogan
v.
Vermont Department of Social and Rehabilitation Services
DOCKET NO. Fair Hearing# 13,474
In the above-entitled cause, the clerk will enter:

Kevin and Diane Hogan appeal from a decision of the Vermont Human Services Board denying their application for federally-funded adoption assistance pursuant to 42 U.S.C. & 673(a). We agree with the Hogans that the Board erred in denying them benefits in connection with their adopted son based on a determination that the child was not eligible for federal Supplemental Security Income (SSI) benefits at the time of the adoption. Accordingly, we reverse.

The relevant facts of the case as found by the Board are not in dispute. The Hogans' adoptive son was born on April 30, 1991, and placed with the petitioners by a private adoption agency less than a month later. The child's birth mother relinquished her parental rights, and the Hogans instituted adoption proceedings before the probate court in Chittenden County in November 1991. The adoption was finalized on January 6, 1992. More than two years later, in the spring of 1994, a psychiatrist diagnosed the child as having "pervasive developmental disability," which the Board characterized as "akin to autism." The Board acknowledged that the child has displayed "disturbing symptoms" of his illness within six months of his birth, but it stressed that no neurological or developmental deficits were diagnosed until the child was nearly three years old.[1]

Although the Vermont Department of Social and Rehabilitation Services (SRS) had notified the private adoption agency about the availability of federally funded adoption assistance benefits under 42 U.S.C. & 673, no one made the Hogans aware of the program during the pendency of the adoption proceedings. The Hogans filed an application for the benefits on December 21, 1994. SRS denied the application, and the Board upheld this determination following an evidentiary hearing. The initial decision of the Board was that a child be found retroactively eligible for adoption assistance and that, rather, there had to be a signed agreement between SRS and the Hogans in place at the time of adoption.

The Hogans' initial appeal to this Court was dismissed on the stipulation of the parties in February 1997 to permit the Board to reconsider its decision in light of written guidance received from the federal Department of Health and Human Services. Specifically, the federal agency advised that (1) the failure of a private adoption agency to notify adoptive parents of the existence of the adoption assistance program during the pendency of the adoption is sufficient grounds for requiring the administrative state agency to conduct a so-called "fair hearing" under 42 U.S.C. & 671(a)(12), and (2) a "special needs" child whose adoptive parents did not receive such notice from the adoption agency is still eligible to receive the adoption assistance benefits as long as the child *"meet[s] the eligibility requirements"* for SSI benefits. [Emphasis added.]

---

[1]The Hogans draw our attention to certain factual assertions that appear to be undisputed but are not contained in the Board's findings. Specifically, they refer to the birth mother's significant history of substance abuse, its connection to the child's medical problems and the adoption agency's failure to inform them of the birth mother's problems prior to the adoption. While these contentions are compelling, we need not consider them in resolving the issues on appeal.

The Board conducted a second evidentiary hearing and, on September 2, 1997, again denied the Hogans' application on the merits. The Hogans claimed two alternative routes to eligibility, one of which required that they show that the child would have been eligible for Supplementary Security Income (SSI) because of disability at the time of the adoption. See 42 U.S.C. & 673(a)(2)(A)(ii). The Board held that, although such a disability has been diagnosed, "it cannot be concluded that *at the time of the adoption* the child could have been diagnosed as having a [qualifying] impairment." This appeal followed.

The circumstances before us are unique. Section 673(a) plainly contemplates that an application for adoption assistance benefits will normally be filed prior to the finalization of adoption. We agree that the child's eligibility under the statute must be determined based on the child's circumstances at that point in time. The question here is how to interpret the eligibility standards when, through no fault of their own, the adoptive parents were deprived of the opportunity to make an application at the proper time.

A careful examination of the position taken by SRS and the federal agency's interpretation as expressed in the letter triggering the previous remand reveals that the two views of the issue are fundamentally inconsistent with one another. If, as the federal Department of Health and Human Services advised SRS, the circumstances of this case justify a post-adoption application for benefits, then it follows that these circumstances also permit a post-adoption application for diagnosis of a condition that meets the SSI disability criteria to substitute for the normal pre-adoption diagnosis of such a condition. Otherwise, the remedy for the failure to inform the parents of the program would be illusory because the parents could not show what the diagnosis would have been if the child had been examined for this purpose at the time. As a simple matter of logic, mitigating the unfair deprivation of an opportunity to seek benefits is useless unless there is also a mitigation of the similar deprivation of an opportunity to build the requisite medical record.

OPINION OF THE SUPREME COURT OF NEBRASKA
Case Title
Jean Schmidt, as guardian and next best friend of Patricia Schmidt, a minor child, Appellant
v.
State of Nebraska, Department of Social Services, Apellee
Case Caption
Schmidt v. State
Filed November 13, 1998. No. S-97-302

Appeal from the District Court for Lancaster County: Earl J. Witthoff, Judge. Judgement vacated and cause remainded with directions to dismiss.

Robert R. Otte and Joseph E. Dalton, of Morrow, Poppe, Otte, Ware-meier and Phillips, P.C. for appellant.

Don Stenberg, Attorney General, and Royce N. Harper for appellee.

Wright, Connolly, Gerrard, Stephan, and McCormack, JJ.

Connolly, J.

The appellant, Jean Schmidt, and her husband Richard Schmidt adopted a child, Patricia Schmidt, without applying for government adoption assistance. Seven years after the adoption was finalized, the appellant on behalf of the child, requested appellee, the then Nebraska Department of Social services (DSS), to find the child eligible for federal adoption assistance, due to her medical conditions. The DSS acting Director, Gerry Oligmueller (the director), determined the child was not eligible for assistance and denied an agency review of the decision. The appellant filed an appeal with the Lancaster County District Court, which upheld DSS' denial of eligibility. The appellant timely appealed. We find that DSS denial was invalid for failure to comply with statutory and regulatory procedure and that the district court and this court lack jurisdiction to review the merits of the appellant's claims. As a result, we vacate the district court's order and remand cause with directions to dismiss.

The child was born on September 16, 1986. Two months later, she was treated for first and second degree burns on her inner thighs at St. Joseph Hospital in Omaha, Nebraska. She was released into foster care after being treated, and the Douglas County Separate Juvenile Court made the child a ward of DSS. On September 1, 1987, both of the child's birth parents relinquished their parental rights. On the same day, the juvenile court placed the child in the custody of the the Nebraska Children's Home Society (NCHS) and relieved DSS of all responsibility.

In October 1987, NCHS placed the child with the appellant and her husband. Medical information the appellant received regarding the child's background was basically limited to her measurements at birth, dates she learned to sit and crawl, and the fact that "[the child] does get a rash from disposable diapers." The appellant was told at placement that the child "seemed hyperactive," but representatives of NCHS told her the condition would improve with a stable environment. The child's hyperactive condition appeared to improve between the time of the placement and the time the adoption was finalized. No one from either NCHS or DSS informed the appellant about existing federal or state adoption assistance programs prior to the adoption's being finalized, and the appellant did not apply for any government assistance prior to finalization of the adoption.

The child's behavioral development was slow. Her allergies, hyperactivity, and behavioral problems led the appellant to quit her full-time job in 1991 to care full time for the child. The child was diagnosed with reactive attachment disorder in 1992. She received 2 months of inpatient therapy and continues to receive therapy for that disorder. She was diagnosed with a seizure disorder in 1992, which continues to cause her sleep difficulties. She was diagnosed with attention deficit hyperactivity disorder in 1993. The appellant stated that they cannot afford to enroll the child in the special school that the child's therapists have recommended.

By September 1994, the appellant confirmed through St. Joseph Hospital records, DSS records, and NCHS personnel that the child was likely neglected and possibly abused by her biological mother, that her biological mother admitted to consuming alcohol during the first trimester of pregnancy, and that her biological mother had been diagnosed with residual schizophrenia. Medical sources in the record state that the child is about 10 times more likely than a member of the general population to develop schizophrenia in her adolescence or adulthood because of her biological mother's schizophrenia.

In a letter to DSS dated May 9, 1955, the appellant requested "a fair hearing to determine [the child's] eligibility for Title IV-E adoption assistance." Title IV-E of the Social Security Act is a federal adoption assistance program administered in Nebraska by DSS. See 42 U.S.C. 670 et seq. (1994): Neb. Rev. Stat. & 43-117.01 (Reissue 1993). DSS scheduled a hearing and docketed it as "In the Matter of the Appeal of Richard and Jean Schmidt, on Behalf of Particia Schmidt."

At the hearing, DSS asserted that the appellant could not receive assistance because (1) state law and DSS regulations provided for assistance only for children who were wards of DSS at the time the adoption was finalized, which the child was not; (2) DSS regulations required the adoption assistance agreement be completed before the adoption was finalized; and (3) DSS regulations required an assessment at the time of the adoption of whether the child was a hard-to-place child with special needs. The appellant contended that (1) state law and DSS regulations in 1988 that restricted benefits to wards of DSS were in violation of federal law and (2) even though she and her husband did not apply for adoption assistance before the adoption was finalized, extenuating circumstances exist to permit consideration of the child's eligibility, specifically, because they were not informed of the adoption assistance program prior to the adoption because they were not told about the child's and her biological mother's medical histories.

In his order, the director held that the child was not eligible for title IV-E adoption assistance because (1) she was not a ward of DSS when her adoption was finalized, as indicated by 474 Neb. Admin. Code, ch. 5 & 023.07 (1983) and (2) nothing in the record indicated that at the time of the adoption, the child had a handicapping condition requiring a subsidy. The director further held that "there are no extenuating circumstances in this case whereby the Nebraska Department of Social Services has to provide a hearing to the Schmidts in regard to their daughter's eligibility for Adoption Assistance." The director held that the federal agency interpretations the appellant presented to support her extenuating circumstances arguments did not apply, because the interpretations applied to reconsiderations for assistance and "a[s] no decision was ever made by the Nebraska Department of Social Services in regard to [the child's] eligibility for subsidized adoption, there can be no reconsideration of an action that never took place." DSS general council Michael Rumbaugh wrote a letter to the appellant with the director's order enclosed, stating "This Finding and Order constitutes the final administrative decision on your case."

The appellant filed a proceeding in the district court for Lancaster County, demanding reversal of the director's order. The district court upheld the director's order. The district court held, inter alia, that (1) the child was never made a ward of the State of Nebraska; (2) the child failed to meet the requirement of 474 Neb. Admin. Code, ch. 4 & 021.01 C2a 2c (1991) (current version at 479 Neb. Admin. Code, ch. 8, && 001.03B1 1d 1995)), because at the time of the hearing she was not a ward of a private nonprofit agency licensed in Nebraska to place children for the purpose of adoption; (3) the child failed to meet the requirements of 474 Neb. Admin. Code, ch. 4 && 021.01 C2a 2a and 021.01 C2b (1991) (current version at 479 Neb. Admin. Code, ch. 8 && 001.03B1 1a and 001.03B2 (1995)), which require for assistance eligibility that a child cannot be adopted without a subsidy, because the child was in fact adopted without a subsidy; (4) "there were no previous requests or denials entitling Plaintiffs to a fair hearing"; and (5) "there were no extenuating circumstances that would allow Plaintiff's [sic] a fair hearing."

Assignments of Error

The appellant assigns the district court erred in finding that (1) the child was at no time made a ward of the state; (2) the child failed to meet the requirement of 474 Neb. Admin. Code, ch. 4 & 021.01 C2a 2c; (3) the child does not meet the criteria for adoption subsidy set forth in 474 Neb. Admin. Code, ch. 4 & 021.01 C2a 2c and 012.01C2b, (4) there were no extenuating circumstances that would allow the appellant a fair hearing; and (5) the child is not now eligible under title IV-E for adoption assistance.

Scope of Review

Before reaching the legal issues presented for review, it is the duty of the appellate court to determine whether it has jurisdiction over the matter before it. *Bonge v. County of Madison*, 253 Neb. 903, 573 N.W. 2d 448 (1998). To the extent the interpretation of statutes and regulations is involved, questions of law are presented, in connection with which an appellate court has an obligation to reach an independent conclusion irrespective of the decision made by the court below. *Inner Harbor Hospitals v. State*, 251 Neb. 793, 559 N.W. 2d 487 (1997).

Analysis

Notwithstanding that the parties have not raised the issue of jurisdiction, this court has a duty to raise and determine the issue of jurisdiction sua sponte, which we now do See, *Bonge v. County of Madison*, supra: In re Interest of D.W., 249 Neb. 133, 542 N.W. 2d 407 (1996). The record indicates that DSS disposed of the appellant's claims in a manner contrary to the express procedure provided in DSS' own regulations and contrary to the procedure required by federal statutes and federal regulations.

First, both the director and the district court expressly found that the appellant had made no application for assistance and that DSS had not denied assistance prior to the appellant's May 9, 1995 request for a fair hearing. The record supports the finding. Despite that fact, DSS granted and held a hearing, after which the director determined the child's ineligibility for title IV-E adoption assistance.

DSS has an explicit procedure on how the agency is to initially determine eligibility for adoption assistance. This procedure was in effect at the time the appellant requested a fair hearing. (Regarding the procedure, the applicable rules are those that were in effect at the time of the appellant's request for the agency hearing and when the hearing was held. *Ventura v. State*, 246 Neb. 116, 517 N.W. 2d 368 (1994): *Durousseau v. Nebraska State Racing Commission*, 194 Neb. 288, 231 N.W. 2d 566 (1975)). To determine a child's eligibility for title IV-E adoption assistance, specific forms need to be completed and forwarded to DSS' adoption specialist. 474 Neb. Admin. Code, ch. 4 & 021.01 C2a 1 (1991) (current version at 479 Neb. Admin. Code, ch. 8, && 001.03B1a (1995)). The adoption specialist determines eligibility, *then* the applicant has a right to a fair hearing in which DSS' director reviews the initial denial. 465 Neb. Admin. Code ch. 2 & 001.02 (1984) (readopted without amendment & 001.02 (1995)). The record is clear that this process, the proper procedure, was not used to determine the child's eligibility.

Second, DSS simultaneously made both an initial and a final determination of the child's eligibility for assistance. As stated, there was no denial of eligibility prior to the hearing that was held. The director stated in his order that the hearing that was held was not a reconsideration. The order was not only the initial DSS determination of the child's eligibility, but also the final DSS determination. By regulation, the DSS director's finding and order after a hearing must be the final agency decision. 465 Neb. Admin. Code, ch. 2 && 006.03A and 006.03D (1984) (current version at & 6-008.02 through 6-008.07 (1995). This was confirmed both by the order in which he purported to deny the appellant a fair hearing and in the letter to the appellant from the DSS' general counsel. However, the regulations provide that every applicant for any program that DSS administers has the *right* to *appeal* to DSS for a fair hearing. 465 Neb. Admin. Code, ch. 2, 001, 11 (1984). Specifically, "[e]very applicant for or recipient of assistance or services provided through [DSS] has the right to appeal any action, inaction, or failure to act with reasonable promptness with regard to assistance or services." 465 Neb. Admin. Code, ch. 2 001.02 (1984) (readopted without amendment 001.02 (1995)). Obviously, one cannot appeal a determination to the director when the director was the person making the initial determination.

Additionally, federal statutes and federal regulations governing title IV-E adoption assistance also require the states to provide an administrative appeal. Title 42 of the U.S. Code requires states to provide "for granting an opportunity for a fair hearing before the State agency to any individual whose claim for benefits available pursuant to this part is denied or is not acted upon with reasonable promptness." 42 U.S.C. 671 (a) (12) (1994). Title 45 C.F.R. 205.10 (a) (5) (1992), made applicable to this program by 45 C.F.R. 1355.30 (k) (1993), amended by 61 Fed. Reg. 58654 (1996), repeats the fair hearing appeal requirement at the agency level. Additionally, at the time the director issued his order, federal statute provided that the denial of the fair hearing right in 42 U.S.C. 671 (a) (12) was grounds for the U.S. Department of Health and Human Services to halt or reduce its payment obligations to the state. 42 U.S.C. 671 (b) (1988), amended by act Oct. 31, 1994 (effective Oct. 1, 1995), 203 (c) (2).

DSS regulations do not provide the authority to initially determine eligibility at a hearing before the director. DSS regulations and federal law do not provide DSS the authority to simultaneously make both an initial and a final determination of an applicant's eligibility for title IV-E adoption assistance and, implicit within that, do not provide the director the authority to deny a fair hearing.

Having found that DSS did not follow proper procedure in determining the appellant's claim, the issue is whether DSS' order in this case is nonetheless valid. We conclude that it is not valid.

Properly adopted and filed agency regulations have the effect of statutory law. *Alexander v. Warehouse*, 253 Neb. 153 N.W. 2d 892 (1997); *Val-Pack of Omaha v. Department of Revenue*, 249 Neb. 776, 545 N.W. 2d 447 (1996). Regulations bind the agency that promulgated them just as they bind individual citizens, even if the adoption of the regulations was discretionary. See, *Accari v. Shaughnessy*, 347 U.S. 260, 74 S. Ct. 499, 98 L. Ed. 2d 681 (1954): *Douglas County Welfare Administration v. Parks*, 204 Neb. 570, 284 N.W. 2d 10 (1979); *Johnson v. Nebraska Environmental Control Council*, 2 Neb. App. 263, 509 N.W. 2d 21 (1993). Regulations governing procedures are just as binding upon both the agency which enacts them and the public, "and the agency does not, as a general rule, have the discretion to waive, suspend, or disregard in a particular case, a validly adopted rule so long as such rule remains in force." *Douglas County Welfare Administration v. Parks*, 204 Neb. at 572, 284 N.W. 2d at 11–12. "To be valid, the action of the agency must conform to its rules which are in effect at the time the action is taken. . . ." *Id.* at 572, 284 N.W. 2d at 12. Se also, *Service v. Dulles*, 354 U.S. 363, 77 S.Ct. 1152, 1 L. Ed. 2d 1403 (1957) (holding that although enactment of pertinent regulations was at agency's discretion, agency's action was invalid when it proceeded without regard to regulations); *Mine Reclamation Corp v. F.E.R.C.*, 30 F. 3d 1519, 1524 (D.C. Cir, 1994) (stating that "an agency' failure to follow its own regulations is fatal to the deviant action").

The court, in *In re Application of Jantzen*, 245 Neb. 81, 511 N.W. 2d 504 (1994), created an exception to the general rule that an agency may not waive application of its own rules and regulations. The court held that if a rule is "but an aid to help the [agency] in its decision," rather than one that "confer[s] procedural benefit upon a party," then the agency's action may depart from that rule. *Id.* at 97, 511 N.W. 2d at 515. In *In re Application of Jantzen*, this court held that an agency could waive a rule that required a party to file a response to a protest within a certain time, given that the plaintiff had the burden of production, even without an answer's being filed, and thus that the regulation conferred no procedural benefit upon the plaintiff.

The *In re Application of Jantzen* exception provides a means to substantively review an agency decision when, although procedure was not followed, no harm was done to the claimant. However, the regulations DSS failed to follow in the instant case conferred procedural benefits upon the appellant. Instead of rejecting the appellant's request for a fair hearing for want of an action to review, DSS responded to the request by docketing a hearing for a denial that never took place. A hearing was held, but the director clearly did not consider the hearing as an appeal of a denial—a "fair hearing." The director rejected at least two of the appellant's legal arguments on grounds that the factual basis for the arguments regarded *reconsiderations* and that the appellant's claim for eligibility was not a reconsideration. The director then purported to deny the appellant a fair hearing. Had DSS followed its regulatory scheme, the appellant could have had the child's eligibility determined administratively and if the decision were unfavorable, could have had that decision reviewed by the director in a "fair hearing," where all extenuating circumstances could have been considered. Instead the appellant got only one bite of apple at the administrative level, and even that one bite was tainted by the director's misunderstanding as to what authority he had and where the appellant's claim was procedurally. The appellant was effectively denied the administrative appeal provided by 465 Neb. Admin. Code, ch. 2 001.02.

Because DSS did not follow its regulatory scheme for determining eligibility for adoption assistance and the appellant was denied a proper determination and review of her claim, we conclude that the director's order denying eligibility for the child is invalid and was not reviewable by the district court. When a lower court does not gain jurisdiction over the case before it, an appellate court also lacks the jurisdiction to review the merits of the claim. *Richdale Dev. Co. v. Mc Neil Co.*, Neb. 694, 508 N.W. 2d 853 (1993), *modified* 244 Neb. 936, 510 N.W. 2d 312 (1994).

Conclusion

The director's finding and order underlying this appeal is invalid. Because the order is invalid, the district court lacked jurisdiction to review the merits of the appellant's claims, and thus this court lacks jurisdiction to review the merits. We vacate the district court's decision in this matter and remand the case to the district court with directions to dismiss DSS' August 14, 1995 order without prejudice to any future applications for assistance.

JUDGMENT VACATED, AND CAUSE
REMANDED
WITH DIRECTIONS TO DISMISS
WHITE, C. J., not participating.

PART IV

INFORMATION RESOURCES

REFERENCES

Babb, L. A., and Laws, R. 1997. *Adopting and advocating for the special needs child: A guide for parents and professionals.* Westport, CT: Bergin & Garvey.

Babb, L. A. (in press). *Ethics in American adoption.* Westport, CT: Bergin & Garvey.

Barth, R. P., and Berry, M. 1988. Adoption and disruption: Rates, risks, and responses. New York: Aldine de Gruyter.

Bower, J. W. 1998. *Achieving permanence for every child.* St. Paul, MN: North American Council Adoptable Children.

Brodzinsky, D. M. 1990. A stress & coping model of adoption adjustment. In *The psychology of adoption,* ed. D. M. Brodzinsky and M. D. Schechter, 3–24. New York: Oxford University Press.

Cohen, J. S., and Westhues, A. 1990. *Well-functioning families for adoptive and foster children.* Toronto: University of Toronto Press.

Cole, E. S., and Donley, K. S. 1990. History, values, and placement policy issues in adoption. In *The psychology of adoption,* ed. D. M. Brodzinsky and M. D. Schechter 273–94. New York: Oxford University Press.

Doss, H. 1954. *The family nobody wanted.* Boston: Little, Brown and Co.

Gilles, T., and Kroll, J. 1992. User's guide to P. L. 96–272: A summarization and codification of administrative ruling. St. Paul, MN: North American Council on Adoptable Children.

Groze, V., Young, J., and Corcran-Rumppe, K. n.d. *Partners: Post adoption resources for training, networking and evaluation services: Working with special needs adoptive families in stress.* Cedar Rapids, IA: Four Oaks.

Laws, R. 1995. Special Needs Adoption Support and Periodicals: A Study of Parent-written and Adoption Professional-written Articles. Ph.D. diss., California Coast University. Research Abstracts International, 20(05), LD-03161.

Laws, R. 1998. The history, elements and ongoing need for adoption support. In *Clinical and practical issues in adoption: Bridging the gap between adoptees placed as infants and as older children*, ed. V. Groza and K. F. Rosenberg, 81–103. Westport, CT: Praeger Publishers.

Marindin, H. 1998. *The handbook for single adoptive parents*. Chevy Chase, MD: National Council for Single Adoptive Parents.

Meaker, P. P. 1990. Post-Placement Needs of Adoptive Families: A Study of Families Who Adopt Through the Texas Department of Human Services. Master's thesis, University of Texas at Arlington, 1989. Masters Abstracts International, 28, 238.

Nelson, K. A. 1985. *On the frontier of adoption: A study of special needs adoptive families*. New York: Child Welfare League of America.

North American Council on Adoptable Children. 1989. Parent group manual: Resources and ideas for adoptive parent support groups. St. Paul, MN: Author.

O'Hanlon, T. 1995. *Accessing federal adoption subsidies after legalization*. Washington, DC: Child Welfare League of America.

O'Hanlon, T. 1998. *Adoption subsidy: A guide for adoptive parents*. Columbus, OH: New Roots.

Oklahoma Choctaw Council. 1983. *Choctaw social and ceremonial life*. Oklahoma City: Oklahoma Choctaw Council.

Rosenthal, J. A., and Groze, V. K. 1992. *Special needs adoption: A study of intact families*. New York: Praeger Publishers.

Ross, M. 1986. The Educational Needs of Adoptive Parents. Ph.D. diss., American University, 1985. Dissertation Abstracts International, A 47, 408A.

Sedlak, Andrea J., and Broadhurst, Diane D. 1993. *Study of adoption assistance impact and outcomes: Final report*. Rockville, MD: Westat Corporation. See also, Cook, Ronna, et al. 1991. *A National Evaluation of Title IV-E Foster Care Independent Living Programs for Youth. Phase 2 Final Report*. Rockville, MD: Westat Corporation [Also published as ERIC Document ED348599].

Tremitiere, B. A. 1992. The large adoptive family: A special kind of normal. Ph.D. diss., Union Institute, 1991. Dissertation Abstracts International, 52, 4094A.

REGIONAL OFFICES U.S. DEPARTMENT OF HEALTH AND HUMAN SERVICES ADMINISTRATION FOR CHILDREN AND FAMILIES

REGION I

Hugh Galligan, RA
JFK Federal Bldg. Rm. 2000
Boston, MA 02203
(617) 565–1020 (voice)
(617) 565–2493 (fax)

STATES

Connecticut
Maine
Massachusetts
New Hampshire
Rhode Island
Vermont

REGION II

Mary Ann Higgins, RA
26 Federal Plaza
Rm. 4049
New York, NY 10278
(212) 264–2890 (ph)
(212) 264–4881 (fax)

New Jersey
New York
Puerto Rico
Virgin Islands

REGION III

David Lett, RA
150 S. Independence
Mall West, Suite 864
Public Ledger Bldg.
Philadelphia, PA 19104–3499
(215) 861–4000 (ph)
(215) 861–4070 (fax)

Delaware
District of Columbia
Maryland
Pennsylvania
Virginia
West Virginia

REGION IV

Steven Golightly, Hub Dir.
ACF Atlanta Fed. Center
61 Forsyth Street, S.W.
Suite 4M60
Atlanta, GA 30303
(404) 562–2900 (ph)
(404) 562–2981 (fax)

Alabama
Florida
Georgia
Kentucky
North Carolina
South Carolina
Tennessee

REGION V

Linda Carson, Hub Dir.   Illinois
105 West Adams St.   Indiana
20th Floor   Michigan
Chicago, IL 60603   Minnesota
(312) 353–4237 (ph)   Ohio
(312) 353–2204 (fax)   Wisconsin

REGION VI

Leon R. McCowan, Hub Dir.   Arkansas
1301 Young Street   Louisiana
Suite 914   New Mexico
Dallas, Texas 75202   Oklahoma
(214) 767–9648 (ph)   Texas
(214) 767–3743 (fax)

REGION VII

Linda Lewis, RA   Iowa
Federal Office Bldg.   Kansas
Rm. 384   Missouri
601 E. 12th St.   Nebraska
Kansas City, MO 64106
(816) 426–3981 (ph)
(816) 426–2888 (fax)

REGION VIII

Beverly Turnbo, RA   Colorado
Federal Office Bldg.   Montana
1961 Stout St., Rm. 1185   North Dakota
Denver, CO 80294–3538   South Dakota
(303) 844–2622 (ph)   Utah
(303) 844–2313 (fax)   Wyoming

REGION IX

Sharon M. Fujii   Arizona
50 United Nations Plaza   California
Rm. 450   Guam
San Francisco, CA 94012   Hawaii
(415) 437–8400 (ph)   Nevada
(415) 437–8444 (fax)   Samoa (American)
                                       Territory of Pacific Islands

REGION X

Stephen Henigson, RA   Alaska
Blanchard Plaza   Idaho
2201 Sixth Ave.   Oregon
Rm. 610-M/S RX-70   Washington
Seattle, Washington 98121
(206) 615–2547 (ph)
(206) 615–2574 (fax)

ADOPTION ASSISTANCE WORLD WIDE WEB SITES

A FEW ESSENTIAL WORLD WIDE WEB SITES FOR ADOPTION ASSISTANCE AND IV-E LEGAL RESEARCH

This list is by no means complete, but it makes a good start.

1. Adoption Policy Resource Center, maintained by Dr. Tim O'Hanlon of Adoption Advocates: http://www.fpsol.com/adoption/advocates.html

Adoption Advocates provides:

* direct advocacy for individual adoptive families

* systemic advocacy for adoption organizations and coalitions

* technical assistance, including case law, to legislators, administrators at all levels of government, and lawyers representing the interests of adoptive families

* policy research and analysis, disseminated through the Adoption Advocates newsletter, Issues in Adoption Advocacy

* the on-line Adoption Policy Resource Center, which offers access to a variety of useful information resources on adoption to a wide audience.

Established by Steven Humerickhouse and Timothy O'Hanlon in 1995, this site supports adoption through direct advocacy for individual adoptive families and provides technical assistance to organizations and professionals.

2. Adoption Information, Laws and Reforms: http://www.webcom.com/~kmc

There are many helpful links from the Adoption Ring. The Adoption Ring is a public service ring dedicated to the best interests of adoption triad members. It is an ever-expanding group of more than 300 pages designed to allow Web surfers to navigate educational adoption sites just by clicking the "Back" and "Next" buttons found on each page.

3. Adoptive Families of America: http://www.adoptivefam.org

Adoptive Families of America (AFA), the publisher of *ADOPTIVE FAMILIES*, is a private, nonprofit membership organization of families and individuals. AFA provides problem-solving assistance and information about the challenges of adoption to members of adoptive and prospective adoptive families. AFA seeks to create opportunities for successful adoptive placement and promotes the health and welfare of children without permanent families.

4. Faces of Adoption: America's Waiting Children: http://nac.adopt.org/adoptqst.html

Faces of Adoption: America's Waiting Children is a computerized photolisting of children with special needs and adoption-related information on the Internet. It is maintained by the National Adoption Center (NAC) and Children Awaiting Parents (CAP Book).

It offers a waiting-child matching resource (find your new son or daughter with on-line photolistings!), an information resource (books and information packets), a mailing list, support services for adoptive families, and much more. Live chat and message boards available through NAC at www.adoptnet.org

5. FindLaw: http://www.findlaw.com/

FindLaw is dedicated to making legal information such as state laws and adoption laws on the Internet easy to find. Maintained by Martin Roscheisen, Tim Stanley, and Stacy Stern, its features include:

the *FindLaw Guide to Internet legal resources.* This comprehensive guide includes links to resources in more than thirty practice areas, case law and codes, legal associations, law schools, law reviews, and more.

the *LawCrawler*—an innovative search tool powered by the Alta Vista™ search engine and database that provides precision by enabling searches to be focused on sites with legal information and within specific domains.

Cases & Codes—search our growing library of case law, including Supreme Court Decisions, and selected state codes.

Law Review Search & Services—you can search law reviews with full text articles on-line, and this is just the beginning.

6. Homes For Kids:http://www.homes4kids.org

This site includes a useful PIQ word-search index, lots of legal and advocacy information, and articles.

Its statement of purpose is to advocate first for the best interests of children without permanent families, next, for the best interests of birth and adoptive parents and families. Based on these, we will advocate for ethical, compassionate adoption practices.

Its goal is to offer information and advocacy support to all who work to provide permanence, safety, and love to the world's waiting children, children who go to bed at night with no one to call "Mom" or "Dad." This site is dedicated to those children, and is founded by Dr. L. Anne Babb and maintained by L. Anne Babb, Rita Laws, and Jody Swarbrick.

7. North American Council on Adoptable Children: http://www.cyfc.umn.edu/Adoptinfo/nacac.html

NACAC is not a placement agency, but a national nonprofit agency that researches adoption issues, educates members of the adoption community and the general public about adoption, and advocates for every child's right to a permanent family. Over the past two decades, NACAC has supported more than 600 adoptive parent groups, published significant research findings, and provided expert testimony to federal and state governments, universities, major foundations, and media representatives. NACAC provides technical consulting to answer parents' and adoption workers' questions about state and federal adoption programs.

8. National Adoption Information Clearinghouse: http://www.calib.com/naic

The National Adoption Information Clearinghouse is a comprehensive resource on all aspects of adoption, including infant, intercountry, and special needs adoption. Established in 1987, NAIC is a service of the Administration for Children, Youth and Families, Department of Health and Human Services. This is *the* place to order free copies of state and federal adoption laws.

9. The Children's Bureau and PIQs: http://www.acf.dhhs.gov/programs/cb/

The oldest federal agency for children, the Children's Bureau (CB) is located within the United States Department of Health and Human Services' Administration for Children and Families, Administration on Children, Youth and Families. It is responsible for assisting states in the delivery of child welfare services—services designed to protect children and strengthen families. The agency provides grants to states, tribes, and communities to operate a range of child welfare services including child protective services (child abuse and neglect), family preservation and support, foster care, adoption and independent living. In addition, the agency makes major investments in staff training, technology and innovative programs.

PIQ Search from ACF Web Server Search: http://www.acf.dhhs.gov/programs/cb/policy/search.htm

If you have trouble locating a certain PIQ, you can go directly to the entire list of available documents and click the one you want. Scroll the entire list to find all of the PIQs available at: http://www.acf.dhhs.gov/programs/cb/policy

10. Thomas: Legislative Information on the Internet: http://thomas.loc.gov/

In the spirit of Thomas Jefferson, this is a service of the U.S. Congress through its library.

Acting under the directive of the leadership of the 104th Congress to make federal legislative information freely available to the Internet public, a Library of Congress team brought the Thomas World Wide Web system on-line in January 1995, at the inception of the 104th Congress. Searching capabilities in Thomas were built on the InQuery information retrieval system, developed by the Center for Intelligent Information Retrieval based at the University of Massachusetts at Amherst, and now available commercially from Sovereign Hill Software.

HOW TO FIND WEB SITES FOR ANY ADOPTION-RELATED TOPIC

International adoption, finding an agency, search and reunion, triad issues, adoption support, research, and information about the homestudy process. All of these adoption-related issues and many others have corresponding Web sites on the World Wide Web. And they are easy to find. Here's how.

Your best helpers are called search tools or search engines but they are really just electronic library card catalogs. Type in a phrase, and the special Web site called a search engine will offer you a list of Web sites that pertain to the phrase you typed in. Click any offering and, instantly, you are there. It's faster than the transporter on "Star Trek."

The oldest and best known of these sites is Yahoo!, the granddaddy of Web indices. But Yahoo! is not the only one, and as big as it is, it doesn't have everything.

The best way to search is to use several search tools for the same word or phrase. You will be amazed how many listings pop up at one search site and not at another. Some search tools specialize in certain types of Web pages, so you will need to know about those, as well. But how do you find the three or four dozen search engines on the Web? How do you search for the search tools?

Happily, it's simple. Just remember this URL or Web address: www.search.com. Search.com brings most of the search engines together in one place so you can use as many different ones as you like. Yahoo! is there, and Excite, Hot Bot (bot is computer talk for robot), Snap, Web Crawler, and on and on. It is the card catalog of card catalogs.

Here's an example. At search.com, if you type in the phrase "adoption homestudy" at the Lycos line, it will return more than 100 links, too many to be practical. If you narrow the search criteria and type in "adoption homestudy in Florida," you will see a return of twenty highly useful links, including a FAQ, or Frequently Asked Questions file. Then, you can type in "adoption homestudy in Florida" at the Alta Vista Web search line, for example. This will return ten more pages of links, some of which were not offered by Lycos. The entire searching process takes less than one minute!

ADOPTION SUPPORT AND RESEARCH—RELATED WEB SITES

AASK America (AASK Midwest)
  http://www.aask.org

Adoption.com
  www.adoption.com

APHSA (formerly APWA)
  www.aphsa.org

Bazelon Center for Mental Health Law (an excellent source of information on the children's SSI program and other issues pertaining to mental health policy and legislation)
  http://www.bazelon.org
  bazelon@nicom.com

Evan B. Donaldson Adoption Institute
  http://www.adoptioninstitute.org

Interethnic Adoption Information Committee
  (Dr. Rita Simon)
  E-mail: rsimon@american.edu
  halstei@umaryland.edu

Institute for children
  www.forchildren.org

National Center for Youth Law
www.youthlaw.org

National Resource Center for Special Needs Adoption (Spaulding for Children)
www.spaulding.org

Resolve Infertility Information
www.resolve.com

Single Adoptive Parents of Los Angeles
home.earthlink.net/~sreben/index.html

Single Parent Adoption Network
members.aol.com/Onemomfor2/index.html

NATIONAL ORGANIZATIONS FOR SPECIAL NEEDS ADOPTIVE FAMILIES AND ADVOCATES

AASK America (Adopt a Special Kid), 287 17th Street, Suite 207, Oakland, CA 94612. Tel.:510–451–1748

Adopt America (formerly AASK Midwest), 1025 N. Reynolds Road, Toledo, OH 43615. Tel.: 419–534–3350, Fax: 419–534–2995, Web site: http://www.aask.org

Adoptive Families of America, Inc. (AFA), 2309 Como Ave., St. Paul, MN 55108. Tel: 651–645–9955, 800–372–3300, Web site: http://www.adoptivefam.org

American Public Human Services Association (APHSA), formerly the American Public Welfare Association (APWA), 810 First Street, N.E., Suite 500, Washington DC 20002–4267. Tel.: 202–682–0100, Fax: 202–289–6555. Issue Brief Series, including adoptive financial assistance

CAP Book (Children Awaiting Parents), 700 Exchange Street, Rochester, NY 14608. Tel.: 716–232–5110, Fax: 716–232–2634, Web site: http://www.ibar.com/adoptions.html. A photolisting book of children awaiting adoption nationwide

Child Welfare League of America, 440 First Street NW, Suite 310, Washington DC 20001–2085. V-mail: 800–407–6273 or 301–617–7825, Fax: 301–206–9789, E-mail: cwla@pmds.com

Dave Thomas Foundation, 4288 West Dublin-Granville Road, Dublin, OH 43017. Tel.: 614–764–3100

Evan B. Donaldson Adoption Institute, 120 Wall Street, 20th Floor, New York, NY 10005. Tel.: 212–269–5080, Fax: 212–269–1962, Web site: http://www.adoptioninstitute.org

Interethnic Adoption Information Committee, School of Social Work, University of Maryland, 525 West Redwood Street, Baltimore, MD 21201–1777. V-mail: 202–885–2907, E-mail: rsimon@american.edu or halstei@umaryland.edu

National Adoption Center, NAC, 1500 Walnut Street, Suite 701, Philadelphia, PA 19102. Tel.: 215–735–9988, Fax: 215–735–9410, E-mail: nac@adopting.org, Web sites: http://www.adopt.org/adopt and www.adoptnet.org. Computer matching of waiting children and prospective adoptive families, chat, message boards

National Adoption Information Clearinghouse, P.O. Box 1182, Washington, DC 20013–1182. Tel.: 888–251–0075 or 703–352–3488, Fax: 703–385–3206, E-mail: naic@calib.com, Web site:http://www.calib.com/naic. Free catalog

National Council for Single Adoptive Parents, P.O. Box 15084, Chevy Chase, MD 20825. Tel.: and Fax: 202–966–6367. Publishes *Handbook for Single Adoptive Parents*.

National Resource Center for Special Needs Adoption (Spaulding for Children), 16250 Northland Drive, Suite 120, Southfield, MI 48075. Tel.: 248–443–7080

North American Council on Adoptable Children, 970 Raymond Avenue, Suite 106, St. Paul, MN 55114–1149. Tel.: 651–644–3036, AAP/Subsidy hotline: 800–470–6665

U.S. Department of Health and Human Services, Children's Bureau, 330 C Street SW, Room 2068, Switzer Bldg., Washington, DC 20447. Tel.: 202–205–8618

Youth Law Center, 114 Sansome Street, Suite 950, San Francisco, CA 94104. Tel.: 415–543–3379

Index

About the Authors

RITA LAWS is the co-author of *Adopting and Advocating for the Special Needs Child* (Bergin & Garvey, 1997) and has written hundreds of articles on adopting and parenting. She has her Ph.D. in psychology and is a NACAC State Representative. She and her nine sons and two daughters by birth and adoption live in Oklahoma.

TIM O'HANLON is a former adoption assistance policy specialist and is the author of *Accessing Federal Adoption Subsidies After Legalization* (1995). Dr. O'Hanlon maintains an adoption advocacy Web site called the "Adoption Policy Resource Center."